SUBSTANCE ABUSE ASSESSMENT, INTERVENTIONS AND TREATMENT

ALCOHOL AND DRUG USE AMONG YOUTH

SUBSTANCE ABUSE ASSESSMENT, INTERVENTIONS AND TREATMENT

Additional books in this series can be found on Nova's website under the Series tab.

Additional E-books in this series can be found on Nova's website under the E-books tab.

SUBSTANCE ABUSE ASSESSMENT, INTERVENTIONS AND TREATMENT

ALCOHOL AND DRUG USE AMONG YOUTH

AGATHA M. PICHLER
EDITOR

Nova Science Publishers, Inc.
New York

Library of Congress Cataloging-in-Publication Data

Alcohol and drug use among youth / editor, Agatha M. Pichler.
   p. cm. -- (Substance abuse assessment, interventions and treatment)
 Includes bibliographical references and index.
 ISBN 978-1-61209-084-9 (hardcover : alk. paper)
 1. Youth--Alcohol use. 2. Youth--Drug use. 3. Youth--Substance use. I. Pichler, Agatha M.
 HV5135.A3859 2011
 362.29'20835--dc22

        2010047538

Published by Nova Science Publishers, Inc. †*New York*

CONTENTS

PREFACE

This book presents and discusses new research findings in the study of alcohol and drug use among youth. Topics discussed include the quantity and frequency of alcohol use among underage drinkers; findings from national surveys on drug use and health; young people who tend to drink and how they are obtaining alcohol and rural middle school counselors' competency for addressing student substance abuse.

Chapter 1 – Alcohol use by persons under age 21 has been identified as a major public health problem. Studies report that it increases the risks for disability and may be detrimental to the developing brain. Minors who drink are more likely to commit suicide, break the law, or be victims of violence. Alcohol is implicated in nearly one-third of youth traffic fatalities. The total annual cost of underage drinking is estimated at $62 billion. On March 6, 2007, the Office of the U.S. Surgeon General issued an official call to increase efforts to curb underage drinking. The prevalence of alcohol consumption by minors is measured by three federally funded national surveys: the National Survey on Drug Use and Health (NSDUH), the Youth Risk Behavior Survey (YRBS), and Monitoring the Future (MTF). There are an estimated 10.8 million underage drinkers in the United States. More than 2 million are classified as heavy drinkers, and nearly 7.2 million are classified as binge drinkers, meaning that they have had more than five drinks on one occasion. Although the consumption of alcohol by youth has dropped steadily over the past decade, recent data suggest that 74.3% of individuals in grades 9-12 have used alcohol on multiple occasions, 43.3% regularly consume alcohol, and 25.5% engage in binge drinking. Underage drinking remains a far more prevalent problem than the use of illicit drugs or tobacco products.

While most underage drinking prevention laws are passed by states, there has been legislative activity and interest at the federal level to support states' efforts to curb the problem. Issues of concern to policy makers include the ineffective enforcement of "zero-tolerance" laws prohibiting underage drinking, and the online sale of alcohol to minors. According to recent research, millions of minors either buy alcohol online or know an underage friend who has done so. In recent years, state and national policy makers have proposed restrictions on home delivery of alcohol ordered from Internet sites.

Chapter 2 – In 2006, a majority (53.9 percent) of American adolescents and young adults aged 12 to 20 had used an alcoholic beverage at least once in their lifetime. Young people aged 12 to 20 consumed approximately 11.2 percent of the alcoholic drinks consumed in the United States in the past month by persons aged 12 or older. Research shows that underage drinkers tend to consume more alcohol per occasion than those over the legal minimum drinking age of 21. Studies also have linked early drinking to heavy alcohol consumption and alcohol-related problems in adulthood. For example, in 2006, 16.3 percent of adults aged 21 or older who had first used alcohol before the age of 15 met the criteria for alcohol dependence or abuse in the past year compared with 2.4 percent of adults who first used alcohol at age 21 or older. Research also shows that early initiation of alcohol use is associated with higher likelihood of involvement in violent behaviors, suicide attempts, unprotected sexual intercourse, and multiple sex partners.

The National Survey on Drug Use and Health (NSDUH) asks persons aged 12 or older to report the frequency and quantity of their alcohol use during the 30 days prior to the interview. Respondents who drank alcohol in the past 30 days also are asked for the number of days they consumed alcohol in the past month and the average number of drinks consumed per day on the days they drank.

This report focuses on the frequency and quantity of past month alcohol use among underage drinkers (i.e., persons aged 12 to 20 who consume alcohol). Comparisons of the quantity and frequency of alcohol use in the past month also are made between underage drinkers and drinkers aged 21 or older. All findings presented in this report are based on combined 2005 and 2006 NSDUH data.

Chapter 3 – Alcohol is the drug of choice among young people in the United States, and alcohol use constitutes one of the principal public health issues for this population. Approximately 5,000 persons under 21 years of age lose their lives each year as a result of underage drinking, and early initiation of alcohol use is associated with increased risk of subsequent alcohol use disorders and increased risk of involvement in violent behaviors, suicide attempts, and a variety of other problematic activities. In response to this issue, this study presents findings from the 2002 to 2006 National Surveys on Drug Use and Health (NSDUHs) on the use of alcohol by persons aged 12 to 20.

NSDUH is an annual survey of the civilian, noninstitutionalized population of the United States aged 12 or older. The survey is sponsored by the Substance Abuse and Mental Health Services Administration (SAMHSA) of the U.S. Department of Health and Human Services and is planned and managed by SAMHSA's Office of Applied Studies (OAS). Data collection is conducted under contract with RTI International, Research Triangle Park, North Carolina.1 Selected key findings from this study are described below.

Chapter 4 – In 2006, more than one in four persons aged 12 to 20 in the United States, or about 10.8 million persons, drank alcohol in the past month (i.e., were current drinkers). Nearly one in five persons aged 18 to 20 drove under the influence of alcohol in the past 12 months in 2006,1 and each year approximately 1,900 people under the age of 21 die as a result of alcohol-involved motor vehicle crashes. In addition, early initiation of alcohol use is associated with increased likelihood of unprotected sexual intercourse and multiple sex partners. The 2006 National Survey on Drug Use and Health (NSDUH) asked past month alcohol users aged 12 to 20 how they obtained the last alcohol they drank and where they were when they consumed it. This issue of The NSDUH Report examines age-related changes in the locations where male and female underage drinkers use alcohol. It also examines differences by college enrollment and living situation for those aged 18 to 20. Findings presented in this report are based on 2006 NSDUH data.

Chapter 5 – A lthough the use of alcohol is illegal for persons under the age of 21, its use constitutes one of the principal public health issues for this age group, and reduction of underage alcohol use is a top public health priority of the Federal Government. Many of the efforts to prevent or reduce underage alcohol use attempt to reduce the availability of alcohol to underage drinkers. Data from the 2006 and 2007 National Surveys on Drug Use and Health (NSDUHs) indicate that even with efforts to reduce availability, underage drinkers are still able to obtain alcohol. This issue of The NSDUH Report examines how current (i.e., "past month") drinkers aged 12 to 20 obtain alcohol, by age group and gender. The 2006 and 2007 NSDUHs included items that asked past month alcohol users aged 12 to 20 how they obtained the last alcohol they drank.

This report also presents data on the prevalence of current underage alcohol use and findings on the average number of drinks that underage drinkers had on their last occasion of alcohol use, depending on where they obtained alcohol. All findings presented are annual averages based on combined 2006 and 2007 NSDUH data.

Chapter 6 – Student substance abuse is a serious concern for middle school personnel. Of all school personnel, counselors are the most likely to deliver mental health services to students which includes substance abuse. There is no research available on the perceived competence of urban, suburban, and rural middle school counselors for addressing student substance abuse concerns. The primary goal of this study was to determine how middle school counselors perceive their training in seven competency areas related to student substance abuse based on urbanicity. This study employed secondary data analysis of a national sample of 274 middle school counselors Findings indicated that urban, suburban and rural school counselors were similar in their perceived competence depending on the specific area of student substance abuse and were clearly able to identify the most important areas for future training. The findings from this study indicate that middle school counselors, regardless of urbanicity, require more training in the area of student substance abuse. Implications for in-service and pre-service training are discussed.

Chapter 7 – School based drugs education and prevention initiatives should be based upon contemporary empirical evidence. These programmes are traditionally developed with evidence gathered from school surveys which collect data on the prevalence estimates of those receiving mainstream education. As a result most education prevention initiatives which are delivered to school aged young people are not based upon evidence of the drug use experiences of those who do not attend mainstream school during adolescence. This paper will report on the drug use experience of the school exclusion sample of the High Risk Booster Sample of the Belfast Youth Development Study (BYDS) and its value for targeted education and prevention initiatives. The drug use behaviours of these high risk young people from the age of 11-16 will be presented in order to provide insights into the key temporal stages of experimental and onset regular illicit drug use. This analysis over a five year period will highlight the key stages for the development and delivery of drug use education and prevention initiatives for those who stop attending mainstream school before the age of 16 years.

In: Alcohol and Drug Use among Youth
Editor: Agatha M. Pichler

ISSN: 978-1-61209-084-9
© 2012 Nova Science Publishers, Inc.

Chapter 1

ALCOHOL USE AMONG YOUTH[*]

Andrew R. Sommers and Ramya Sundararaman

ABSTRACT

Alcohol use by persons under age 21 has been identified as a major public health problem. Studies report that it increases the risks for disability and may be detrimental to the developing brain. Minors who drink are more likely to commit suicide, break the law, or be victims of violence. Alcohol is implicated in nearly one-third of youth traffic fatalities. The total annual cost of underage drinking is estimated at $62 billion. On March 6, 2007, the Office of the U.S. Surgeon General issued an official call to increase efforts to curb underage drinking. The prevalence of alcohol consumption by minors is measured by three federally funded national surveys: the National Survey on Drug Use and Health (NSDUH), the Youth Risk Behavior Survey (YRBS), and Monitoring the Future (MTF). There are an estimated 10.8 million underage drinkers in the United States. More than 2 million are classified as heavy drinkers, and nearly 7.2 million are classified as binge drinkers, meaning that they have had more than five drinks on one occasion. Although the consumption of alcohol by youth has dropped steadily over the past decade, recent data suggest that 74.3% of individuals in grades 9-12 have used alcohol on multiple occasions, 43.3% regularly consume alcohol, and 25.5% engage in binge drinking. Underage drinking remains a far more prevalent problem than the use of illicit drugs or tobacco products.

While most underage drinking prevention laws are passed by states, there has been legislative activity and interest at the federal level to support states' efforts to curb the problem. Issues of concern to policy makers include the ineffective enforcement of "zero-tolerance" laws prohibiting underage drinking, and the online sale of alcohol to minors. According to recent research, millions of minors either buy alcohol online or know an underage friend who has done so. In recent years, state and national policy makers have proposed restrictions on home delivery of alcohol ordered from Internet sites.

This report describes the extent of alcohol use by youth, federal surveillance systems for monitoring underage drinking, judicial and legislative activity on this issue, and various policy implications. As new data become available, this report will be updated.

---

[*] This is an edited, reformatted and augmented version of Congressional Research Service Report RL34344, dated January 30, 2008.

INTRODUCTION

On March 6, 2007, the Office of the U.S. Surgeon General issued an official call to increase efforts to curb underage drinking [1]. "We can no longer ignore what alcohol is doing to our children," said Acting Surgeon General Kenneth Moritsugu. "Alcohol," he continued, "is the most heavily abused substance by America's youth." [2]. The nation, he implored, must "attempt to change attitudes toward drinking."

In light of recent research demonstrating that alcohol may harm the adolescent brain and that individuals who start drinking before the age of 15 are five times more likely to have alcohol- related problems later in life, the Acting Surgeon General announced six basic goals:

- Fostering changes in American society that facilitate healthy adolescent development and help prevent and reduce underage drinking.
- Engaging youth and all social systems that interface with youth in a coordinated effort to prevent and reduce drinking and its consequences.
- Promoting understanding of underage drinking in the context of development and maturation that considers individual adolescent characteristics and environmental, ethnic, cultural, and gender differences.
- Conducting additional research on adolescent alcohol use and its relationship to development.
- Improving surveillance on underage drinking and its risk factors.
- Ensuring that all policies are consistent with the goal of preventing and reducing underage alcohol consumption.

Although drinking by persons under the age of 21 is illegal in all states, people aged 12-20 drink almost 20% of alcohol consumed in the United States [3]. In 2004, there were more than 142,000 emergency room visits by youth aged 12-20 as a result of injuries and other conditions linked to alcohol consumption [4]. Each year, data suggest, approximately 5,000 young people under the age of 21 die as a result of underage drinking.

The economic toll of underage drinking in the United States in 2001 was an estimated $61.9 billion [5]. It has been reported that medical care, work loss, and pain and suffering directly associated with underage drinking cost $2,207 annually for each young person in the United States [6]. Low educational achievement and high absenteeism rates are common among underage students who drink alcohol. These youth often have problems with social integration, are more prone to fighting, and are often disinclined to participate in healthier activities such as intramural sports. They have a higher risk of being engaged in illegal activities and participating in unprotected sex [7]

SURVEILLANCE

Although many national surveys collect information about alcohol consumption, three federally funded studies most comprehensively cover aspects of underage drinking.

National Survey on Drug Use and Health (NSDUH)

NSDUH is the primary source of statistical information on illegal drug use by the U.S. population. Sponsored by the Substance Abuse and Mental Health Services Administration (SAMHSA), NSDUH collects data in interviews at each respondent's place of residence. Survey items aim to provide the drug prevention, treatment, and research communities with current, relevant information on the status of the nation's drug usage, including national and state-level estimates of the past month, past year, and lifetime use of alcohol. NSDUH tracks trends in the use of alcohol and helps identify the consequences of underage alcohol use and the groups who are at greatest risk.

Youth Risk Behavior Survey (YRBS)

The YRBS monitors health risk behaviors, including underage drinking, that contribute to mortality, disability, and social problems among youth in the United States. The YRBS is a national school-based survey fielded by the Centers for Disease Control and Prevention (CDC) and supplemented with data collected by state and local education and health agencies. It is conducted every two years during the spring semester and provides data representative of 9th- through 12th-grade students in public and private schools throughout the United States.

Monitoring the Future (MTF)

Funded by the National Institute on Drug Abuse, MTF annually surveys 8th, 10th, and 12th graders about substance use, including alcohol consumption. Respondents are asked about daily and monthly alcohol use, the quantity of alcohol consumed, and the number of episodes of heavy drinking in the past month. Unlike NSDUH or YRBS, MTF also explores issues of risk and ethics by asking, "How much do you think people risk harming themselves (physically or in other ways)" if they drink daily or if they drink heavily on the weekends. Similarly, survey participants are asked whether they "disapprove" of these behaviors. Each year, a random sample of 12th grade MTF participants is selected for follow-up studies. These individuals are surveyed by mail every other year until age 30, then every fifth year until age 45. Data from these follow-up surveys allow researchers to investigate questions about the effects of alcohol use over time, such as the following:

- How do different social contexts (e.g., military service, civilian employment, college, unemployment) and social roles (e.g., marital status, parenthood) affect alcohol use by individuals?
- How does the life course of individuals who used alcohol as teens differ from those who did not?

PREVALENCE

The consumption of alcohol by youth has dropped steadily over the past decade. Data from 2005 suggest that 74.3% of individuals in grades 9-12 have used alcohol on multiple occasions, 43.3% regularly consume alcohol, and 25.5% engage in binge drinking (see Figure 1) [8].

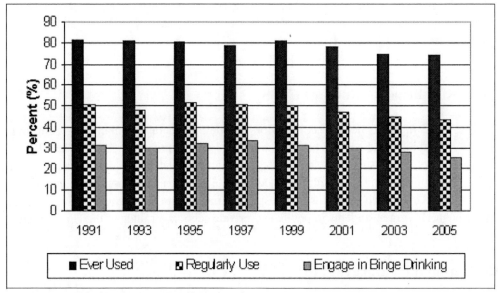

Source: Centers for Disease Control and Prevention, 2005 Youth Risk Behavior Survey; data available at http://www.cdc.gov/yrbss.

Figure 1. Underage Use of Alcohol, 1991-2005.

These figures represent absolute declines of 4.8, 7.5, and 7.9 percentage points, respectively, since 1997. Still, underage drinking remains a far more prevalent problem than the use of illicit drugs or tobacco products. According to Monitoring the Future, U.S. high school seniors are 50% more likely to have consumed alcohol more than once than to have ever tried illicit drugs or to have smoked tobacco [9].

There are an estimated 10.8 million underage drinkers in the United States. More than 2.0 million are classified as heavy drinkers, and nearly 7.2 million are classified as binge drinkers, meaning that they have had more than five drinks on one occasion [10]. Rates of alcohol consumption differ by gender among individuals aged 12-20. In 2006, drinking was more common among boys than girls in this age category, with males reporting more current alcohol use (29.2% vs. 27.4% for girls), more frequent binge drinking (21.3% vs. 16.5%), and more frequent heavy drinking (7.9% vs. 4.3%). Racial and ethnic differences were also evident. Rates of binge drinking were highest among American Indian/Alaskan Native (23.6%) and white youth (22.7%), followed by Hispanic youth (16.5%), Asian American youth (11.8%), and African American youth (8.6%) [11]

Underage drinking varies by geographic region. Since 2002, it has been higher in the Northeast (32.0%) and Midwest (29.7%) than in the West (28.1%) and South (25.8%) [12]. According to the most recent NSDUH data, underage drinking rates in 2006 were similar in small metropolitan (28.9%), large metropolitan (27.8%), and non-metropolitan areas (29. 1%) [13]. Unlike in previous years, the rate in rural areas has increased to 28.2% and now exceeds the underage drinking rate seen in large metropolitan areas [14].

While NSDUH and YRBS ask many similar questions regarding underage drinking, the Youth Risk Behavior Survey includes several unique, noteworthy findings. Among high school students surveyed in 2005, 26% had their first alcoholic drink before age 13; one in three had ridden with a driver who had been drinking alcohol; and over the course of the past month, 10% had consumed alcohol while operating a motor vehicle, and 4.3% had done so while on school property [15]

LEGAL PERSPECTIVES

The 21st Amendment to the U.S. Constitution gives states the primary authority to regulate the sale and distribution of alcohol within their borders. Hence, most underage drinking prevention laws are passed by states. Today, all states have set the minimum legal drinking at age 21 and have passed zero-tolerance laws that make it illegal for people under age 21 to drive after drinking any alcohol. Despite their demonstrated benefits, legal drinking age laws and zero- tolerance laws generally have not been vigorously enforced [16]. Alcohol purchase laws aimed at sellers and buyers also can be effective, but experts believe that more resources need to be made available for enforcing these laws [17]

Online Sales of Alcohol

Millions of minors either buy alcohol online or know an underage friend who does, according to an April 2006 study conducted by Teen Research Unlimited (TRU) [18]. This survey analyzed a nationally representative sample of youth. Its finding suggest that at least 551,000 individuals (2%) aged 14-20 have purchased alcohol over the Internet; 3.1 million minors (12%) in this age bracket report having at least one friend who has purchased alcohol online. Moreover, nearly 8.9 million Americans (33%) aged 14-20 believe it is possible that they will make an online alcohol purchase before age 21.

The Wine and Spirits Wholesalers of America (WSWA), a trade association representing U.S. alcohol wholesalers, argues that the TRU study underscores the dangers of permitting wine and other alcoholic beverages to be sold online. It is important to note that WSWA has a vested interest in limiting Internet sales of alcohol and ensuring that wine and liquor continue to be sent from distillers or brewers to the distributors it represents, not to the doorsteps of consumers—be they adults or teenagers. The TRU numbers suggest that in 2004 only 9% of teens had visited a website that sells alcohol. However, this 9% figure may be more substantial than is initially evident. Because only 34% of survey respondents reported knowing that it was "possible to purchase alcohol online," another way to frame this finding is that more than 25% of 14-to-20- year-olds who knew alcohol could be purchased via the Internet visited websites that sell beer, wine, or liquor.

Viewed in this light, the TRU study's estimate that 68% of 14-to-20-year-olds report that their parents make no attempt to control online activity, and the report that 75% say their parents are unable to control what they do online, leads some analysts to believe that more minors can be expected to purchase alcohol online in the future [19]. This suggestion is consistent with a 2003 report by the Institute of Medicine, which found that underage individuals are increasingly buying alcohol online and concluded that greater use of the Internet in the future will likely exacerbate this problem [20]. It is also supported by the significant number of teenagers who are being given credit/debit cards by their parents (or guardians) [21]

In recent years, state and national policy makers have proposed restrictions on home delivery of alcohol ordered from Internet sites. It is unclear, however, whether debates over alcohol sales from the Internet are driven primarily by the desire to reduce youth access to alcohol, because prohibitions of home delivery from local retail outlets have not been included in the policy debates on Internet sales. This omission has led some political observers to conclude that policy attention to Internet sales of alcohol may reflect the varying economic interests of local versus national alcohol distributors and retailers—rather than concerns about teen access to alcohol [22].

Judicial Activity Regarding Internet Wine Sales

In May 2005, the Supreme Court issued a 5-4 opinion in Granholm v. Heald (03-1116) 544 U.S. 460 (2005), and consolidated cases [23]. This opinion held that Michigan's and New York's regulatory schemes, which permit in-state wineries to ship alcohol directly to consumers, but restrict the ability of out-of-state wineries to do so, violate the Constitution's Commerce Clause. While the facts of these cases involved wine sales, the Court's opinion has made it more difficult for states to regulate businesses that engage in Internet-based commerce.

At issue was the 21st Amendment, which ended Prohibition in 1933 and granted states the authority to regulate alcohol sales. Nearly half the states subsequently passed laws requiring out- of-state wineries to sell their products through licensed in-state wholesalers, resulting in millions of dollars in state alcohol taxes. However, the Commerce Clause generally prohibits state laws that unreasonably discriminate against out-of-state businesses. That led to the challenges to the Michigan and New York laws.

Justice Anthony Kennedy, who wrote the majority opinion, stated, "States have broad power to regulate liquor. This power, however, does not allow States to ban, or severely limit, the direct shipment of out-of-state wine while simultaneously authorizing direct shipment by in-state producers." The Majority continued, "The differential treatment between in-state and out-of-state wineries constitutes explicit discrimination against interstate commerce," that is "neither authorized nor permitted by the Twenty-first Amendment." Justice Kennedy's opinion was joined by Justices Antonin Scalia, David H. Souter, Ruth Bader Ginsburg, and Stephen G. Breyer.

New York and Michigan defended their laws as necessary to prevent underage drinkers from buying wine without having to show proper proof of age, as well as to prevent tax evasion. The majority rejected these arguments, finding that the states "provide little concrete evidence for the sweeping assertion that they cannot police direct shipments by out-of-state wineries." Justice Kennedy also said that the states' concerns did not justify discrimination. "Minors are just as likely to order wine from in-state producers as from out-of-state ones."

Moreover, he noted, minors are no more likely to purchase and consume wine than beer or wine coolers or hard liquor. Finally, the Majority asserted that minors who choose to disobey laws governing alcohol purchase/consumption have more direct means of gaining access to alcohol than methods that involve direct shipping.

Given the decision in *Granholm*, it is anticipated that any effort to regulate online sales of alcohol will face considerable political and legal hurdles, because the Court has ostensibly ruled that the only way to limit Internet sales of alcohol is to treat out-of-state direct sellers (such as Internet- based sales) and in-state direct sellers equally [24]

POLICY PERSPECTIVES

Legislative Activity

At the federal level, legislative activity has been aimed primarily at coordinating and supporting the states' efforts. The following underage drinking prevention laws have been passed since the 106th Congress:

- Sober Truth on Preventing Underage Drinking Act (STOP Act), 2006: Mandates the Secretary of Health and Human Services to formally enhance the efforts of the Interagency Coordinating Committee on the Prevention of Underage Drinking [25]
- Science, State, Justice, Commerce, and Related Agencies Appropriations Act, 2006: [26] Provides $25 million for grants to states to enforce minimum drinking age laws, and for technical assistance.
- Consolidated Appropriations Act, 2005: [27] Provides $25 million for grants to states to enforce minimum drinking age laws, and for technical assistance.
- No Child Left Behind Act, 2001: [28] Authorizes the Substance Abuse and Mental Health Services Administration to award grants to local educational agencies to develop and implement programs to reduce alcohol abuse in secondary schools.
- National Police Athletic League Youth Enrichment Act, 2000: [29] Provides for expansion of Police Athletic League Chapters to conduct underage drinking prevention activities in non-school hours.
- District of Columbia Appropriations Act, 2001: [30] Provides $25 million for grants to states to enforce minimum drinking age laws, and for technical assistance.
- Missing, Exploited, and Runaway Children Protection Act, 1999: [31] Provides funding for community-based alcohol and drug abuse prevention and education services to street youth.

Although no legislation directly addressing the sale of alcohol over the Internet has been signed into law, the 106th Congress did consider a bill that indirectly dealt with this topic: S. 577, the Twenty-First Amendment Enforcement Act. Introduced by Senator Orrin Hatch (R-UT), this bill would have amended the Webb-Kenyon Act to authorize a state attorney general to deal with the consequences of new distribution channels for the sale of alcohol. S.577 was concerned with "the interstate sale of alcohol," which included purchases made on the Internet and delivered by direct mail. By permitting states to bring actions in federal court for violation of state alcohol laws, it sought to give state attorneys more power to enforce underage drinking laws and to ensure payment of state and local taxes on the sale of alcohol.

In addition, Senator Dianne Feinstein (D-CA) inserted into The Violent and Repeat Juvenile Offender Accountability and Rehabilitation Act of 1999 (S. 254/H.R. 1501, 106th Congress) a provision that would have amended liquor trafficking prohibitions to (1) require persons who ship alcoholic beverages in interstate commerce to label the packages as containing alcohol, (2) require shipping companies to obtain the signature of the person receiving delivery of packages containing alcohol, and (3) verify that that person is of legal age for the purchase of alcohol beverages within the receiving state. None of the aforementioned bills from the 106th Congress were signed into law.

Following the release of the Acting Surgeon General's *Call to Action to Prevent and Reduce Underage Drinking* (March 2007), [32] the 110th Congress has considered one bill directly addressing alcohol consumption by minors: H.R. 4453, the Underage Drinking Prevention Act of 2007.

Sponsored by Representative Edolphus Towns (D-NY), this bill proposes a grant program to support enforcement of laws that prohibit underage drinking, to improve the collection and reporting of data on underage drinking, and to establish dedicated funding designed to increase parental involvement in school-based efforts to reduce alcohol consumption. H.R. 4453, however, does not address the commercial aspects of alcohol sales to minors. Rather, it concerns itself primarily with situations where minors are consuming alcohol that has been garnered by consenting parents or other adults. H.R. 4453 was referred to the House Committees on Education and Labor, and Energy and Commerce on December 11, 2007.

Institute of Medicine Recommendations

The 2003 Institute of Medicine (IOM) report on reducing underage drinking concluded that underage drinking cannot be successfully addressed by focusing on youth alone [33]. Because minors "usually obtain alcohol—directly or indirectly—from adults," the IOM contended, efforts to reduce drinking among teens should also be aimed at adults and industry. The IOM's recommendations, discussed below, included community-based interventions and policy options to limit or prevent underage alcohol consumption.

Prohibit Alcohol Advertisements from Targeting Youth

Long-term exposure to alcohol advertising and promotion increases the likelihood that children will drink. The IOM has called on the alcohol and entertainment industries to shield youth from unsuitable messages about drinking by ensuring that programs do not portray underage drinking in a favorable light. The IOM also suggested that Congress consider restrictions on the alcohol industry, analogous to those placed on the tobacco companies, to prevent marketing practices that disproportionately appeal to minors.

Increase Alcohol Prices Through Excise Taxes

The current tax on alcohol has not kept pace with inflation, observed the IOM, thus reducing the real price of alcohol over time. Thus, alcoholic beverages are cheaper today in real dollars than they were in the 1960s and 1970s. Research indicates that increases in alcohol price are associated with decreased underage drinking.34 Increasing excise taxes on alcohol, according to the IOM, could provide revenue for strategies to reduce underage drinking [35]

Public Awareness

Educating the public about the consequences of underage drinking, as well as the existing laws regarding alcohol consumption by minors, could curtail underage drinking. The IOM recommended that the federal government fund and support development of a national media effort as a major component of an adult-oriented campaign to reduce underage drinking. For these public education efforts to be effective, said the IOM, they would need to be combined with better enforcement of existing laws.

Enforcement

The IOM suggested that states or the federal government could consider criminalizing the use of falsified or fraudulent identification in an attempt to purchase alcoholic beverages, as well as criminalizing the provision of any alcohol to minors by adults, except to their own children in their own residences.

REFERENCES

[1]   U.S. Department of Health and Human Services, *The Surgeon General's Call to Action to Prevent and Reduce Underage Drinking*, United States Department of Health and Human Services, Office of the Surgeon General, 2007, at http://www.surgeon general.gov/topics/underagedrinking/calltoaction.pdf.

[2]   U.S. Department of Health and Human Services Press Office, *Acting Surgeon General Issues National Call to Action on Underage Drinking*, Office of the Surgeon General, March 6, 2007, at http://www.hhs.gov/news/press/2007pres/ 20070306.html.

[3]   Susan E. Foster et al., "Alcohol Consumption and Expenditure for Underage Drinking and Adult Excessive Drinking," *Journal of the American Medical Association*, vol. 289, no. 8 (2003), pp. 989-95.

[4]   Office of Applied Studies, "Emergency Department Visits Involving Underage Drinking," The New DAWN Report, Issue 1, Rockville, MD: SAMSHA, 2006, at https://dawninfo.samhsa.gov/files/tndr02underagedrinking.htm.

[5]   Excluding pain and suffering from these costs, the direct costs of underage drinking incurred exceed $20.3 billion each year; Ted R. Miller, David T. Levy, Rebecca S. Spicer, and Dexter M. Taylor, "Societal Costs of Underage Drinking," *Journal of Studies on Alcohol*, vol. 67 (2006), pp. 5 19-528.

[6]   For alcohol-related fatalities, the costs of pain and suffering were computed based on the monetary values that people ascribed in experimental settings to not being killed. Similarly, the pain and suffering costs of nonfatal injuries were based on the values associated with different dimensions of functioning, cognition, mobility, sensation, and

pain. Methodology details are outlined at http://www.udetc.org/documents/ UnderageMethods.pdf.

[7]   See http://www.cdc.gov/alcohol/quickstats/underage_drinking.htm.

[8]   Centers for Disease Control and Prevention, 2005, Youth Risk Behavior Survey, available at http://www.cdc.gov/ yrbss.

[9]   Lloyd D. Johnston, Patrick M. O'Malley, Jerald G. Bachman, et al., *Monitoring the Future national survey results on drug use, 1975-2005. Volume I: Secondary school students*, NIH Publication No. 06-5883, Bethesda, MD: National Institute on Drug Abuse, 2006

[10] SAMHSA, *Results from the 2006 National Survey on Drug Use and Health: National Findings*, NSDUH Series H30, HHS Pub. No. SMA 06-4194. Rockville, MD: SAMHSA, Office of Applied Studies, 2006.

[11] NSDUH, 2006, at http://www.oas.samhsa.gov/nsduh/2k6nsduh/2k6Results.pdf.

[12] U.S. Census regions are defined as follows: Northeast—Maine, New Hampshire, Vermont, Massachusetts, Rhode Island, Connecticut, New York, New Jersey, Pennsylvania; Midwest—Ohio, Indiana, Illinois, Michigan, Wisconsin, Minnesota, Iowa, Missouri, North Dakota, South Dakota, Nebraska, Kansas; *South*—Delaware, Maryland, District of Columbia, Virginia, West Virginia, North Carolina, South Carolina, Georgia, Florida, Kentucky, Tennessee, Alabama, Mississippi, Arkansas, Louisiana, Oklahoma, Texas; West—Montana, Idaho, Wyoming, Colorado, New Mexico, Arizona, Utah, Nevada, Washington, Oregon, California, Alaska, Hawaii.

[13] Large metropolitan (large metro) areas have a population of 1 million or more. Small metropolitan (small metro) areas have a population fewer than 1 million, but more than 2,500. Nonmetropolitan (nonmetro) areas are outside of "metropolitan statistical areas," which are geographic clusters defined by the United States Census Bureau that have 2,500 or more individuals and include either a city of at least 50,000 people or an urbanized area of at least 100,000 people.

[14] NSDUH , 2006, at http://www.oas.samhsa.gov/nsduh/2k6nsduh/2k6Results.pdf.

[15] Centers for Disease Control and Prevention, *2005 Youth Risk Behavior Survey*, 2005.

[16] Ralph K. Jones and John H. Lacey, *Alcohol and Highway Safety 2001: A Review of the State of Knowledge*, DOT HS 809 383, Washington, DC: National Highway Traffic Safety Administration, 2001, at http://www.nhtsa.dot.gov/people/injury/research/ AlcoholHighway.

[17] David F. Preusser, A.F. Williams, and H.B. Weinstein, "Policing Underage Alcohol Sales," *Journal of Safety Research*, vol. 25, pp. 127-133, 1994.

[18] David Carney, "Supreme Court Rules in Internet Wine Sales Case," *Tech Law Journal*, May 17, 2005, available at http://www.techlawjournal.com/alert/2005/05/17.asp.

[19] Richard J. Bonnie and Mary Ellen O'Connell (eds.), *Reducing Underage Drinking: A Collective Responsibility*, Institute of Medicine, Committee on Developing a Strategy to Reduce and Prevent Underage Drinking, Washington, DC: National Research Council and the Institute of Medicine, 2003, at http://www.nap.edu/catalog/10729.html.

[20] In 2005, 11.1% of teens had their own credit cards. Credit card ownership increases steadily with age. Only 6.2% of teens aged 13-14 own credit cards, compared with 13.1% of teens aged 17. Among teens 18 years of age and older, 20.5% have their own credit cards. See the Junior Achievement Interprise Poll on *Teens and Personal*

Finance 2005, April 4, 2005, at http://www.ja.org/files/polls/personal_finance_ 2005.pdf.

[21]   Kelli A. Komro and Traci L. Toomey, "Strategies to Prevent Underage Drinking," *Alcohol Research & Health*, vol. 26, no. 1 (2002), pp. 5-14.

[22]   When two or more cases have common questions of law or arise of a common dispute, the Court may "consolidate" such cases and hear them simultaneously. In this instance, the Court consolidated *Granholm v. Heald* (03-1116), *Michigan Beer & Wine Wholesalers v. Heald* (03-1120), and *Swedenburg v. Kelly* (03-1274)18 This study was funded by the Wine and Spirits Wholesalers of America, Inc.

[23]   Carney, "Supreme Court Rules in Internet Wine Sales Case," May 17, 2005.

[24]   P.L. 109-422, Sec. 2(c)(1), 120 Stat. 2891

[25]   P.L. 109-108, Sec. 5(c), 119 Stat. 2300.

[26]   P.L. 108-447, Sec. 2, Division B, Title I, 118 Stat. 2866.

[27]   P.L. 107-110, Title IV, Sec. 4129, 115 Stat. 1757.

[28]   P.L. 106-367, Sec. 6(a)(2)(B)(I), 114 Stat. 1414.

[29]   P.L. 106-553, Appendix B, Title I, 114, Stat. 2762A-65. P.L. 106-553.

[30]   P.L. 106-71, Sec. 3(b)(1), 113 Stat. 1042.

[31]   U.S. Department of Health and Human Services, 2007, at http://www.surgeon general.gov/topics/underagedrinking/ calltoaction.pdf

[32]   Richard J. Bonnie and Mary Ellen O'Connell (eds.), *Reducing Underage Drinking: A Collective Responsibility*, Institute of Medicine, Committee on Developing a Strategy to Reduce and Prevent Underage Drinking, Washington, DC: National Research Council and the Institute of Medicine, 2003, available at http://www.nap.edu/catalog/ 10729.html.

[33]   Frank J. Chaloupka, Michael Grossman, and Henry Saffer, "The effects of price on alcohol consumption and alcohol-related problems," *Alcohol Research and Health*, vol. 26, no. 1, pp. 22-34, 2002.

[34]   If this policy option were pursued, the IOM emphasized that alcohol taxes would have to be indexed to the consumer price index to ensure that they keep pace with inflation.

In: Alcohol and Drug Use among Youth
Editor: Agatha M. Pichler

ISSN: 978-1-61209-084-9
© 2012 Nova Science Publishers, Inc.

Chapter 2

QUANTITY AND FREQUENCY OF ALCOHOL USE AMONG UNDERAGE DRINKERS[*]

National Survey on Drug Use and Health

IN BRIEF

- Combined 2005 and 2006 data indicate that an annual average of 28.3 percent of persons aged 12 to 20 in the United States (an estimated 10.8 million persons annually) drank alcohol in the past month
- Past month alcohol users aged 12 to 20 drank on an average of 5.9 days in the past month and consumed an average of 4.9 drinks per day on the days they drank in the past month
- Underage drinkers aged 12 to 20 consumed, on average, more drinks per day on the days they drank in the past month than persons aged 21 or older (4.9 vs. 2.8 drinks)

In 2006, a majority (53.9 percent) of American adolescents and young adults aged 12 to 20 had used an alcoholic beverage at least once in their lifetime [1]. Young people aged 12 to 20 consumed approximately 11.2 percent of the alcoholic drinks consumed in the United States in the past month by persons aged 12 or older [2]. Research shows that underage drinkers tend to consume more alcohol per occasion than those over the legal minimum drinking age of 21 [3]. Studies also have linked early drinking to heavy alcohol consumption and alcohol-related problems in adulthood [4,5]. For example, in 2006, 16.3 percent of adults aged 21 or older who had first used alcohol before the age of 15 met the criteria for alcohol dependence or abuse in the past year compared with 2.4 percent of adults who first used alcohol at age 21 or older [6]. Research also shows that early initiation of alcohol use is asso-ciated with higher likelihood of involvement in violent behaviors, suicide attempts, unprotected sexual intercourse, and multiple sex partners [7,8]

---

[*] This is an edited, reformatted and augmented version of a National Survey on Drug Use and Health Report, dated March 31, 2008.

The National Survey on Drug Use and Health (NSDUH) asks persons aged 12 or older to report the frequency and quantity of their alcohol use during the 30 days prior to the interview. Respondents who drank alcohol in the past 30 days also are asked for the number of days they consumed alcohol in the past month and the average number of drinks consumed per day on the days they drank [9].

This report focuses on the frequency and quantity of past month alcohol use among underage drinkers (i.e., persons aged 12 to 20 who consume alcohol). Comparisons of the quantity and frequency of alcohol use in the past month also are made between underage drinkers and drinkers aged 21 or older. All findings presented in this report are based on combined 2005 and 2006 NSDUH data.

PAST MONTH ALCOHOL USE

Combined 2005 and 2006 data indicate that an annual average of 28.3 percent of persons aged 12 to 20 in the United States (an estimated 10.8 million persons annually) drank alcohol in the past month. Rates of past month alcohol use among persons aged 12 to 20 varied by demographic characteristics. Young adults aged 18 to 20 were 3 times as likely as youths aged 12 to 17 to have used alcohol in the past month (51.4 vs. 16.6 percent) (Table 1). Underage males were more likely than their female counterparts to have drunk alcohol in the past month (29.1 vs. 27.5 percent). Across racial/ethnic groups, the rate of past month alcohol use among persons aged 12 to 20 ranged from 17.6 percent among Asians to 32.3 percent among whites [10]

Table 1. Percentages of Past Month Alcohol Use among Persons Aged 12 to 20, by Demographic Characteristics: 2005-2006

Demographic Characteristic	Past Month Alcohol Use	
	%	SE*
Total Aged 12 to 20	28.3	0.31
Age Group		
12 to 17	16.6	0.23
18 to 20	51.4	0.58
Gender		
Male	29.1	0.39
Female	27.5	0.40
*Race/Ethnicity**￼		
White	32.3	0.39
Black or African American	18.8	0.58
American Indian or Alaska Native	26.4	2.43
Native Hawaiian or Other Pacific Islander	18.0	3.76
Asian	17.6	1.59
Two or More Races	25.7	1.82
Hispanic or Latino	25.6	0.69

Source: SAMHSA, 2005 and 2006 NSDUHs.

• Standard error (SE) is a measure of the sampling variability or precision of an estimate, where smaller values represent greater precision and larger values represent less precision.
•• See End Note 10.

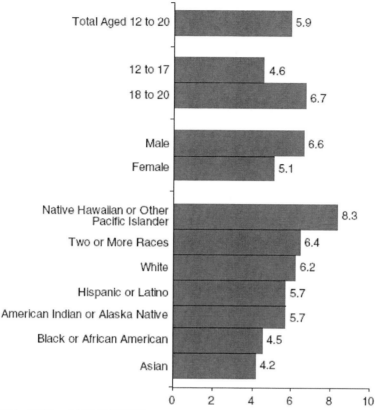

Source: SAMHSA, 2005 and 2006 NSDUHs.

Figure 1. Average Number of Days of Alcohol Use in the Past Month among Past Month Alcohol Users Aged 12 to 20, by Demographic Characteristics: 2005-2006.

NUMBER OF DAYS OF ALCOHOL USE IN THE PAST MONTH

Past month alcohol users aged 12 to 20 drank on an average of 5.9 days in the past month (Figure 1). Underage drinkers aged 18 to 20 consumed alcohol on more days in the past month than those aged 12 to 17 (6.7 vs. 4.6 days). Male underage drinkers used alcohol on more days in the past month than their female counterparts (6.6 vs. 5.1 days). The number of days of alcohol use in the past month varied by race/ethnicity, ranging from an average of 4.2 days among Asians to an average of 8.3 days in the past month among Native Hawaiians or Other Pacific Islanders.

NUMBER OF DRINKS PER DAY IN THE PAST MONTH

Past month alcohol users aged 12 to 20 consumed an average of 4.9 drinks per day on the days they drank in the past month (Figure 2). The average number of drinks consumed per day varied by demographic characteristics. Past month alcohol users aged 18 to 20 averaged more drinks per day than their counterparts aged 12 to 17 (5.2 vs. 4.5 drinks). Among underage past month alcohol users, males consumed an average of 5.8 drinks per day on the days they drank in the past month, and females consumed an average of 4.0 drinks per day on the days they drank. Among underage past month drinkers, the average number of drinks consumed per day ranged from 2.8 drinks per day among blacks to 6.4 drinks per day among Native Hawaiians or Other Pacific Islanders.2008

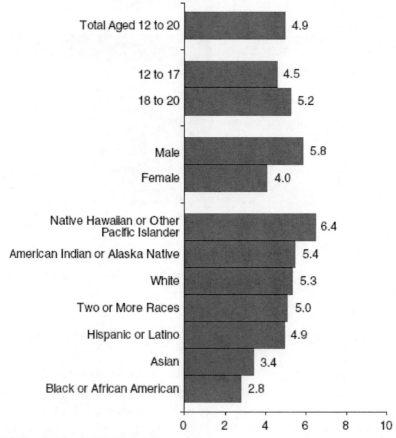

Source: SAMHSA, 2005 and 2006 NSDUHs.

Figure 2. Average Number of Drinks Consumed per Day on the Days Used Alcohol in the Past Month among Past Month Alcohol Users Aged 12 to 20, by Demographic Characteristics: 2005-2006.

UNDERAGE DRINKERS VERSUS DRINKERS OF LEGAL AGE

Among past month alcohol users, drinkers aged 21 or older averaged more days of alcohol consumption in the past month than underage drinkers (8.7 vs. 5.9 days). However, underage drinkers consumed, on average, more drinks per day on the days they drank in the past month than drinkers aged 21 or older (4.9 vs. 2.8 drinks).

RESEARCH FINDINGS FROM THE SAMHSA 2005 AND 2006 NATIONAL SURVEYS ON DRUG USE AND HEALTH (NSDUHS)

- Combined 2005 and 2006 data indicate that an annual average of 28.3 percent of persons aged 12 to 20 in the United States (an estimated 10.8 million persons annually) drank alcohol in the past month
- Past month alcohol users aged 12 to 20 drank on an average of 5.9 days in the past month and consumed an average of 4.9 drinks per day on the days they drank in the past month
- Underage drinkers aged 12 to 20 consumed, on average, more drinks per day on the days they drank in the past month than persons aged 21 or older (4.9 vs. 2.8 drinks)

The National Survey on Drug Use and Health (NSDUH) is an annual survey sponsored by the Substance Abuse and Mental Health Services Administration (SAMHSA). The 2005 and 2006 data used in this report are based on information obtained from 62,602 persons aged 12 to 20. The survey collects data by administering questionnaires to a representative sample of the population through face-to-face interviews at their place of residence.

The NSDUH Report is prepared by the Office of Applied Studies (OAS), SAMHSA, and by RTI International in Research Triangle Park, North Carolina. (RTI International is a trade name of Research Triangle Institute.)

Information on the most recent NSDUH is available in the following publication:

Office of Applied Studies. (2007). Results from the 2006 National Survey on Drug Use and Health: National findings (DHHS Publication No. SMA 07-4293, NSDUH Series H-32). Rockville, MD: Substance Abuse and Mental Health Services Administration.

Information for the earlier NSDUH is available in the following publication:

2005 NSDUH: (DHHS Publication No. SMA 06-4194, NSDUH Series H-30).

Also available online: http://oas.samhsa.gov.

Because of improvements and modifications to the 2002 NSDUH, estimates from the 2002 through 2006 surveys should not be compared with estimates from the 2001 or earlier versions of the survey to examine changes over time.

U.S. DEPARTMENT OF HEALTH & HUMAN SERVICES

END NOTES

[1] Office of Applied Studies. (2007). *Results from the 2006 National Survey on Drug Use and Health: National findings* (DHHS Publication No. SMA 07-4293, NSDUH Series H-32). Rockville, MD: Substance Abuse and Mental HealthServices Administration.

[2] Office of Applied Studies, Substance Abuse and Mental Health Services Administration. (2006, September 28). Table 7.7B: Alcohol use in the past month and measures of past month alcohol consumption, by detailed age category: 2005. Retrieved March 13, 2008, fromhttp://oas.samhsa.gov/NSDUH/2k5NSDUH/tabs/Sect7peTabs1to66.htm#Tab7.7B.

[3] Institute of Medicine (Bonnie, R. J., & O'Connell, M. E., Eds.). (2004). Reducing underage drinking: A collective responsibility. Washington, DC: The National Academies Press. [Available at http://www.nap.edu/catalog.php?record_id=10729]

[4] Hingson, R. W., Heeren, T., Zakocs, R. C., Kopstein, A., & Wechsler, H. (2002). Magnitude of alcohol-related mortality and morbidity among U.S. college students ages 18-24. *Journal of Studies on Alcohol*, 63(2), 136-144.

[5] Grant, B. F., Stinson, F. S, & Harford, T. C. (2001). Age at onset of alcohol use and DSM–IV alcohol abuse and dependence: A 12-year follow-up. *Journal of Substance Abuse,* 13, 493-504.

[6] Office of Applied Studies, Substance Abuse and Mental Health Services Administration. (2007, October 18). Table 7.36B: Alcohol dependence or abuse in the past year among persons aged 21 or older, by age first used alcohol and age group: Percentages, 2005 and 2006. Retrieved March 13, 2008, from http://oas.samhsa.gov/NSDUH/2K6NSDUH/tabs/Sect7peTabs1to47.htm#Tab7.36B

[7] Swahn, M. H., Bossarte, R. M., & Sullivent, E. E.,3rd (2008). Age of alcohol use initiation, suicidal behavior, and peer and dating violence victimization and perpetration among high-risk, seventh-grade adolescents. *Pediatrics,* 121, 297-305.

[8] Stueve, A.,& O'Donnell, L. N. (2005). Early alcohol initiation and subsequent sexual and alcohol risk behaviors among urban youths. *American Journal of Public Health*, 95, 887-893.

[9] Respondents with unknown or missing information regarding the number of alcoholic drinks consumed per day on the days that they drank were excluded from this analysis.

[10] Race/ethnicity categories are determined by combining the responses from two separate questions. For this report, respondents identifying themselves as Hispanic were assigned to the Hispanic group regardless of their racial identification. Respondents identifying themselves as non-Hispanic were grouped according to their racial identification. Thus, "white" refers to those identifying themselves as non-Hispanic and white.

In: Alcohol and Drug Use among Youth
Editor: Agatha M. Pichler

ISSN: 978-1-61209-084-9
© 2012 Nova Science Publishers, Inc.

Chapter 3

UNDERAGE ALCOHOL USE: FINDINGS FROM THE 2002-2006 NATIONAL SURVEYS ON DRUG USE AND HEALTH[*]

Michael R. Pemberton, James D. Colliver, Tania M. Robbins and Joseph C. Gfroerer

HIGHLIGHTS

Alcohol is the drug of choice among young people in the United States, and alcohol use constitutes one of the principal public health issues for this population. Approximately 5,000 persons under 21 years of age lose their lives each year as a result of underage drinking, and early initiation of alcohol use is associated with increased risk of subsequent alcohol use disorders and increased risk of involvement in violent behaviors, suicide attempts, and a variety of other problematic activities. In response to this issue, this study presents findings from the 2002 to 2006 National Surveys on Drug Use and Health (NSDUHs) on the use of alcohol by persons aged 12 to 20.

NSDUH is an annual survey of the civilian, noninstitutionalized population of the United States aged 12 or older. The survey is sponsored by the Substance Abuse and Mental Health Services Administration (SAMHSA) of the U.S. Department of Health and Human Services and is planned and managed by SAMHSA's Office of Applied Studies (OAS). Data collection is conducted under contract with RTI[1] International, Research Triangle Park, North Carolina.1 Selected key findings from this study are described below.

---

[1] RTI International is a trade name of Research Triangle Institute.

[*] This is an edited, reformatted and augmented version of the Department of Health and Human Services, Substance Abuse and Mental Health Services Administration Office of Applied Studies, dated June 2008.

Prevalence of Underage Drinking Behaviors in 2006

- In 2006, more than half (53.9 percent) of persons aged 12 to 20 (20.6 million persons) had used alcohol in their lifetime, almost half (46.1 percent, 17.6 million) had used it in the past year, and more than a quarter (28.3 percent, 10.8 million) had used it in the past month (current use). One in five persons in this age group (19.0 percent, 7.2 million) engaged in binge alcohol use, meaning they had consumed five or more drinks of alcohol on at least one occasion in the past month. This includes 2.4 million (6.2 percent of persons aged 12 to 20) who drank heavily, defined as 5 or more days of binge alcohol use in the past month.

Trends in Underage Current and Binge Drinking

- Between 2002 and 2006, rates of current and binge drinking among those aged 12 to 20 remained stable. Current use among underage persons was 28.8 percent in 2002 and 28.3 percent in 2006, while binge use was 19.3 percent in 2002 and 19.0 percent in 2006.
- There were varying trends by age. Among youths aged 12 to 14, there was no change in current or binge alcohol use between 2002 and 2006, but past year use declined from 17.6 to 16.2 percent. Among 15 to 17 year olds, the rates declined from 2002 to 2006 for past year use (from 52.3 to 48.7 percent) and current use (from 28.3 to 26.1 percent), but binge use remained stable. There were no changes for 18 to 20 year olds in any of these alcohol use measures from 2002 to 2006.

Sociodemographic and Geographic Differences in Underage Drinking

- Combined data from 2002 to 2006 indicated that rates of current (past month) alcohol use were 7.0 percent for youths aged 12 to 14, 27.5 percent for youths aged 15 to 17, and 51.3 percent for 18 to 20 year olds. Binge alcohol use rates for these age groups were 3.3, 17.8, and 36.3 percent, respectively.
- Underage males were more likely than underage females to be current alcohol users (29.4 percent for males, 27.8 percent for females) and binge drinkers (21.6 percent for males, 16.5 percent for females). Among youths aged 12 to 14, the rate of current drinking was higher for females (7.7 percent) than males (6.3 percent), but there was no gender difference in the rate of binge drinking. For those aged 15 to 17, males and females did not differ in the rate of current alcohol use, but binge drinking was higher for males than females (19.0 vs. 16.5 percent). Among those aged 18 to 20, males had higher rates of current and binge drinking than females.
- Past month underage alcohol use was higher among non-Hispanic whites (32.6 percent) than Hispanics (25.7 percent), who in turn had a higher rate than blacks (18.8 percent). Underage current drinking rates were 27.2 percent among American Indians or Alaska Natives and 17.1 percent among Asians.

- One third (33.9 percent) of persons aged 12 to 20 whose family income was less than $20,000 consumed alcohol in the past month, higher than the rate among those with a family income in any category over $20,000. The rate of current alcohol use among underage persons in the highest income category ($75,000 or more) was 28.6 percent, higher than the rate for those with a family income of $20,000 to $49,999 (26.0 percent) and $50,000 to $74,999 (26.4 percent). A similar pattern was found for binge drinking.
- Underage persons who lived in nonmetropolitan areas were more likely than those who lived in metropolitan areas to engage in binge drinking (20.8 percent in nonmetropolitan areas, 18.8 percent in metropolitan areas). The rate of current drinking among underage persons was 29.4 percent among those who lived in nonmetropolitan areas and 28.5 percent among those who lived in metropolitan areas, though this difference was not statistically significant.
- Among underage persons who lived in metropolitan areas, the prevalence of current drinking was higher for non-Hispanic whites (33.2 percent) than for Hispanics (25.3 percent). Among those who lived in rural areas, however, Hispanics had a higher prevalence of current drinking (32.4 percent) than whites (28.9 percent).

Rates of current and binge alcohol use among 12 to 20 year olds were higher in the Northeast and Midwest than in the South or West. For example, 21.4 percent of those in the Northeast and 21.8 percent of those in the Midwest engaged in binge drinking compared with 17.3 percent of those in the South and 17.8 percent of those in the West. Among the 10 States with the highest rates of binge drinking, 4 were in the Midwest (Iowa, North Dakota, South Dakota, and Wisconsin), and 4 were in the Northeast (Massachusetts, New Hampshire, Rhode Island, and Vermont).

Alcohol Use Disorders among Persons Aged 12 to 20

- Combined data from 2002 to 2006 indicated that an annual average of 9.4 percent of persons aged 12 to 20 (3.5 million persons in that age range) met the diagnostic criteria for an alcohol use disorder (dependence or abuse) in the past year.
- Among all persons aged 12 to 20, a higher percentage of males (10.3 percent) than females (8.5 percent) had an alcohol use disorder, though this pattern varied by age group. Among youths aged 12 to 14, a higher percentage of females (2.2 percent) than males (1.6 percent) were classified with an alcohol use disorder. In contrast, among 18 to 20 year olds, a higher percentage of males (19.6 percent) than females (13.4 percent) were classified with an alcohol use disorder.
- The rate of past year alcohol use disorder among persons aged 12 to 20 was higher for American Indians or Alaska Natives (14.9 percent) than for whites (10.9 percent), blacks (4.6 percent), Hispanics (8.7 percent), and Asians (4.9 percent). One in eight Native Hawaiians or Other Pacific Islanders (12.7 percent) met the criteria for an alcohol use disorder.

Association of Underage Drinking with Parental Alcohol Use

- Rates of current and binge alcohol use among underage persons were higher among persons aged 12 to 20 who lived with a mother or father who had consumed alcohol in the past year compared with those who lived with a mother or father who had not consumed alcohol in the past year. For example, rates of binge drinking among underage persons were 17.6 percent for those whose mother was a past year drinker versus 9.3 percent for those whose mother was not a past year drinker, and 16.5 percent for those whose father was a past year drinker versus 10.2 percent for those whose father was not a past year drinker. Rates of underage binge drinking were also higher among those aged 12 to 20 who lived with a mother (21.3 percent) or father (19.5 percent) who was a binge drinker than among those whose mother (17.5 percent) or father (15.4 percent) was a current drinker but not a binge drinker.

Social Context of Last Alcohol Use

- In 2006, 80.9 percent of persons aged 12 to 20 who had consumed alcohol in the past month were with two or more people the last time they drank alcohol, 14.3 percent were with one other person the last time they drank, and 4.9 percent were alone. Underage persons who drank with two or more other people on the last occasion in the past month had more drinks on the last occasion on average (4.9 drinks) than those who drank with one other person (3.1 drinks) or those who drank alone (2.9 drinks).

Among current drinkers, youths aged 12 to 14 were more likely to have been alone (9.0 percent) or with one other person (21.9 percent) the last time they drank compared with youths aged 15 to 17 (5.2 percent alone and 14.6 percent with one other person) or 18 to 20 year olds (4.2 percent alone and 13.2 percent with one other person)

Location of Last Alcohol Use

- A majority of underage current drinkers in 2006 reported that when they last used alcohol they were either in someone else's home (53.4 percent) or their own home (30.3 percent).
- Drinkers aged 12 to 14 were more likely to have been in their own home the last time they drank (38.8 percent) and less likely to have been in someone else's home (45.0 percent) compared with underage drinkers in older age groups (26.0 and 60.9 percent, respectively, for those aged 15 to 17, and 31.4 and 50.7 percent, respectively, for those aged 18 to 20). Drinkers aged 18 to 20 were more likely than those in younger age groups to have been in a restaurant, bar, or club on their last drinking occasion (12.9 percent for those aged 18 to 20 vs. 4.6 percent for those aged 12 to 14 and 3.7 percent for those aged 15 to 17).

Sources of Alcohol

- Among all underage current drinkers, 31.0 percent paid for the alcohol the last time they drank, including 9.3 percent who purchased the alcohol themselves and 21.6 percent who gave money to someone else to purchase it. Underage persons who paid for alcohol themselves consumed more drinks on their last drinking occasion (average of 5.9 drinks) than did those who did not pay for the alcohol themselves (average of 3.9 drinks).

- More than one in four underage drinkers (25.8 percent) indicated that on their last drinking occasion they were given alcohol for free by an unrelated person aged 21 or older. One in sixteen (6.4 percent) got the alcohol from a parent or guardian, 8.3 percent got it from another family member aged 21 or older, and 3.9 percent took it from their own home.

- Underage persons in older age groups were more likely to have paid for alcohol themselves on their last drinking occasion, with 37.6 percent of 18 to 20 year olds paying for it themselves compared with 23.5 percent of 15 to 17 year olds and 6.6 percent of 12 to 14 year olds. Among underage drinkers, males were more likely to have paid for alcohol themselves on their last drinking occasion (36.7 percent) than were females (24.5 percent).

Underage Drinking and Illicit Drug Use

- In 2006, more than one third (35.8 percent) of persons aged 12 to 20 who used alcohol in the past month also had used an illicit drug in the past month, and 16.0 percent of underage drinkers used an illicit drug within 2 hours of using alcohol on their last occasion of alcohol use.

Marijuana was the illicit drug most used by underage drinkers, with nearly one third (30.0 percent) having used marijuana in the past month, and 15.0 percent having used marijuana within 2 hours of their last alcohol use.

1. INTRODUCTION

This report presents findings from the 2002 to 2006 National Surveys on Drug Use and Health (NSDUHs) on the use of alcohol by persons aged 12 to 20, that is, those who are under the minimum legal age for alcohol use. NSDUH is an annual survey of the civilian, noninstitutionalized population of the United States aged 12 or older and is conducted by the Substance Abuse and Mental Health Services Administration (SAMHSA). This report examines trends in alcohol use from 2002 to 2006 among underage persons and variations in underage drinking and alcohol use disorders across demographic groups and geographic areas. The discussion is based on measures of alcohol use in the past month, past year, and lifetime included in NSDUH, as well as questions that allow for the classification of past year dependence on or abuse of alcohol. Findings also are presented from items added to the 2006

NSDUH regarding the social context and location of underage drinking, the sources for alcohol among underage drinkers, and the co-occurrence of underage alcohol use and illicit drug use.

1.1. Background

Alcohol is the drug of choice among young people in the United States, and alcohol use constitutes one of the principal public health issues for this population (National Institute on Alcohol Abuse and Alcoholism [NIAAA], 2006). Each year, approximately 5,000 young people under the age of 21 die as a result of underage drinking, including about 1,900 deaths from motor vehicle crashes (Hingson & Kenkel, 2004). Drinking drivers under age 21 are involved in fatal crashes at twice the rate of adult drivers (National Highway Traffic Safety Administration [NHTSA], 2002). Early initiation of alcohol use is associated with higher likelihood of involvement in violent behaviors, suicide attempts, unprotected sexual intercourse, and multiple sex partners (Stueve & O'Donnell, 2005; Swahn, Bossarte, & Sullivent, 2008).

In addition, early initiation of alcohol use has been linked to higher rates of alcohol dependence or abuse in later life (Grant & Dawson, 1997). In the 2006 NSDUH, for example, the rate of alcohol abuse or dependence among adults aged 21 or older was 2.4 percent for those who first used alcohol at age 21 or older compared with 9.6 percent among those who initiated alcohol use prior to age 21 and 16.3 percent among those who first used alcohol before age 15 (Office of Applied Studies [OAS], 2007a). An estimated 38.7 percent of adults age 21 or older with past year alcohol dependence or abuse initiated alcohol use before age 15 (OAS, 2007b).

Information from several national sources indicates that underage alcohol use is widespread. According to the 2006 NSDUH, about 10.8 million persons aged 12 to 20 (28.3 percent of this age group) reported drinking in the past month (OAS, 2007a). Approximately 7.2 million (19.0 percent) were binge drinkers (consumed five or more drinks at the same time or within a couple of hours of each other on at least 1 day in the past 30 days), and 2.4 million (6.2 percent) were heavy drinkers (five or more drinks on the same occasion on each of 5 or more days in the past 30 days). The percentage of underage persons reporting past month alcohol use was similar from 2002 to 2006, according to the 2006 NSDUH. The 2006 Monitoring the Future (MTF), a survey of 8th, 10th, and 12th graders that also includes a follow-up of persons who had participated in the survey as high school seniors, indicated that 17.2 percent of 8th graders, 33.8 percent of 10th graders, 45.3 percent of 12th graders, and 57.6 percent of those aged 19 or 20 had consumed alcohol in the past month (Johnston, O'Malley, Bachman, & Schulenberg, 2007a, 2007b). Furthermore, 6.2 percent of 8th graders indicated that they had been drunk in the past month, as did 18.8 percent of 10th graders, 30.0 percent of 12 graders, and 42.5 percent of those aged 19 or 20. Data from the Treatment Episode Data Set (TEDS) indicate that in 2006 there were over 61,000 admissions to substance abuse treatment among persons aged 12 to 20 in which alcohol was the primary substance of abuse, a number that represented 24.1 percent of all substance abuse treatment admissions for this age group (Substance Abuse and Mental Health Data Archive [SAMHDA], 2008).

Reduction of underage alcohol use has been highlighted as a top health priority of the Federal Government. In 2007, the Surgeon General issued a Call to Action to Prevent and Reduce Underage Drinking to highlight the nature and extent of underage drinking and to focus the attention of the public on this enduring problem (U.S. Department of Health and Human Services [DHHS], 2007). As part of SAMHSA's leadership role to coordinate the Federal effort to address this problem, the agency has issued A Comprehensive Plan for Preventing and Reducing Underage Drinking that outlines a detailed, goal-driven plan to reduce underage drinking (DHHS, 2006). Currently, SAMHSA sponsors two workgroups that address the underage drinking problem, one internal to SAMHSA and the other involving other agencies. SAMHSA's internal workgroup coordinates the agency's activities with regard to the prevention and treatment of alcohol-related problems and addresses such topics as the prevention of underage drinking, adolescent treatment, the prevention of excessive drinking by those of legal age, and alcohol treatment in general. The Interagency Coordinating Committee on the Prevention of Underage Drinking, which includes members from NIAAA, NHTSA, and other agencies in addition to SAMHSA, was responsible for developing SAMHSA's Report to Congress on the Prevention and Reduction of Underage Drinking.

This analytic series report, the first full-length NSDUH report to focus solely on underage drinking, complements these recent and ongoing efforts. NSDUH's large sample of the population aged 12 to 20 (more than 158,000 respondents in this age range from 2002 to 2006 combined), its inclusion of items to measure alcohol use and alcohol use disorders, and the added items on the context, location, and co-occurrence of alcohol use and illicit drug use make the survey a unique source of data to address the issue of underage alcohol use. NSDUH provides estimates that are representative at both the national level and within each State. It has sufficient sample size to examine the prevalence of rare drug use patterns, to study trends from 2002 to 2006, and to investigate differences in prevalence and other indicators across demographic groups, socioeconomic circumstances, and geographic areas.

1.2. General Information about NSDUH

NSDUH is the primary source of statistical information on the use of alcohol and illicit drug use by the U.S. civilian, noninstitutionalized population aged 12 or older. Conducted by the Federal Government since 1971, the survey collects data by administering questionnaires to a representative sample of the population through face-to-face interviews at their places of residence. The survey, which has been repeated annually since 1990, is sponsored by SAMHSA, an operating division of the DHHS, and is planned and managed by OAS within SAMHSA. Data collection is conducted under contract with RTI International, Research Triangle Park, North Carolina [1]. This section briefly describes the survey methodology; a more complete description is provided in Appendices A and B.

Prior to 2002, the survey was called the National Household Survey on Drug Abuse (NHSDA). Because of improvements to the survey in 2002, the 2002 data constitute a new baseline for tracking trends in substance use and other measures. Estimates from 2002 to 2006 included in this report should not be compared with estimates from the 2001 or earlier versions of the survey to examine changes in underage alcohol use over time.

Particular strengths of the NSDUH data for reporting on underage alcohol use in the United States include, but are not limited to, the probability sampling design and large sample sizes (see below). Data are weighted to allow inferences to be made for the civilian, noninstitutionalized population aged 12 or older in the United States and for specific demographic subgroups (such as those aged 12 to 20) and geographic subgroups within the United States. Large sample sizes and probability sampling yielding representative estimates in each of the 50 States and the District of Columbia ensure coverage of even relatively rare behaviors and provide a high level of precision in the national estimates, particularly when survey data are pooled across multiple years.

NSDUH collects information from residents of households, noninstitutional group quarters (e.g., shelters, rooming houses, dormitories), and civilians living on military bases. The survey does not include homeless persons who do not use shelters, military personnel on active duty, and residents of institutional group quarters, such as jails and hospitals.

Since 1999, the NSDUH interview has been carried out using computer-assisted interviewing (CAI). Most of the questions are administered with audio computer-assisted self-interviewing (ACASI). ACASI is designed to provide the respondent with a highly private and confidential means of responding to questions to increase the level of honest reporting of illicit drug use and other sensitive behaviors. Less sensitive items are administered by interviewers using computer-assisted personal interviewing (CAPI).

The 2002 to 2006 NSDUHs employed a State-based design with an independent, multistage area probability sample within each State and the District of Columbia. The eight States with the largest population (California, Florida, Illinois, Michigan, New York, Ohio, Pennsylvania, and Texas), which together account for 48 percent of the total U.S. population aged 12 or older) were designated as large sample States. For the remaining 42 States and the District of Columbia, smaller, but adequate, samples were selected. In this report, State variations are studied using direct, weighted, and design-based estimates from the sample. For these estimates, 5 years of data (2002 to 2006) were combined to obtain sample sizes sufficient to produce State estimates and estimates for small demographic groups that met the precision criteria for publication (see Appendix A). The NSDUH design also oversampled persons aged 12 to 17 and those aged 18 to 25, so that each State's sample was approximately equally distributed among three major age groups: 12 to 17 years, 18 to 25 years, and 26 years or older.

Each year's survey was conducted from January through December of that calendar year (e.g., January through December 2006 for the 2006 NSDUH). Sampled dwelling units were screened to identify eligible residents aged 12 or older. Up to two persons per dwelling unit were selected to be interviewed. In each year, respondents were given an incentive payment of $30 for completing the interview.

Weighted response rates for household screening ranged from 90.6 to 91.3 percent for these 5 survey years. Weighted response rates for interviewing ranged from 74.2 to 78.9 percent. Sample sizes were 68,126 in 2002, 67,784 in 2003, 67,760 in 2004, 68,308 in 2005, and 67,802 in 2006, for a total of 339,780 completed interviews for all those aged 12 or older across the 5 years. Sample sizes just for those aged 12 to 20 were 32,787 in 2002, 31,475 in 2003, 31,235 in 2004, 31,282 in 2005, and 31,320 in 2006, for a total of 158,099 completed interviews for those aged 12 to 20 across the 5 years. The weighted response rates for interviewing among those aged 12 to 20 were 89.2 percent in 2002, 88.5 percent in 2003, 88.0 percent in 2004, 86.8 percent in 2005, and 84.9 percent in 2006.

1.3. Measures of Alcohol Use and Disorders

NSDUH includes questions about the recency and frequency of consumption of alcoholic beverages, such as beer, wine, whiskey, brandy, and mixed drinks. An extensive list of examples of the kinds of beverages covered is given to respondents prior to the question administration. A "drink" is defined as a can or bottle of beer, a glass of wine or a wine cooler, a shot of liquor, or a mixed drink with liquor in it. Times when the respondent only had a sip or two from a drink are not considered to be consumption.

For this report, estimates for the prevalence of alcohol use are reported primarily at five levels defined for both males and females and for all ages as follows:

- *Lifetime use* – Use of alcohol at least once in the respondent's lifetime. This measure includes respondents who also reported last using alcohol in the past 30 days or past 12 months.
- *Past year use* – Use of alcohol in the 12 months prior to the interview. This definition includes those respondents who last used alcohol in the 30 days prior to the interview. Respondents who indicated past year use of alcohol also were classified as lifetime users.
- *Current (past month) use* – At least one drink in the past 30 days (includes binge and heavy use).
- *Binge use* – Five or more drinks on the same occasion (i.e., at the same time or within a couple of hours of each other) on at least 1 day in the past 30 days (includes heavy use).
- *Heavy use* – Five or more drinks on the same occasion on each of 5 or more days in the past 30 days.

NSDUH includes questions designed to measure dependence on and abuse of alcohol based on the criteria in the *Diagnostic and Statistical Manual of Mental Disorders*, 4th edition (DSM-IV) (American Psychiatric Association [APA], 1994). A respondent was defined as having dependence on alcohol if he or she met three or more of the following seven dependence criteria:

1. Spent a great deal of time over a period of a month getting, using, or getting over the effects of alcohol.
2. Used alcohol more often than intended or was unable to keep set limits on the alcohol use.
3. Needed to use alcohol more than before to get desired effects or noticed that the same amount of alcohol had less effect than before.
4. Inability to cut down or stop using alcohol every time tried or wanted to.
5. Continued to use alcohol even though it was causing problems with emotions, nerves, mental health, or physical problems.
6. Alcohol use reduced or eliminated involvement or participation in important activities.
7. Experienced withdrawal symptoms (e.g., having trouble sleeping, cramps, hands tremble).

A respondent was defined as having abused alcohol if he or she met one or more of the following four abuse criteria and was determined not to be dependent on alcohol in the past year:

1. Serious problems at home, work, or school caused by alcohol, such as neglecting your children, missing work or school, doing a poor job at work or school, or losing a job or dropping out of school.
2. Used alcohol regularly and then did something that might have put you in physical danger.
3. Use of alcohol caused you to do things that repeatedly got you in trouble with the law.
4. Had problems with family or friends that were probably caused by using alcohol and continued to use alcohol even though you thought alcohol use caused these problems.

Criteria used to determine whether a respondent was asked the dependence and abuse questions included responses from the core alcohol use questions and the frequency of alcohol use questions, as well as the noncore alcohol use questions. Missing or incomplete responses in the core alcohol use and frequency of use questions were imputed. However, the imputation process did not take into account reported data in the noncore questions, including those on dependence and abuse. Respondents with missing information on dependence or abuse (3.5 percent of past year users aged 12 to 20) were included in the analyses, but they were not counted as having dependence or abuse.

1.4. New Alcohol Use Items in the 2006 NSDUH

The 2006 NSDUH included a new module on consumption of alcohol that asked for additional information about respondents' last use of alcohol for those who indicated that they had consumed alcohol at least once in the past month. In this module, past month drinkers were asked to think about the last time they used alcohol and then were asked to provide the following information about their last drinking occasion:

-   the number of drinks they had when they last drank;
-   their use of illicit drugs while using alcohol or within 2 hours of using alcohol the last time they drank;
-   for those aged 12 to 20, the social context of their last drinking occasion (i.e., whether they were alone, with one other person, or with two or more other people when they last drank);
-   for those aged 12 to 20, the location of their last drinking occasion (in a car or other vehicle; at home; at someone else's home; at a park, on a beach, or in a parking lot; at a restaurant, bar, or club; at a concert or sports game; at school; or at some other place); and
-   for those aged 12 to 20, their source for obtaining the alcohol the last time they drank (e.g., whether or not they paid for the alcohol; if they paid for it, whether they

purchased it themselves or gave money to somebody else to purchase the alcohol for them; and if they did not pay for it, who it was who gave them the alcohol).

In addition, respondents of all ages who indicated that they had binged on alcohol at least once in their life also were asked about their age when they first binged on alcohol. Respondents who indicated an age of first binge episode that was the same as their current age or 1 year younger than their current age were then asked to give the month and year when they first binged, which enabled a measure of initiation of binge alcohol use in the year prior to the survey.

Moreover, females who were lifetime drinkers were asked whether they had ever had four or more drinks on the same occasion, as well as their age when they first had four or more drinks on the same occasion. These two questions enable a comparison of binge drinking rates based on the definition used previously by NSDUH, which was five or more drinks on the same occasion for both males and females, and an alternative definition used by the NIAAA (2004), which is five or more drinks on the same occasion for males and four or more drinks on the same occasion for females.

Findings based on most of the items in the new consumption of alcohol module are presented in Chapter 4 and the tables in Appendix C. Section B.4 of Appendix B presents additional technical information and findings from items in this module.

1.5. Measures of Demographic and Geographic Characteristics

Data are presented for racial/ethnic groups in several categorizations, based on current standards for collecting and reporting race and ethnicity data (Office of Management and Budget [OMB], 1997) and on the level of detail permitted by the sample. Because respondents were allowed to choose more than one racial group, a "two or more races" category is presented that includes persons who reported more than one category among the seven basic groups listed in the survey question (white, black or African American, American Indian or Alaska Native, Native Hawaiian, Other Pacific Islander, Asian, Other). It should be noted that, except for the "Hispanic or Latino" group, the racial/ethnic groups discussed in this report include only non- Hispanics. The category "Hispanic or Latino" includes Hispanics of any race. Also, more detailed categories describing specific subgroups were obtained from survey respondents if they reported either Asian race or Hispanic ethnicity. Data on Native Hawaiians and Other Pacific Islanders are combined in this report.

Data also are presented for four U.S. geographic regions in this report. These regions and the nine geographic divisions within those regions, as defined by the U.S. Census Bureau, consist of the following groups of States:

Northeast Region - New England Division: Connecticut, Maine, Massachusetts, New Hampshire, Rhode Island, Vermont; *Middle Atlantic Division:* New Jersey, New York, Pennsylvania.

Midwest Region - East North Central Division: Illinois, Indiana, Michigan, Ohio, Wisconsin; *West North Central Division:* Iowa, Kansas, Minnesota, Missouri, Nebraska, North Dakota, South Dakota.

South Region - South Atlantic Division: Delaware, District of Columbia, Florida, Georgia, Maryland, North Carolina, South Carolina, Virginia, West Virginia; *East South Central Division:* Alabama, Kentucky, Mississippi, Tennessee; *West South Central Division:* Arkansas, Louisiana, Oklahoma, Texas.

West Region - Mountain Division: Arizona, Colorado, Idaho, Montana, Nevada, New Mexico, Utah, Wyoming; *Pacific Division:* Alaska, California, Hawaii, Oregon, Washington.

Geographic comparisons also are made based on county type, which reflects different levels of urbanicity and metropolitan area inclusion of counties, based on metropolitan area definitions issued by the OMB in June 2003 (OMB, 2003). For this purpose, counties are grouped based on the 2003 rural-urban continuum codes. These codes were originally developed by the U.S. Department of Agriculture (Butler & Beale, 1994). Each county is either inside or outside a metropolitan statistical area (MSA), as defined by the OMB.

Large metropolitan areas have a population of 1 million or more. Small metropolitan areas have a population of fewer than 1 million. Small metropolitan areas are further classified based on whether they have a population of 250,000 or more. Nonmetropolitan areas are areas outside MSAs. Counties in nonmetropolitan areas are further classified based on the number of people in the county who live in an urbanized area, as defined by the U.S. Census Bureau at the subcounty level. "Urbanized" counties have 20,000 or more population in urbanized areas, "less urbanized" counties have at least 2,500 but fewer than 20,000 population in urbanized areas, and "completely rural" counties have fewer than 2,500 population in urbanized areas.

1.6. Organization of This Report

This report contains separate chapters that discuss the following topics related to the use of alcohol by persons aged 12 to 20: trends in underage alcohol use and disorders from 2002 to 2006 (Chapter 2); patterns of underage alcohol use and alcohol use disorders by demographic and geographic groups (Chapter 3); and the social context and location of underage drinking, the sources of alcohol for underage drinkers, and the co-occurrence of underage drinking and illicit drug use (Chapter 4). Most analyses are presented for all underage persons aged 12 to 20 and by gender and age group (12 to 14, 15 to 17, 18 to 20). Technical appendices describe NSDUH (Appendix A) and its statistical methods and measurement (Appendix B). Appendix C contains the tables of estimates referenced in Chapters 2 through 4. Tables showing standard errors for the estimated numbers and percentages in the tables in Appendix C are available on the SAMHSA/OAS website at http://oas.samhsa.gov/WebOnly.htm.

Tables, text, and figures present prevalence measures for the population in terms of both the number of alcohol users and the rate of alcohol use for those aged 12 to 20. The tables and figures for Chapter 2 include trend data that are based on comparisons of single-year estimates between 2002 to 2006. In these tables and figures showing trend data, significant differences between estimates from 2006 and previous years of the survey are indicated. The tables and figures for Chapter 3 are based on averages for 2002 to 2006; combining data from these 5 survey years increases the sample sizes to support detailed estimates. The tables and figures for Chapter 4 are based on new items added to NSDUH in 2006.

Statistical tests have been conducted for all statements appearing in the text of the report that compare estimates between years or subgroups of the population. Unless explicitly stated that a difference is not statistically significant, all statements that describe differences are significant at the .05 level. Statistically significant differences are described using terms such as "higher," "lower," "increased," and "decreased." Statements that use terms such as "similar," "no difference," "same," or "remained steady" to describe the relationship between estimates denote that a difference is not statistically significant. In addition, a set of estimates for survey years or population subgroups may be presented without a statement of comparison, in which case a statistically significant difference between these estimates is not implied and testing was not conducted.

All estimates presented in the report have met the criteria for statistical reliability (see Appendix B). Estimates that do not meet these criteria are suppressed and do not appear in tables, figures, or text. Also, subgroups with suppressed estimates are not included in statistical tests of comparisons. For example, a statement that "whites had the highest prevalence" means that the rate among whites was higher than the rate among all nonsuppressed racial/ethnic subgroups, but not necessarily higher than the rate among a subgroup for which the estimate was suppressed.

2. TRENDS IN UNDERAGE DRINKING: 2002-2006

This chapter presents 2002 to 2006 data on the prevalence of alcohol use and alcohol dependence and abuse among persons aged 12 to 20. Findings are presented overall and by age group and gender. The trends are based on single years of data from the 2002 to 2006 National Surveys on Drug Use and Health (NSDUHs). This chapter includes estimates of lifetime, past year, and current (past month) alcohol use, binge alcohol use, heavy alcohol use, and alcohol dependence or abuse in the past year.

2.1. Overall Trends

In each year from 2002 to 2006, more than half of all persons aged 12 to 20 had consumed at least one drink of alcohol in their lifetime. In 2006, an estimated 53.9 percent of underage persons (20.6 million persons) had used alcohol in their lifetime, which was lower than the percentage in 2003 (55.8 percent) or 2002 (56.2 percent) (Figure 2.1; also see Table 2.1 in Appendix C). Lifetime alcohol use among underage persons was stable from 2004 to 2006.

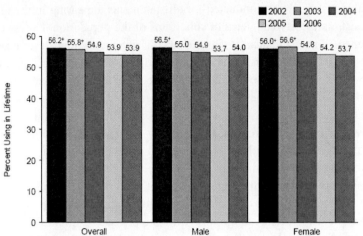

+ Difference between estimate and 2006 estimate is statistically significant at the 0.05 level.

Figure 2.1. Lifetime Alcohol Use among Persons Aged 12 to 20, by Gender: 2002-2006.

In 2006, about 17.6 million (46.1 percent) underage persons used alcohol in the past year, 10.8 million (28.3 percent) used in the past month, 7.2 million (19.0 percent) engaged in binge alcohol use, and 2.4 million (6.2 percent) engaged in heavy alcohol use. Also in 2006, about 3.5 million (9.1 percent) underage persons were classified with alcohol dependence or abuse in the past year. In this overall age group, rates of past year use, current use, binge use, heavy use, or past year dependence or abuse remained stable from 2002 to 2006. For example, current use among underage persons was 28.8 percent in 2002 and 28.3 percent in 2006, while binge use was 19.3 percent in 2002 and 19.0 percent in 2006.

2.2. Trends, by Age

Among youths aged 12 to 14 and youths aged 15 to 17, the prevalence of lifetime alcohol use was lower in 2006 compared with 2002, 2003, or 2004 (Table 2.2). For example, the rate of lifetime alcohol use for 12 to 14 year olds declined from 24.9 percent in 2002 to 22.1 percent in 2006, and the rate of lifetime use for 15 to 17 year olds declined from 62.7 percent in 2002 to 57.7 percent in 2006. The prevalence of past year drinking was lower in 2006 (16.2 percent) than in 2002 (17.6 percent) for youths aged 12 to 14, and it was lower in 2006 (48.7 percent) compared with 2002 (52.3 percent), 2003 (51.6 percent), or 2004 (50.9 percent) for youths aged 15 to 17 (Figure 2.2). Among 15 to 17 year olds, the prevalence of past month alcohol use was lower in 2006 (26.1 percent) compared with 2002 (28.3 percent), 2003 (28.2 percent), or 2004 (28.3 percent). Among 15 to 17 year olds, the rates of binge drinking and alcohol use disorders in 2006 were not different from the rates in 2002. However, the rate of binge drinking among 15 to 17 year olds was lower in 2006 (17.1 percent) than in 2004 (19.1 percent), and past year dependence or abuse also decreased from 10.1 percent in 2004 to 8.8 percent in 2006. There were no changes in any measures of alcohol use from 2002 to 2006 for 18 to 20 year olds.

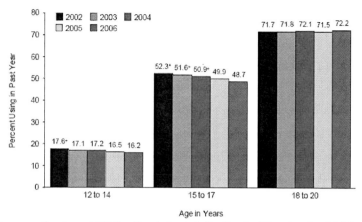

+ Difference between estimate and 2006 estimate is statistically significant at the 0.05 level.

Figure 2.2. Past Year Alcohol Use among Persons Aged 12 to 20, by Age: 2002-2006.

2.3. Trends, by Gender

Among both males and females aged 12 to 20, rates of lifetime alcohol use decreased between 2002 and 2006 (Figure 2.1 and Table 2.1). Rates of lifetime alcohol use decreased from 56.5 percent in 2002 to 54.0 percent in 2006 for underage males and from 56.0 to 53.7 percent for underage females. Among underage males, the prevalence of past year dependence or abuse was lower in 2006 (9.6 percent) than in 2004 (10.8 percent) or 2002 (10.9 percent). Among underage females, the prevalence of past year alcohol use was lower in 2006 (46.2 percent) than in 2003 (48.0 percent). There were no differences between 2006 and the previous 4 years of the survey for either males or females on past month alcohol use, binge use, or heavy use.

3. PATTERNS OF UNDERAGE ALCOHOL USE AND DISORDERS:2002-2006

This chapter presents estimates of alcohol use and alcohol dependence or abuse among persons aged 12 to 20 based on annual averages for the combined 2002 to 2006 National Surveys on Drug Use and Health (NSDUHs). Combining data from these 5 survey years increases the sample size to support detailed estimates and is particularly useful for examining demographic and geographic correlates of alcohol use and alcohol use disorders.

The first section in this chapter presents estimates of alcohol use by demographic group, including age group, gender, race/ethnicity, income level, county type, and geographic area. Variations by State also are presented. The alcohol use measures include current (i.e., past month) use, binge use, and heavy use. The second section presents estimates of alcohol use disorders, defined as alcohol dependence or abuse in the past year, by demographic group and geographic area. The third section presents associations between underage drinking and parent alcohol use using data from households in which both a person aged 12 to 20 and his or her mother or father was interviewed.

3.1. Alcohol Use

In 2002 to 2006, more than one in four persons aged 12 to 20 (28.6 percent) had consumed alcohol in the past month, corresponding to an estimated 10.8 million underage current alcohol users (see Table 3.1 in Appendix C). Within this age group, 7.2 million (19.2 percent) engaged in binge alcohol use, and 2.3 million (6.2 percent) were heavy drinkers.

3.1.1. Age

The prevalence of current, binge, and heavy alcohol use among persons aged 12 to 20 was higher for older age groups than for younger age groups (Figure 3.1). For example, current drinking was reported by 7.0 percent of youths aged 12 to 14 (Table 3.3), 27.5 percent of youths aged 15 to 17 (Table 3.4), and 51.3 percent of 18 to 20 year olds (Table 3.5). In addition, 3.3 percent of persons aged 12 to 14, 17.8 percent of persons aged 15 to 17, and 36.3 percent of persons aged 18 to 20 were binge alcohol users. The prevalence of heavy drinking was 0.5 percent for 12 to 14 year olds, 4.5 percent for 15 to 17 year olds, and 13.4 percent for 18 to 20 year olds. Thus, more than one in three persons aged 18 to 20 was a binge drinker, and more than one in eight was a heavy drinker.

3.1.2. Gender

Among all underage persons, males were more likely than females to be current alcohol users (29.4 percent for males, 27.8 percent for females), binge drinkers, (21.6 percent for males, 16.5 percent for females), and heavy drinkers (7.9 percent for males, 4.3 percent for females) (Table 3.1)

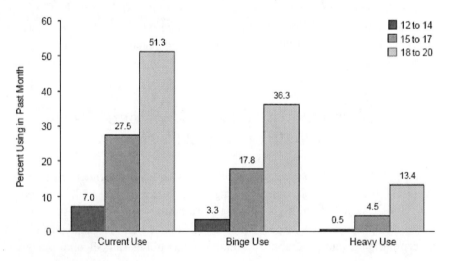

Figure 3.1. Current, Binge, and Heavy Alcohol Use among Persons Aged 12 to 20, by Age: Annual Averages, 2002-2006.

3.1.3. Race/Ethnicity

Among persons aged 12 to 20, non-Hispanic whites had higher rates of current and heavy alcohol use than any other racial/ethnic group, and they had a higher rate of binge use than non- Hispanic blacks, Asians, or Hispanics (Table 3.2). For example, approximately one third

(32.6 percent) of whites were current users compared with 27.2 percent of American Indians or Alaska Natives, 25.7 percent of Hispanics, 24.3 percent of Native Hawaiians or Other Pacific Islanders, 18.8 percent of blacks, and 17.1 percent of Asians (Figure 3.2). Blacks had lower rates of current, binge, and heavy drinking compared with whites or Hispanics.

Among underage Hispanics, Cubans had a higher rate of current alcohol use (32.0 percent) than Central or South Americans (26.0 percent), Puerto Ricans (25.0 percent), or Mexicans (24.9 percent) (Table 3.2). There were no differences between Hispanic groups for binge or heavy alcohol use. Among underage Asians, rates of binge alcohol use were higher among Japanese (12.9 percent), Koreans (12.9 percent), and Filipinos (12.0 percent) than among Chinese (7.2 percent) or Vietnamese (5.2 percent). Koreans and Filipinos also had higher rates of binge alcohol use than Asian Indians (7.1 percent).

3.1.4. Gender, by Age Group

The pattern of differences between males and females in the prevalence of current drinking differed by age group. Among youths aged 12 to 14, the rate of current drinking was higher for females (7.7 percent) than for males (6.3 percent) (Table 3.3 and Figure 3.3). For those aged 18 to 20, however, the rate of current drinking was higher for males (54.4 percent) than for females (47.9 percent) (Table 3.5). There was no difference in the rate of current drinking for males and females among persons aged 15 to 17 (Table 3.4). For binge and heavy drinking, there were no gender differences for those aged 12 to 14, whereas for those aged 15 to 17 or 18 to 20, males had higher rates than females. For example, the rates of binge drinking were higher for males than for females for those aged 15 to 17 (19.0 percent for males, 16.5 percent for females) and those aged 18 to 20 (42.6 percent for males, 29.7 percent for females).

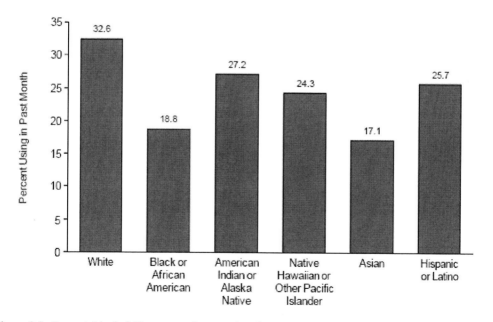

Figure 3.2. Current Alcohol Use among Persons Aged 12 to 20, by Race/Ethnicity: Annual Averages, 2002-2006.

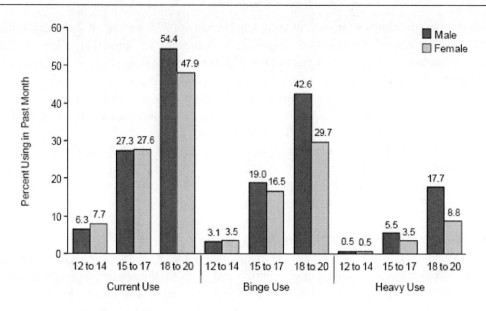

Figure 3.3. Current, Binge, and Heavy Alcohol Use among Persons Aged 12 to 20, by Age Group and Gender: Annual Averages, 2002-2006.

3.1.5. Race/Ethnicity, by Age Group

Among youths aged 12 to 14, non-Hispanic whites had a higher prevalence of current, binge, and heavy alcohol use compared with blacks or Asians (Table 3.3). For example, 7.5 percent of whites in this age group had consumed alcohol in the past month compared with 4.7 percent of blacks and 3.2 percent of Asians. However, rates of binge drinking for those aged 12 to 14 were lower for whites (3.4 percent) than for American Indians or Alaska Natives (8.1 percent) or for Hispanics (4.3 percent).

The pattern of racial/ethnic differences for those aged 15 to 17 was similar to that for those aged 12 to 14, with a higher percentage of non-Hispanic whites engaging in current, binge, and heavy alcohol use than blacks or Asians (Table 3.4). In contrast to the findings for those 12 to 14, a higher percentage of whites than Hispanics aged 15 to 17 engaged in current alcohol use (31.4 percent for whites, 26.0 percent for Hispanics), binge alcohol use (21.0 percent for whites, 17.1 percent for Hispanics), and heavy alcohol use (5.8 percent for whites, 3.7 percent for Hispanics). Within this age group, rates of current and binge alcohol use were also higher among whites (31.4 percent current users, 21.0 percent binge users) compared with Native Hawaiians or Other Pacific Islanders (17.4 percent current users, 9.1 percent binge users).

There were also differences between non-Hispanic whites and other racial/ethnic groups in alcohol consumption among persons aged 18 to 20. A higher percentage of whites in this age group were current or heavy drinkers compared with those in any other racial/ethnic group, though this difference was not statistically significant for those who reported being two or more races (Table 3.5). For example, 17.4 percent of whites in this age group were heavy drinkers compared with 8.8 percent of Hispanics, 7.9 percent of American Indians or Alaska Natives, 7.4 percent of Native Hawaiians or Other Pacific Islanders, 4.3 percent of Asians, and 4.1 percent of blacks. A similar pattern was found for binge drinking, which was more prevalent among whites (42.9 percent) than among American Indians or Alaska Natives (35.4 percent), Hispanics (31.3 percent), blacks (18.6 percent), or Asians (18.4 percent).

3.1.6. Income Level

As shown in Table 3.6 and Figure 3.4, persons aged 12 to 20 whose family income was less than $20,000 had higher rates of current (33.9 percent), binge (23.7 percent), and heavy drinking (8.7 percent) compared with those whose family income was $20,000 or higher. In addition, persons in this age group whose family income was $75,000 or higher were more likely to have engaged in current, binge, and heavy alcohol use than those whose family income was $20,000 to $49,000 or those whose family income was $50,000 to $74,999. For example, 28.6 percent of persons aged 12 to 20 whose family income was $75,000 or higher were current drinkers compared with 26.0 percent for those with a family income of $20,000 to $49,999 and 26.4 percent for those with a family income of $50,000 to $74,999.

3.1.7. County Type

There was considerable variation in the rates of alcohol use among persons aged 12 to 20 by county type. Underage persons who lived in counties in nonmetropolitan areas were more likely than those who lived in counties in metropolitan areas to engage in binge drinking (20.8 percent in nonmetropolitan areas, 18.8 percent in metropolitan areas) and heavy drinking (6.9 percent in nonmetropolitan areas, 6.0 percent in metropolitan areas) (Table 3.6 and Figure 3.5). The rate of current drinking among underage persons was 29.4 percent among those who lived in nonmetropolitan areas and 28.5 percent among those who lived in metropolitan areas, though this difference was not statistically significant. Underage persons who lived in counties in small metropolitan areas (population less than 1 million) had higher rates of current, binge, and heavy drinking than those who lived in counties in large metropolitan areas (population of 1 million or more). Furthermore, persons aged 12 to 20 who lived in urbanized nonmetropolitan counties had higher rates of current, binge, and heavy drinking than those who lived in counties in large metropolitan areas, counties in small metropolitan areas, or rural counties. For example, 22.2 percent of underage persons who lived in urbanized nonmetropolitan counties were binge drinkers compared with 17.7 percent of those who lived in counties in large metropolitan areas, 20.8 percent in small metropolitan areas, and 19.8 percent in rural counties.

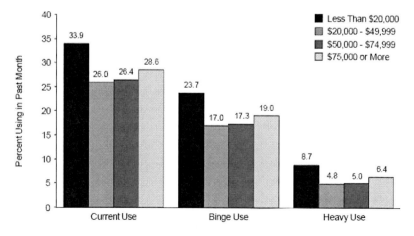

Figure 3.4. Current, Binge, and Heavy Alcohol Use among Persons Aged 12 to 20, by Family Income: Annual Averages, 2002-2006.

3.1.8. Demographic Differences within County Type

Across county types, underage persons in younger age groups had lower rates of current, binge, and heavy alcohol use compared with older age groups. For example, the prevalence of current drinking in counties in metropolitan areas was 6.7 percent for 12 to 14 year olds, 27.1 percent for 15 to 17 year olds, and 51.5 percent for 18 to 20 year olds (Table 3.7). Within rural counties, the prevalence of current drinking was 8.7 percent for 12 to 14 year olds, 30.0 percent for 15 to 17 year olds, and 46.1 percent for 18 to 20 year olds (Table 3.9).

There was little variation in the pattern of alcohol use among males and females by county type. For example, the rate of current alcohol use among those who lived in counties in metropolitan areas was higher for males (29.1 percent) than females (27.8 percent), and current drinking was also more prevalent among males in rural counties (30.0 percent) than among females (26.0 percent).

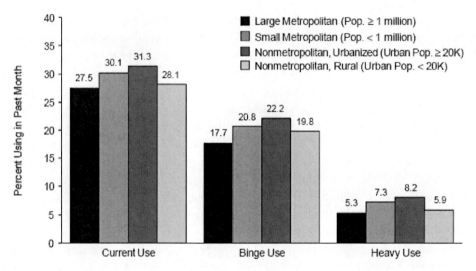

Figure 3.5. Current, Binge, and Heavy Alcohol Use among Persons Aged 12 to 20, by County Type: Annual Averages, 2002-2006.

There was considerable variation in the pattern of alcohol use by race/ethnicity between counties in metropolitan areas and rural counties. For example, among persons aged 12 to 20 who lived in counties in metropolitan areas, the prevalence of current drinking was higher for non-Hispanic whites (33.2 percent in metropolitan areas) than for Hispanics (25.3 percent) (Table 3.7 and Figure 3.6). In rural counties, however, underage Hispanics had a higher prevalence of current drinking (32.4 percent) than underage whites (28.9 percent) (Table 3.9). This pattern was similar for binge drinking, with a higher percentage of whites (22.9 percent) than Hispanics (17.0 percent) who lived in metropolitan areas reporting binge drinking, and a higher percentage of Hispanics (24.7 percent) than whites (20.7 percent) in rural counties reporting binge drinking. Whites aged 12 to 20 who lived in counties in metropolitan areas also were more likely to drink heavily (8.2 percent) than were Hispanics (4.1 percent), though there was no difference in the prevalence of heavy drinking between whites and Hispanics in rural counties. Within each county type, blacks were less likely to be current, binge, or heavy drinkers than either whites or Hispanics.

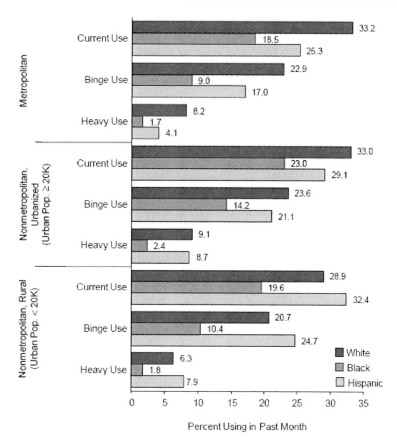

Figure 3.6. Current, Binge, and Heavy Alcohol Use among Persons Aged 12 to 20, by Race/Ethnicity and County Type: Annual Averages, 2002-2006.

3.1.9. Geographic Regions

For each of the three measures of past month alcohol use, rates among 12 to 20 year olds were higher in the Northeast and Midwest than in the South or West (Table 3.6 and Figure 3.7). For example, 21.4 percent of those in the Northeast and 21.8 percent of those in the Midwest engaged in binge drinking compared with 17.3 percent of those in the South and 17.8 percent of those in the West.

3.1.10. States

There was substantial variation among States in the prevalence of underage alcohol consumption. In 2002 to 2006, the rate of current alcohol use among those aged 12 to 20 ranged from a high of 41.2 percent in North Dakota to a low of 19.3 percent in Utah (Table 3.10 and Figure 3.8). Among the States in the highest fifth for current drinking, four were in the Midwest (Nebraska, North Dakota, South Dakota, and Wisconsin), four were in the Northeast (Massachusetts, New Hampshire, Rhode Island, and Vermont), and two were in the West (Montana and Wyoming). Among the States in the lowest fifth for current drinking, six were in the South (Alabama, Georgia, Mississippi, North Carolina, South Carolina, and Tennessee), three were in the West (California, Idaho, and Utah), and one was in the Midwest (Indiana).

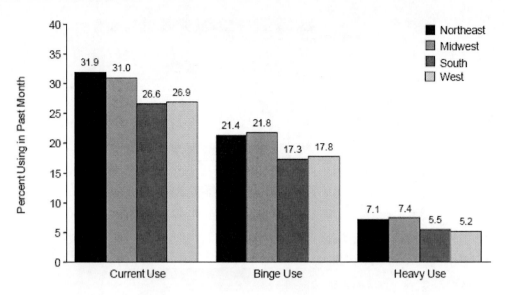

Figure 3.7. Current, Binge, and Heavy Alcohol Use among Persons Aged 12 to 20, by Geographic Region: Annual Averages, 2002-2006.

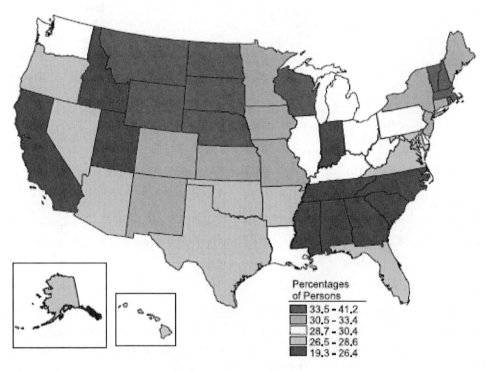

Figure 3.8. Current Alcohol Use among Persons Aged 12 to 20, by State: Annual Averages, 2002-2006.

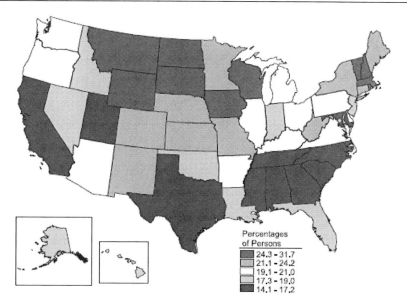

Figure 3.9. Binge Alcohol Use among Persons Aged 12 to 20, by State: Annual Averages, 2002-2006.

The distribution of underage binge drinking by State was similar to the pattern of current use, ranging from a high of 31.7 percent in North Dakota to a low of 14.1 percent in Utah (Table 3.10 and Figure 3.9). Among the States in the highest fifth for binge drinking, four were in the Midwest (Iowa, North Dakota, South Dakota, and Wisconsin), four were in the Northeast (Massachusetts, New Hampshire, Rhode Island, and Vermont), and two were in the West (Montana and Wyoming). Among the States in the lowest fifth for binge drinking, eight were in the South (Alabama, Georgia, Maryland, Mississippi, North Carolina, South Carolina, Tennessee, and Texas), and two were in the West (California and Utah).

3.2. Alcohol Dependence or Abuse

This section presents differences by demographic group and geographic area in the prevalence of underage persons who met the criteria for alcohol use disorders, defined as alcohol dependence or abuse in the past year. The prevalence rates cited are averages based on combined data from the 2002 to 2006 NSDUHs. In 2002 to 2006, an annual average of 3.5 million persons aged 12 to 20 met the criteria for alcohol dependence or abuse in the past year (9.4 percent of all persons in this age range) (Table 3.1).

3.2.1. Age
As was the case with the prevalence of alcohol use, the prevalence of past year alcohol dependence or abuse among persons aged 12 to 20 was higher for older persons than for younger persons. Only 0.5 percent of 12 year olds were classified with alcohol use disorders compared with 10.0 percent of those aged 16 and 17.7 percent of those aged 19 or 20 (Table 3.1).

3.2.2. Gender

Among all 12 to 20 year olds, a higher percentage of males (10.3 percent) than females (8.5 percent) met the criteria for past year alcohol dependence or abuse (Table 3.1).

3.2.3. Race/Ethnicity

Dependence or abuse among underage persons varied considerably by race/ethnicity. Among underage persons, more than one in seven American Indians or Alaska Natives (14.9 percent) and one in eight Native Hawaiians or other Pacific Islanders (12.7 percent) met the criteria for an alcohol use disorder (Table 3.2 and Figure 3.10). This rate of alcohol use disorders for underage American Indians or Alaska Natives was higher than the rate for whites (10.9 percent), blacks (4.6 percent), Hispanics (8.7 percent), or Asians (4.9 percent). Furthermore, Native Hawaiians or Other Pacific Islanders had a higher prevalence of alcohol use disorders than non-Hispanic blacks or Asians, and whites had a higher prevalence of alcohol use disorders than non-Hispanic blacks, Hispanics, or Asians.

Among Hispanics, the rate of alcohol use disorders among 12 to 20 year olds was lower among Puerto Ricans (6.8 percent) than among Mexicans (8.9 percent) (Table 3.2). Among Asians, the rate of alcohol use disorders was higher among Koreans (9.3 percent) than among any other Asian subgroup except for Filipinos.

3.2.4. Gender, by Age Group

Differences between males and females in the percentage of underage persons who met the criteria for alcohol use disorders in the past year varied considerably by age group. Among youths aged 12 to 14, a higher percentage of females (2.2 percent) than males (1.6 percent) were classified with an alcohol use disorder (Table 3.3 and Figure 3.11). In contrast, among those aged 18 to 20, a higher percentage of males (19.6 percent) than females (13.4 percent) was classified with an alcohol use disorder (Table 3.5). For youths aged 15 to 17, there was no difference between males and females in alcohol dependence or abuse.

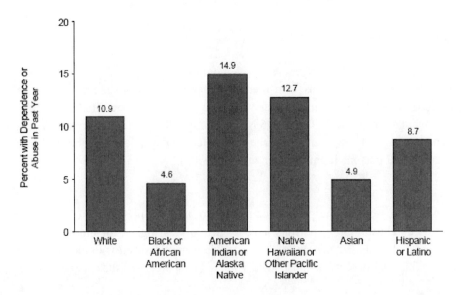

Figure 3.10. Alcohol Dependence or Abuse in the Past Year among Persons Aged 12 to 20, by Race/Ethnicity: Annual Averages, 2002-2006.

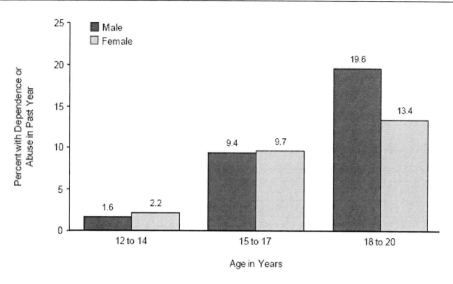

Figure 3.11. Alcohol Dependence or Abuse in the Past Year among Persons Aged 12 to 20, by Gender and Age: Annual Averages, 2002-2006.

3.2.5. Race/Ethnicity, by Age Group

The pattern of alcohol dependence or abuse in the past year among racial/ethnic groups was similar for those aged 12 to 14 or aged 15 to 17. Among youths aged 12 to 14, the percentage of American Indians or Alaska Natives classified with alcohol dependence or abuse (4.2 percent) was higher than among non-Hispanic whites, blacks, or Asians (Table 3.3). Among youths aged 15 to 17, the percentage of American Indians or Alaska Natives classified with alcohol dependence or abuse (19.0 percent) was higher than among whites, blacks, Native Hawaiians or Other Pacific Islanders, Asians, or Hispanics (Table 3.4). Blacks and Asians aged 12 to 14 or 15 to 17 had a similar prevalence of alcohol use disorders as Native Hawaiians or Other Pacific Islanders, but they had a lower prevalence than any other racial/ethnic group. Similarly, for persons aged 18 to 20, the prevalence of alcohol use disorders was lower among blacks (9.2 percent) and Asians (9.6 percent) than among whites (19.2 percent), American Indians or Alaska Natives (22.1 percent), Native Hawaiians or Other Pacific Islanders (24.5 percent), persons reporting two or more races (22.4 percent), or Hispanics (14.5 percent) (Table 3.5). These data indicate that nearly one out of four American Indians or Alaska Natives, Native Hawaiians or Other Pacific Islanders, or persons aged 18 to 20 reporting two or more races met the criteria for an alcohol use disorder.

3.2.6. Income Level

As shown in Table 3.6, persons aged 12 to 20 whose family income was less than $20,000 had higher rates of past year alcohol dependence or abuse (11.6 percent) compared with those whose family income was $20,000 to $49,999 (8.4 percent), $50,000 to $74,999 (8.5 percent), or $75,000 or higher (9.2 percent).

3.2.7. County Type

Among underage persons, those who lived in counties in nonmetropolitan areas were more likely than those who lived in counties in metropolitan areas to meet the criteria for alcohol dependence or abuse in the past year (10.6 percent in nonmetropolitan areas, 9.1

percent in metropolitan areas) (Table 3.6). Underage persons who lived in small metropolitan areas had higher rates of alcohol use disorder (10.3 percent) than those who lived in large metropolitan areas (8.5 percent). Furthermore, persons aged 12 to 20 who lived in urbanized nonmetropolitan counties had higher rates of alcohol use disorders (11.7 percent) than those who lived in counties in large metropolitan areas (8.5 percent), small metropolitan areas (10.3 percent), or rural counties (9.8 percent).

3.2.8. Demographic Differences within County Type

As was the case with the prevalence of alcohol use, the pattern of alcohol use disorder by age group and gender was similar across county types. In each county type, those in older age groups were more likely to be classified with alcohol dependence or abuse than younger age groups, and males were more likely to be classified with alcohol dependence or abuse than females (Tables 3.7 to 3.9). However, there was considerable variation in the pattern of alcohol use disorders by race/ethnicity between counties in metropolitan areas and rural counties. Among persons aged 12 to 20 who lived in counties in metropolitan areas, the prevalence of alcohol dependence or abuse in the past year was higher for non-Hispanic whites (10.9 percent in metropolitan areas) than for Hispanics (8.4 percent) (Table 3.7 and Figure 3.12). In contrast, there were no statistically significant differences in the prevalence of alcohol use disorders among underage whites and Hispanics who lived in either urbanized nonmetropolitan counties or in rural counties. Within each county type, blacks were less likely to be classified with alcohol dependence or abuse in the past year than either whites or Hispanics, though this difference did not reach statistical significance for those who lived in urbanized nonmetropolitan counties.

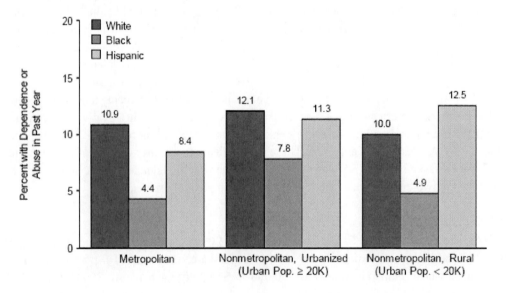

Figure 3.12. Alcohol Dependence or Abuse in the Past Year among Persons Aged 12 to 20, by Race/Ethnicity and County Type: Annual Averages, 2002-2006.

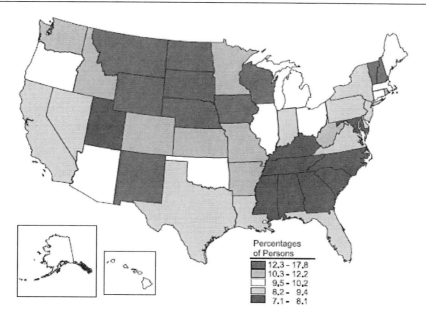

Figure 3.13. Alcohol Dependence or Abuse in the Past Year among Persons Aged 12 to 20, by State: Annual Averages, 2002-2006.

3.2.9. Geographic Regions

Persons aged 12 to 20 who lived in the Midwest had higher rates of alcohol dependence or abuse (10.7 percent) than those who lived in the Northeast (9.5 percent), West (9.5 percent), or South (8.4 percent) (Table 3.6). The prevalence of alcohol use disorders among underage persons in the South was lower than for any other region.

3.2.10. States

In 2002 to 2006, the rates of alcohol dependence or abuse in the past year among those aged 12 to 20 ranged from a high of 17.8 percent in Montana to a low of 7.1 percent in Mississippi (Table 3.10 and Figure 3.13). Of the States in the top fifth in the prevalence of alcohol use disorders, five were in the Midwest (Iowa, Nebraska, North Dakota, South Dakota, and Wisconsin), three were in the West (Montana, New Mexico, and Wyoming), and two were in the Northeast (New Hampshire and Vermont). Of the States in the bottom fifth, nine were in the South (Alabama, District of Columbia, Georgia, Kentucky, Maryland, Mississippi, North Carolina, South Carolina, and Tennessee), and one was in the West (Utah).

3.3. Association of Underage Drinking and Parental Alcohol Use

This section presents information on the association between drinking by persons aged 12 to 20 and drinking by their parents. The prevalence rates cited are averages from the 2002 to 2006 NSDUHs, utilizing data from households in which both a person aged 12 to 20 and his or her mother or father was interviewed.

3.3.1. Alcohol Use

In 2002 to 2006, there was a clear association between current drinking by persons aged 12 to 20 and past year drinking by their parents. Rates of current alcohol use, binge use, and heavy use among underage persons were considerably higher among persons aged 12 to 20 who lived with a parent who had consumed alcohol in the past year compared with those who lived with a parent who had not consumed alcohol in the past year (Table 3.11). For example, rates of binge drinking among underage persons were higher for those who lived with a parent who had consumed alcohol in the past year, whether that parent was a mother (17.6 percent for those whose mother was a past year drinker vs. 9.3 percent for those whose mother was not a past year drinker) or a father (16.5 percent for those whose father was a past year drinker vs. 10.2 percent for those whose father was not a past year drinker) (Figure 3.14). Furthermore, rates of underage binge drinking were higher among those who lived with a mother who was a binge drinker (21.3 percent) than among those whose mother had used alcohol in the past month but had not binged (17.5 percent). Similarly, 19.5 percent of underage persons whose father had binged in the past month were binge drinkers compared with 15.4 percent among those whose fathers had used alcohol in the past month but had not binged.

Household Structure. The comparisons of drinking patterns of underage persons and their parents can be further examined by the number of parents living in the household. Mother-child pairs are more likely than father-child pairs to come from single-parent households (22.3 vs. 5.3 percent). For both one-parent and two-parent households, rates of binge and heavy alcohol use were higher among underage persons who lived with a mother or father who had consumed alcohol in the past year compared with those who lived with a mother or father who did not drink in the past year (Table 3.12). In addition, for underage persons who lived in two- parent households, rates of binge drinking were higher among those who lived with a mother who had binged on alcohol in the past month compared with those who lived with a mother who had consumed alcohol in the past month but had not binged. Rates of heavy drinking were higher among those who lived with a father who had binged on alcohol in the past month compared with those who lived with a father who was a current drinker but was not a binge drinker.

3.3.2. Dependence or Abuse in the Past Year

As was the case for alcohol use, there was a clear association between the prevalence of alcohol use disorders among 12 to 20 year olds and drinking by their parents. Underage person whose parents had consumed alcohol in the past year had a higher prevalence of alcohol use disorders in the past year whether that parent was a mother (7.9 percent for those whose mother was a past year drinker vs. 5.2 percent for those whose mother was not a past year drinker) or a father (8.0 percent for those whose father was a past year drinker vs. 5.2 percent for those whose father was not a past year drinker) (Table 3.11 and Figure 3.15). A similar pattern was found for fathers who binged on alcohol during the past month, with higher rates of alcohol use disorders among underage persons whose fathers were binge drinkers versus those whose fathers were past month users but were not binge drinkers (10.2 and 7.1 percent, respectively). There was no significant difference in alcohol use disorders between underage persons whose mothers were binge drinkers and those whose mothers were past month drinkers but were not binge drinkers.

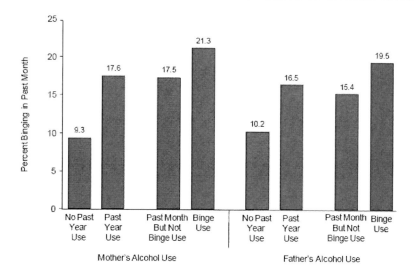

Figure 3.14. Binge Alcohol Use among Persons Aged 12 to 20, by Parental Alcohol Use: Annual Averages, 2002-2006.

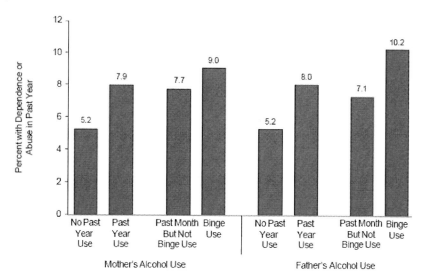

Figure 3.15. Dependence or Abuse in the Past Year among Persons Aged 12 to 20, by Parental Alcohol Use: Annual Averages, 2002-2006.

Household Structure. Analyses of the link between alcohol use disorders among underage persons and alcohol use by their parents for one-parent and two-parent households are limited by small sample sizes, especially for fathers in one-parent households. Looking just at two-parent households, underage persons whose mothers had consumed alcohol in the past year were more likely to meet the criteria for alcohol dependence or abuse (7.6 percent) than those whose mothers did not drink in the past year (4.8 percent) (Table 3.12). This pattern held for fathers as well, with 7.9 percent of underage persons whose fathers had drunk alcohol in the past year meeting the criteria for an alcohol use disorder compared with 5.4 percent of those whose fathers did not drink in the past year. In addition, 12 to 20 year olds in two-parent households had a higher rate of past year alcohol use disorder if their father was a binge drinker (9.9 percent) than if their father was a past month drinker but was not a binge drinker (6.9 percent). There was no significant difference in alcohol use disorders between underage persons in two-parent households whose mothers were binge drinkers and those whose mothers were past month drinkers but were not binge drinkers.

3.4. Summary

Combined data from 2002 to 2006 indicated that among persons aged 12 to 20, rates of current (past month), binge, and heavy alcohol use were higher for those who were older than for those who were younger and for males than for females. Among all persons aged 12 to 20, non- Hispanic whites had higher rates of current and heavy alcohol use than any other racial/ethnic group. Whites aged 12 to 14 had a lower rate of binge drinking than Hispanics and American Indians or Alaska Natives, but among those aged 15 to 17 or those aged 18 to 20, whites had higher rates of current, binge, and heavy drinking compared with Hispanics. Underage persons whose family income was less than $20,000 or $75,000 or higher had higher rates of current, binge, and heavy drinking compared with those whose family income was $20,000 to $74,999. Underage persons who lived in urbanized nonmetropolitan counties had higher rates of current, binge, and heavy drinking than those who lived in counties in large metropolitan areas, counties in small metropolitan areas, or rural areas. The pattern of underage alcohol use by racial/ethnic group differed between county types, with a higher rate for current drinking among non-Hispanic whites (33.2 percent) than among Hispanics (25.3 percent) in metropolitan areas. In rural areas, however, the rate for current drinking was higher among Hispanics (32.4 percent) than among whites (28.9 percent).

Among youths aged 12 to 14, a higher percentage of females (2.2 percent) than males (1.6 percent) were classified with an alcohol use disorder. This pattern was reversed for those aged 18 to 20, with a higher percentage of males (19.6 percent) than females (13.4 percent) who were classified with an alcohol use disorder. Among all persons aged 12 to 20, more than one in seven American Indians or Alaska Natives (14.9 percent) and one in eight Native Hawaiians or Other Pacific Islanders (12.7 percent) met the criteria for an alcohol use disorder. As was the case with alcohol use, persons aged 12 to 20 who lived in urbanized nonmetropolitan counties had higher rates of alcohol use disorders than those who lived in counties in large metropolitan areas, small metropolitan areas, or rural areas. Also, the prevalence of alcohol dependence or abuse in the past year among those who lived in counties in metropolitan areas was higher for non-Hispanic whites (10.9 percent) than for Hispanics (8.4 percent). However, there were no statistically significant differences in the prevalence of alcohol use disorders between underage whites and Hispanics who lived in urbanized metropolitan counties or rural counties. Within counties in metropolitan or rural areas, blacks were less likely to be classified with alcohol dependence or abuse in the past year than either whites or Hispanics.

Among underage persons, rates of current alcohol use, binge use, and heavy use, as well as rates of alcohol use disorders, were higher among persons who lived with a parent who had consumed alcohol in the past year compared with those who lived with a parent who had not consumed alcohol in the past year. Furthermore, rates of underage binge drinking were higher among those who lived with a mother or father who was a binge drinker than among those whose mother or father had used alcohol in the past month but had not binged. Underage persons who lived with a father who was a binge drinker also had higher rates of alcohol use disorders in the past year compared with those whose father was a current drinker but was not a binge drinker whereas there was no difference in alcohol use disorders between those whose mothers were binge drinkers and those whose mothers were current drinkers but were not binge drinkers.

4. CHARACTERISTICS OF RECENT DRINKING EPISODES

This chapter presents information on the social context and location of underage drinking, the sources of alcohol for underage drinkers, and the co-occurrence of underage drinking and illicit drug use. These estimates are based on new items from the 2006 National Survey on Drug Use and Health (NSDUH) and include only data from current (past month) drinkers aged 12 to 20. Findings are presented by age group and gender.

4.1. Social Context of Alcohol Use

Among persons aged 12 to 20 who had used alcohol in the past month, most (80.9 percent) were with two or more people the last time they drank alcohol, 14.3 percent were with one other person the last time they drank, and 4.9 percent were alone (see Table 4.1 in Appendix C). Underage persons who drank with two or more other people on the last occasion in the past month had more drinks on the last occasion on average (4.9 drinks) than those who drank with one other person (3.1 drinks) or those who drank alone (2.9 drinks) (Table 4.2).

4.1.1. Age
In 2006, the majority of underage current drinkers in each age group (i.e., those aged 12 to 14, 15 to 17, and 18 to 20) consumed alcohol with two or more other people the last time they drank (Table 4.1 and Figure 4.1). Among current drinkers, youths aged 12 to 14 were more likely to have been alone (9.0 percent) or with one other person (21.9 percent) the last time they drank compared with youths aged 15 to 17 (5.2 percent alone and 14.6 percent with one other person) or 18 to 20 year olds (4.2 percent alone and 13.2 percent with one other person).

Current drinkers aged 12 to 14 who drank with two or more other people the last time they drank averaged more drinks on the last occasion (3.1 drinks) than those who drank with one other person (2.0 drinks) (Table 4.2 and Figure 4.2). Among current drinkers aged either 15 to 17 or 18 to 20, those who drank with two or more people on the last occasion consumed more drinks on average than those who drank either with one other person or by themselves.

4.1.2. Gender
Among underage drinkers, the majority of both males and females were with two or more other people on their last drinking occasion (Table 4.1). However, female drinkers were more likely to have been with two or people the last time they drank (83.6 percent) than were male

drinkers (78.4 percent). Conversely, male drinkers were more likely to have been alone the last time they drank (6.3 percent) than were female drinkers (3.3 percent).

For both males and females, underage persons who drank with two or more other people on the last occasion consumed more drinks on average than those who drank alone or with one other person (Table 4.2 and Figure 4.3). Males and females who drank alone on the last occasion reported a similar number of drinks on their last drinking occasion (3.1 drinks for males, 2.6 drinks for females), but males consumed more drinks than females when the last occasion was with one other person (3.5 drinks for males, 2.5 drinks for females) or with two or more people (5.8 drinks for males, 3.9 drinks for females).

4.2. Location of Alcohol Use

Overall, a majority of underage drinkers in 2006 reported that when they last used alcohol they were either in someone else's home (53.4 percent) or their own home (30.3 percent) (Table 4.1 and Figure 4.4).

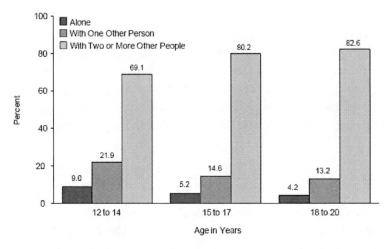

Figure 4.1. Social Context of Last Alcohol Use in the Past Month among Current Drinkers Aged 12 to 20, by Age: 2006.

The next most popular drinking locations for this age group were at a restaurant, bar, or club (9.4 percent); in a car or vehicle (5.5 percent); or at a park, on a beach, or in a parking lot (4.8 percent). Underage drinkers whose last drinking occasion was at someone else's home consumed an average of 4.9 drinks, while those whose last drinking occasion was at their own home consumed an average of 4.0 drinks (Table 4.2 and Figure 4.5). Among the next most popular drinking locations, underage current drinkers whose last alcohol use was at a restaurant or bar averaged 4.6 drinks, and those whose last alcohol use was at school, in a car or vehicle, or at a park, on a beach, or in a parking lot averaged 5.1 drinks. Current drinkers aged 12 to 20 who last drank at a concert or sports game (1.6 percent of all underage drinkers) consumed an average of 6.0 drinks on their last drinking occasion.

4.2.1. Age

More than 80 percent of underage drinkers in each age group (i.e., those aged 12 to 14, 15 to 17, or 18 to 20) drank at their own or someone else's home when they last used alcohol. However, there were differences in drinking locations between these age groups. Current drinkers aged 12 to 14 were more likely to have been at their own home the last time they drank (38.8 percent) and less likely to have been at someone else's home (45.0 percent) compared with those aged 15 to 17 (26.0 and 60.9 percent, respectively) or those aged 18 to 20 (31.4 and 50.7 percent, respectively) (Table 4.1 and Figure 4.6). In addition, drinkers aged 18 to 20 were more likely than younger age groups to have been in a restaurant, bar, or club on their last drinking occasion (12.9 percent for those aged 18 to 20 vs. 4.6 percent for those aged 12 to 14 and 3.7 percent for those aged 15 to 17), and they were less likely than younger age groups to have been at a park, on the beach, or in a parking lot on their last drinking occasion (2.9 percent for those aged 18 to 20 vs. 8.3 percent for those aged 12 to 14 and 7.7 percent for those aged 15 to 17).

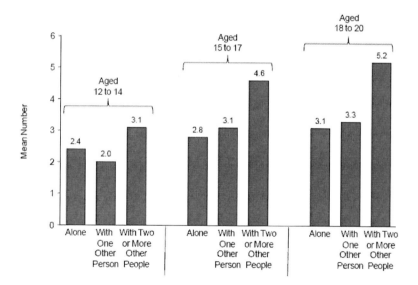

Figure 4.2. Drinks Consumed on Last Occasion of Alcohol Use in the Past Month among Current Drinkers Aged 12 to 20, by Social Context and Age: 2006.

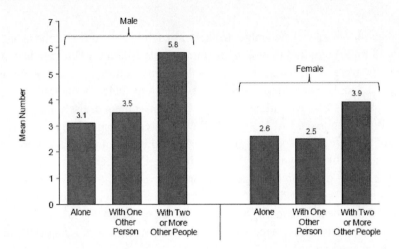

Figure 4.3. Drinks Consumed on Last Occasion of Alcohol Use in the Past Month among Current Drinkers Aged 12 to 20, by Social Context and Gender: 2006.

Current drinkers aged 12 to 14 who last drank at home consumed an average of 2.2 drinks on their last drinking occasion, whereas those who last drank at someone else's home consumed an average of 3.4 drinks on their last occasion (Table 4.2). This pattern was similar for youths aged 15 to 17 (average of 3.6 drinks if they last drank in their own home, 4.7 drinks if they last drank in someone else's home) and 18 to 20 year olds (average of 4.4 drinks if they last drank in their own home, 5.2 drinks if they last drank in someone else's home)

4.2.2. Gender

Among underage current drinkers, males were more likely than females to have been in their own home on their last drinking occasion (32.2 percent for males, 28.1 for females), whereas females were more likely than males to have been in a restaurant, bar, or club on their last drinking occasion (12.0 percent for females, 7.2 percent for males) (Table 4.1).

Underage male drinkers who last drank alcohol at their own home consumed more drinks on average on their last drinking occasion (4.6 drinks) than underage female drinkers who last drank at their own home (3.3 drinks) (Table 4.2). The pattern was similar for underage drinkers who last drank at someone else's home, with males averaging 5.8 drinks on this last drinking occasion and females averaging 4.0 drinks.

4.3. Sources of Alcohol among Underage Drinkers

This section provides information on the source of last alcohol use in the past month among current drinkers aged 12 to 20 in 2006. The sources of last alcohol use are divided into two categories: (a) underage drinker paid (he or she purchased it or gave someone else money to purchase it) and (b) underage drinker did not pay (he or she received it for free from someone or took it from his or her own or someone else's home)

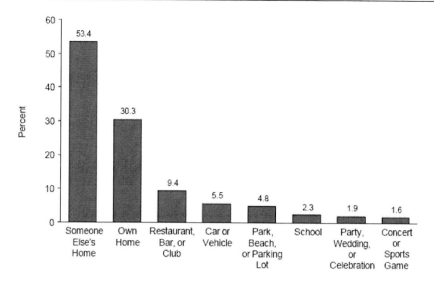

Figure 4.4. Location of Last Alcohol Use in the Past Month among Current Drinkers Aged 12 to 20: 2006.

Among all underage current drinkers, 31.0 percent paid for the alcohol the last time they drank, including 9.3 percent who purchased the alcohol themselves and 21.6 percent who gave money to someone else to purchase it (Table 4.3). The remaining 69.0 percent of underage drinkers did not pay for the alcohol on their last drinking occasion. More than one in four underage drinkers (25.8 percent) indicated that on their last drinking occasion they were given alcohol for free by an unrelated person aged 21 or older. Nearly one in five underage drinkers were given alcohol for free by a member of their family or took the alcohol from their own home on their last drinking occasion, including 6.4 percent who were given alcohol by their parent or guardian, 8.3 percent who were given alcohol by another family member aged 21 or older, and 3.9 percent who took it from their own home.

Persons aged 12 to 20 who paid for alcohol themselves consumed more drinks on their last drinking occasion (5.9 drinks) than did those who did not pay for the alcohol themselves (3.9 drinks) (Table 4.4).

4.3.1. Age

The most common sources of alcohol among underage current drinkers varied substantially by age group. For youths aged 12 to 14, the most common sources were receiving it for free from someone under the age of 21 (17.5 percent), receiving it from a parent or guardian (17.1 percent), or taking it from their own home (15.0 percent) (Table 4.3 and Figure 4.7). For youths aged 15 to 17, the most common sources were receiving it for free from an unrelated person aged 21 or older (20.1 percent), receiving it from someone under the age of 21 (19.9 percent), and giving somebody else money to purchase the alcohol (17.9 percent). For persons aged 18 to 20, the majority of current drinkers either received alcohol for free from an unrelated person aged 21 or older (30.0 percent) or gave somebody else money to purchase the alcohol (25.3 percent).

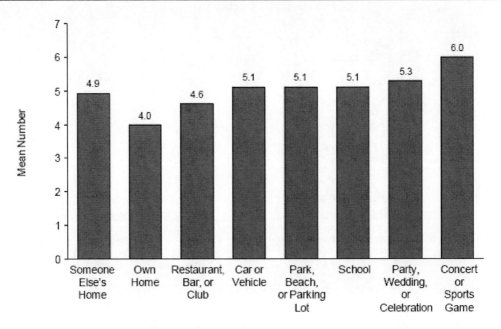

Figure 4.5. Drinks Consumed on Last Alcohol Use in the Past Month among Current Drinkers Aged 12 to 20, by Location of Last Alcohol Use: 2006.

Those in older age groups were more likely to have paid for alcohol themselves on their last drinking occasion, with 37.6 percent of 18 to 20 year olds paying for it themselves compared with 23.5 percent of 15 to 17 year olds and 6.6 percent of 12 to 14 year olds.

Within each of these age groups, persons who paid for alcohol themselves on the last occasion had more drinks on average than those who did not pay for alcohol themselves (Table 4.4 and Figure 4.8). For example, youths aged 12 to 14 had 4.8 drinks when they paid for their own drinks, but they had 2.7 drinks when they did not pay for them.

4.3.2. Gender

Among underage current drinkers, males were more likely to have paid for alcohol themselves on their last drinking occasion (36.7 percent) than were females (24.5 percent) (Table 4.3). That is, female drinkers aged 12 to 20 were more likely to have others give them alcohol for free than were male drinkers in this age group. Among underage drinkers, similar percentages of females and males reported getting alcohol from their parent or guardian, another family member aged 21 or older, or from their own home. However, underage females were more likely than underage males to have received alcohol without paying from someone not related aged 21 or older (29.8 percent for females, 22.2 percent for males) or from someone under the age of 21 (16.0 percent for females, 12.5 percent for males).

Among both underage males and females, persons who paid for alcohol themselves on the last occasion had more drinks on average (6.8 drinks for males, 4.5 drinks for females) than those who did not pay for alcohol themselves (4.4 drinks for males, 3.4 drinks for females) (Table 4.4).

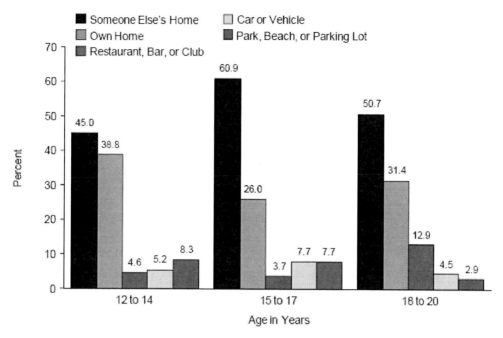

Figure 4.6. Location of Last Alcohol Use in the Past Month among Current Drinkers Aged 12 to 20, by Age: 2006.

4.4. Use of Illicit Drugs with Alcohol

In 2006, more than one third (35.8 percent) of persons aged 12 to 20 who used alcohol in the past month also had used an illicit drug in the past month (Table 4.5). Among underage drinkers, marijuana was the drug most often used in the past month (30.0 percent), followed by pain relievers (8.8 percent). Furthermore, 16.0 percent of underage drinkers had used an illicit drug within 2 hours of using alcohol on their last occasion of alcohol use in the past month (Table 4.5). The drug most often used within 2 hours of their last alcohol use in the past month was marijuana (15.0 percent), followed by pain relievers (1.2 percent).

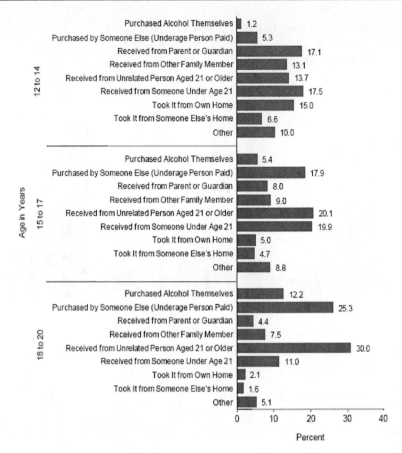

Figure 4.7. Source of Alcohol Used in the Past Month among Current Drinkers Aged 12 to 20, by Age: 2006.

4.4.1. Age

Approximately one in four youths aged 12 to 14 who had used alcohol in the past month had also used an illicit drug in the past month (25.2 percent), as had more than one in three current drinkers aged 15 to 17 (37.0 percent) and those aged 18 to 20 (36.4 percent) (Table 4.5). Current drinkers aged 12 to 14 were less likely to have used marijuana in the past month (15.5 percent) compared with those aged 15 to 17 (31.0 percent) or those aged 18 to 20 (31.2 percent); however, 12- to 14-year-old drinkers used illicit drugs other than marijuana at a similar rate (15.2 percent) as those aged 15 to 17 (15.3 percent).

Among current drinkers, 5.4 percent of 12 to 14 year olds had used an illicit drug within 2 hours of alcohol use on their last drinking occasion, as did 15.7 percent of 15 to 17 year olds and 17.4 percent of 18 to 20 year olds (Table 4.5 and Figure 4.9). For all three age groups, marijuana was used more often with alcohol than any other illicit drug. Drinkers aged 12 to 14 were less likely to have used illicit drugs other than marijuana within 2 hours of their last alcohol use (1.1 percent) than those aged 18 to 20 (2.9 percent).

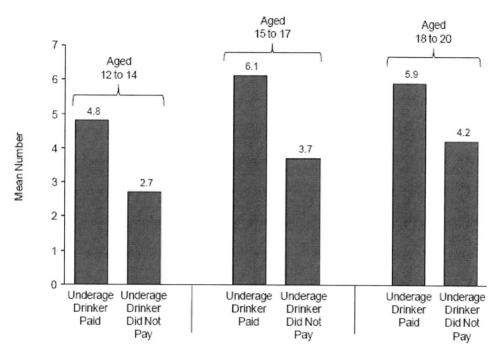

Figure 4.8. Drinks Consumed on Last Occasion of Alcohol Use in the Past Month among Current Drinkers Aged 12 to 20, by Source of Last Alcohol Used and Age: 2006.

4.4.2. Gender

Among underage drinkers, males were more likely than females to have used an illicit drug in the past month (37.3 percent for males, 34.0 percent for females) or to have used an illicit drug within 2 hours of their last alcohol use in the past month (18.3 percent for males, 13.4 percent for females) (Table 4.5). Among underage drinkers, males were more likely than females to have used marijuana within 2 hours of their last alcohol use in the past month (17.2 percent for males, 12.6 percent for females), but males and females had similar rates of use of illicit drugs other than marijuana within 2 hours of drinking in the past month

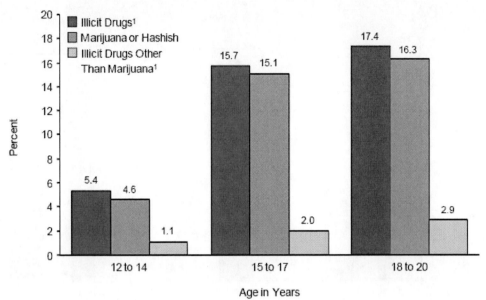

¹Illicit Drugs include marijuana/hashish, cocaine (including crack), heroin, hallucinogens, inhalants, or prescription-type psychotherapeutics used nonmedically. Illicit Drugs Other Than Marijuana include cocaine (including crack), heroin, hallucinogens, inhalants, or prescription-type psychotherapeutics used nonmedically. These summary estimates do not include data from the methamphetamine use items added in 2005 and 2006.

Figure 4.9. Illicit Drug Use within 2 Hours of Alcohol Use in the Past Month among Current Drinkers Aged 12 to 20, by Age: 2006.

4.5. Summary

In 2006, most (80.9 percent) of the persons aged 12 to 20 who had consumed alcohol in the past month were with two or more people the last time they drank alcohol, 14.3 percent were with one other person the last time they drank, and 4.9 percent were alone. Among underage drinkers, females were more likely to have been with two or people the last time they drank (83.6 percent) than were males (78.4 percent), whereas males were more likely to have been alone the last time they drank (6.3 percent) than were females (3.3 percent). Males and females who drank alone on the last occasion reported a similar number of drinks on their last drinking occasion (3.1 drinks for males, 2.6 drinks for females), but males consumed more drinks than females did when their last drinking occasion was with one other person (3.5 drinks for males, 2.5 drinks for females) or with two or more people (5.8 drinks for males, 3.9 drinks for females). A majority of underage drinkers reported that when they last used alcohol they were either in someone else's home (53.4 percent) or their own home (30.3 percent). Drinkers aged 12 to 14 were more likely to have been at their own home the last time they drank and less likely to have been at someone else's home compared with drinkers in older age groups, and drinkers aged 18 to 20 were more likely than those in younger age groups to have been in a restaurant, bar, or club on their last drinking occasion.

Among all underage current drinkers, 9.3 percent purchased the alcohol themselves, and 21.6 percent gave money to someone else to purchase it. Underage persons who paid for alcohol themselves consumed more drinks on their last drinking occasion (average of 5.9 drinks) than did those who did not pay for the alcohol themselves (average of 3.9 drinks). More than one in four underage drinkers (25.8 percent) indicated that on their last drinking occasion they were given alcohol for free by an unrelated person aged 21 or older. Among underage drinkers, males were more likely to have paid for alcohol themselves on their last drinking occasion (36.7 percent) than were females (24.5 percent).

In 2006, more than one third (35.8 percent) of persons aged 12 to 20 who used alcohol in the past month also had used an illicit drug in the past month, and 16.0 percent of underage drinkers used an illicit drug with alcohol or within 2 hours of alcohol use on their last occasion of alcohol use in the past month. Marijuana was the illicit drug most used by underage drinkers, with nearly one third (30.0 percent) having used marijuana in the past month, and 15.0 percent having used marijuana with alcohol or within 2 hours of their last alcohol use. Males were more likely than females to have used an illicit drug within 2 hours of their last alcohol use in the past month (18.3 percent for males, 13.4 percent for females)

ACKNOWLEDGMENTS

This report was prepared by the Division of Population Surveys, Office of Applied Studies, Substance Abuse and Mental Health Services Administration (SAMHSA), and by RTI International, a trade name of Research Triangle Institute, Research Triangle Park, North Carolina. Work by RTI was performed under Contract No. 283-2004-00022. At RTI, the report was authored by Michael R. Pemberton, and all statistical analyses were conducted by Tania M. Robbins. Other contributors and reviewers at RTI listed alphabetically include Jeremy Aldworth, Justine Allpress, Teresa R. Davis, David C. Heller, Larry A. Kroutil, Mary Ellen Marsden, Lisa Packer, and Kathryn Spagnola. At SAMHSA, the report was coauthored by James D. Colliver, conceptualized by Joseph C. Gfroerer, and reviewed by Joel Kennet. Also at RTI, report and web production staff listed alphabetically include Teresa G. Bass, Wendy Broome, Cassandra M. Carter, Joyce Clay-Brooks, Diane G. Eckard, Shari B. Lambert, Danny Occoquan, Brenda K. Porter, Pamela Couch Prevatt, and Richard S. Straw. Final report production was provided by Beatrice Rouse, Coleen Sanderson, and Jane Feldmann at SAMHSA.

APPENDIX A: DESCRIPTION OF THE SURVEYS

A.1. Sample Design

The designs for the 2002 to 2006 National Surveys on Drug Use and Health (NSDUH) [1] are part of coordinated sample designs providing estimates for all 50 States plus the District of Columbia. Survey years 2002 to 2004 come from a coordinated 5-year design for the 1999 through 2004 surveys, while the 2005 and 2006 designs are from a coordinated 5-year design for the 2005 through 2009 NSDUHs. The respondent universe is the civilian, noninstitutionalized population aged 12 years old or older residing within the 50 States and the District of Columbia. The survey includes persons living in noninstitutionalized group quarters (e.g., shelters, rooming/boarding houses, college dormitories, migratory workers' camps, halfway houses), and civilians living on military bases. Persons excluded from NSDUH include persons with no fixed household address (e.g., homeless and/or transient persons not in shelters), active-duty military personnel, and residents of institutional group quarters, such as correctional facilities, nursing homes, mental institutions, and long-term hospitals.

For the 50-State design, 8 States were designated as large sample States (California, Florida, Illinois, Michigan, New York, Ohio, Pennsylvania, and Texas) with samples large enough to support direct State estimates. In 2006, sample sizes in these States ranged from 3,512 to 3,671. For the remaining 42 States and the District of Columbia, smaller, but adequate, samples were selected to support State estimates using small area estimation (SAE) [2]. Sample sizes in these States ranged from 862 to 1,000 in 2006.

In 2005 and 2006, States were first stratified into a total of 900 State sampling (SS) regions (48 regions in each large sample State and 12 regions in each small sample State). These regions were contiguous geographic areas designed to yield the same number of interviews on average [3]. Unlike the 2002 through 2004 NSDUHs in which the first-stage sampling units were clusters of census blocks called "area segments," the first stage of selection for the 2005 through 2009 NSDUHs was census tracts [4] This stage was included to contain sample segments within a single census tract to the extent possible [5]

For each SS region, 48 census tracts were selected with probability proportional to size. Within sampled census tracts, adjacent census blocks were combined to form the second-stage sampling units or area segments. One area segment was selected within each sampled census tract with probability proportional to population size to support the 5-year sample and any supplemental studies that the Substance Abuse and Mental Health Services Administration (SAMHSA) may choose to field [6]. Of these segments, 24 were designated for the coordinated 5- year sample and 24 were designated as "reserve" segments. Eight sample segments per SS region were fielded during the 2006 survey year.

These sampled segments were allocated equally into four separate samples, one for each 3-month period (calendar quarter) during the year, so that the survey was essentially continuous in the field. In each of these area segments, a listing of all addresses was constructed and used as the frame for selecting a sample of addresses. Selected addresses were determined to be eligible sample units or to be ineligible. In the eligible sample units (which can be either households or units within group quarters), sample persons were randomly selected using an automated screening procedure programmed in a handheld computer carried by the interviewers. Persons aged 12 to 17 years and those aged 18 to 25 years were oversampled at this stage. Because of the large sample sizes in each year, there was no need to oversample racial/ethnic groups, as was done on surveys prior to 1999. Consistent with previous surveys in this series, the final respondent samples in each survey year were representative of the U.S. general population (since 1991, the civilian, noninstitutionalized population) aged 12 or older. In addition, State samples were representative of their respective State populations. More detailed information on the disposition of the national screening and interview samples can be found in Appendix B.

NSDUH covers residents of households (living in houses/townhouses, apartments, condominiums, etc.), persons in noninstitutional group quarters (e.g., shelters, rooming/boarding houses, college dormitories, migratory workers' camps, halfway houses), and civilians living on military bases. Although the survey covers residents of these types of units (they are given a nonzero probability of selection), the sample sizes of most specific groups are too small to provide separate estimates.

More information on the sample design can be found in the 2006 NSDUH sample design report by Morton et al. (2007) on the Office of Applied Studies (OAS) website (available at http://oas.samhsa.gov/nsduh/methods.cfm).

A.2. Data Collection Methodology

The data collection method used in NSDUH involves in-person interviews with sample persons, incorporating procedures designed to maximize respondents' cooperation and willingness to report honestly about their illicit drug use behavior. Confidentiality is stressed in all written and oral communications with potential respondents. Respondents' names are not collected with the data, and computer-assisted interviewing (CAI) methods, including audio computer-assisted self-interviewing (ACASI), are used to provide a private and confidential setting to complete the interview.

Introductory letters are sent to sampled addresses, followed by an interviewer visit. A 5-minute screening procedure using a handheld computer involves listing all household members along with their basic demographic data. The computer uses the demographic data in a preprogrammed selection algorithm to select zero, one, or two sample person(s), depending on the composition of the household. This selection process is designed to provide the necessary sample sizes for the specified population age groupings and to select a subsample of pairs of individual respondents within the same households.

Interviewers immediately attempt to conduct the NSDUH interview with each selected person in the household. The interviewer requests the selected respondent to identify a private area in the home to conduct the interview away from other household members. The interview averages about an hour and includes a combination of CAPI (computer-assisted personal interviewing, in which the interviewer reads the questions) and ACASI (which is self- administered by the respondent).

The NSDUH interview consists of a core and supplemental sections. A core set of questions critical for basic trend measurement of prevalence estimates remains in the survey every year and comprises the first part of the interview. Supplemental questions, or modules, that can be revised, dropped, or added from year to year make up the remainder of the interview. The core consists of initial demographic items (which are interviewer-administered) and self- administered questions pertaining to the use of tobacco, alcohol, marijuana, cocaine, crack cocaine, heroin, hallucinogens, inhalants, pain relievers, tranquilizers, stimulants, and sedatives. Supplemental topics in the remaining self-administered sections include (but are not limited to) injection drug use, perceived risks of substance use, substance dependence or abuse, arrests, treatment for substance use problems, pregnancy and health care issues, and mental health issues. Supplemental demographic questions (which are interviewer-administered and follow the ACASI questions) address such topics as immigration, current school enrollment, employment and workplace issues, health insurance coverage, and income. It should be noted that some of the supplemental portions of the interview have remained in the survey, relatively unchanged, from year to year (e.g., current health insurance coverage, employment).

Thus, the interview begins in CAPI mode with the field interviewer (FI) reading the questions from the computer screen and entering the respondent's replies into the computer. The interview then transitions to the ACASI mode for the sensitive questions. In this mode, the respondent can read the questions silently on the computer screen and/or listen to the questions read through headphones and enter his or her responses directly into the computer. At the conclusion of the ACASI section, the interview returns to the CAPI mode with the interviewer completing the questionnaire. Each respondent who completes a full interview is given a $30.00 cash payment as a token of appreciation for his or her time.

No personal identifying information is captured in the CAI record for the respondent. Interviewers transmit the completed interview data to RTI in Research Triangle Park, North Carolina, via home telephone lines.

A.3. Data Processing

Computers at RTI direct the information to a raw data file that consists of one record for each completed interview. Even though editing and consistency checks are done by the CAI program during the interview, additional, more complex edits and consistency checks are completed at RTI. Cases are retained only if respondents provided data on lifetime use of cigarettes and at least nine other substances in the core section of the questionnaire. An important aspect of subsequent editing routines involves assignment of codes when respondents legitimately were skipped out of questions that definitely did not apply to them (e.g., if respondents never used a drug of interest). For key alcohol and other drug use measures, the editing procedures identify inconsistencies between related variables. Inconsistencies in variables pertaining to the most recent period that respondents used alcohol or other drugs are edited by assigning an "indefinite" period of use (e.g., use at some point in the lifetime, which could mean use in the past 30 days or past 12 months). Inconsistencies in other key substance use variables are edited by assigning missing data codes. These inconsistencies then are resolved through statistical imputation procedures, as discussed in Section A.3.1.

In addition, an important principle that was followed in editing NSDUH data was that data from core substance use modules (i.e., tobacco through sedatives, and including the core alcohol module) generally were not used to edit data in noncore modules, such as the consumption of alcohol module that was the source of estimates in some chapters of this report. In particular, noncore self-administered data (including the consumption of alcohol module in 2006) were never used to edit related variables in the core self-administered modules, such as alcohol. Consequently, variables in noncore sections of the interview could be inconsistent with variables in core sections. For example, respondents could report in the core alcohol module that they did not engage in binge alcohol use in the past 30 days (i.e., consumed five or more drinks in a single occasion on 0 days in the past 30 days), but they also could report in the noncore consumption of alcohol module that they had five or more drinks the last time they drank alcohol in the past 30 days. No further editing was done to make these core and noncore reports about binge alcohol use consistent with one another.

In an exception to the principle that items from noncore modules not be used to edit core variables, new methamphetamine items added to the special drugs noncore module in 2005 and 2006 were considered in the estimates of methamphetamine use in the past year among past year alcohol users in the top section of Table 4.5 in Appendix C. These methamphetamine items were added to better account for how methamphetamine is supplied and obtained. Unlike other stimulants that are available by prescription, most methamphetamine in the United States is supplied through illicit manufacturing and trafficking rather than through the conventional prescription drug distribution process. Therefore, one concern is that methamphetamine use may have been underestimated in NSDUH due to its inclusion within a set of questions about prescription-type drugs. Specifically, survey respondents who used methamphetamine might not have reported its use when questions about it were asked in the context of other questions about prescription pharmaceuticals. Section B.4.6 in Appendix B of the 2006 NSDUH national findings report (Office of Applied Studies [OAS], 2007a) provides a discussion of the new items and the process used to generate the prevalence estimates based on them.

A.3.1. Statistical Imputation

For some key variables that still had missing or ambiguous values after editing, statistical imputation was used to replace these values with appropriate response codes. For example, the response is ambiguous if the editing procedures assigned a respondent's most recent use of alcohol or other drugs to "use at some point in the lifetime," with no definite period within the lifetime. In this case, the imputation procedures assign a definite value for when the respondent last used the substance (e.g., in the past 30 days, more than 30 days ago but within the past 12 months, more than 12 months ago). Similarly, if a response is completely missing, the imputation procedures replace missing values with nonmissing ones.

In most cases, missing or ambiguous values are imputed in NSDUH using a methodology called predictive mean neighborhoods (PMN), which was developed specifically for the 1999 survey and used in all subsequent survey years. The PMN method offers a rigorous and flexible method that was implemented to improve the quality of estimates and allow more variables to be imputed. Some of the key reasons for implementing this method include the following: (1) the ability to use covariates to determine donors is far greater than that offered in the hot deck, (2) the relative importance of covariates can be determined by standard estimating equation techniques, (3) the correlations across response variables can be accounted for by making the imputation multivariate, and (4) sampling weights can be easily incorporated in the models. The PMN method has some similarity with the predictive mean matching method of Rubin (1986) except that, for the donor records, Rubin used the observed variable value (not the predictive mean) to compute the distance function. Also, the well-known method of nearest neighbor imputation is similar to PMN, except that the distance function is in terms of the original predictor variables and often requires somewhat arbitrary scaling of discrete variables. PMN is a combination of a model-assisted imputation methodology and a random nearest neighbor hot- deck procedure. The hot-deck procedure is set up in such a way that imputed values are made consistent with preexisting nonmis sing values for other variables. Whenever feasible, the imputation of variables using PMN is multivariate, in which imputation is accomplished on several response variables at once. Variables requiring imputation using PMN are the core demographic variables, core alcohol and other drug use variables (recency of use, frequency of use, and age at first use), income, health insurance, and noncore demographic variables for work status, immigrant status, and the household roster.

In the modeling stage of PMN, the model chosen depends on the nature of the response variable Y. In the 2006 NSDUH, the models included binomial logistic regression, multinomial logistic regression, Poisson regression, and ordinary linear regression, where the models incorporated the sampling design weights.

In general, hot-deck imputation replaces an item nonresponse (missing or ambiguous value) with a recorded response that is donated from a "similar" respondent who has nonmissing data. For random nearest neighbor hot-deck imputation, the missing or ambiguous value is replaced by a responding value from a donor randomly selected from a set of potential donors. Potential donors are those defined to be "close" to the unit with the missing or ambiguous value according to a predefined function called a distance metric. In the hot-deck stage of PMN, the set of candidate donors (the "neighborhood") consists of respondents with complete data who have a predicted mean close to that of the item nonrespondent. The predicted means are computed both for respondents with and without missing data, which differs from Rubin's method where predicted means are not computed for the donor respondent (Rubin, 1986). In particular, the neighborhood consists of either the set of the closest 30 respondents or the set of respondents with a predicted mean (or means) within 5 percent of the predicted mean(s) of the item nonrespondent, whichever set is smaller. If no respondents are available who have a predicted mean (or means) within 5 percent of the item nonrespondent, the respondent with the predicted mean(s) closest to that of the item nonrespondent is selected as the donor.

In the univariate case (where only one variable is imputed using PMN), the neighborhood of potential donors is determined by calculating the relative distance between the predicted mean for an item nonrespondent and the predicted mean for each potential donor, then choosing those means defined by the distance metric. The pool of donors is restricted further to satisfy logical constraints whenever necessary (e.g., age at first crack use must not be less than age at first cocaine use).

Whenever possible, missing or ambiguous values for more than one response variable are considered at a time. In this (multivariate) case, the distance metric is a Mahalanobis distance (Manly, 1986) rather than a relative Euclidean distance. Whether the imputation is univariate or multivariate, only missing or ambiguous values are replaced, and donors are restricted to be logically consistent with the response variables that are not missing. Furthermore, donors are restricted to satisfy "likeness constraints" whenever possible. That is, donors are required to have the same values for variables highly correlated with the response. If no donors are available who meet these conditions, these likeness constraints can be loosened. For example, donors for the age at first use variable are required to be of the same age as recipients, if at all possible. Further details on the PMN methodology are provided in RTI International (2008) and by Singh, Grau, and Folsom (2001, 2002).

Although statistical imputation could not proceed separately within each State due to insufficient pools of donors, information about each respondent's State of residence was incorporated in the modeling and hot-deck steps. For most drugs, respondents were separated into three "State usage" categories as follows: respondents from States with high usage of a given drug were placed in one category, respondents from States with medium usage into another, and the remainder into a third category. This categorical "State rank" variable was used as one set of covariates in the imputation models. In addition, eligible donors for each item nonrespondent were restricted to be of the same State usage category (i.e., the same "State rank") as the nonrespondent.

A.3.2. Development of Analysis Weights

The general approach to developing and calibrating analysis weights involved developing design-based weights, dk, as the product of the inverse of the selection probabilities at each selection stage. The 2005 and 2006 NSDUHs used a four-stage sample selection scheme in which an extra selection stage of census tracts was added before the selection of a segment.

Thus, the design-based weights, dk, for the 2005 and 2006 NSDUHs incorporated the extra layer of sampling selection to reflect the change in sample design relative to the 2002 to 2004 NSDUHs. Adjustment factors, ak(λ), then were applied to the design-based weights to adjust for nonresponse, to poststratify to known population control totals, and to control for extreme weights when necessary. In view of the importance of State-level estimates with the 50-State design, it was necessary to control for a much larger number of known population totals. Several other modifications to the general weight adjustment strategy that had been used in past surveys also were implemented for the first time beginning with the 1999 CAI sample.

Weight adjustments were based on a generalization of Deville and Särndal's (1992) logit model. This generalized exponential model (GEM) (Folsom & Singh, 2000) incorporates unit- specific bounds (Rk, uk), k0s, for the adjustment factor ak(X) as follows

$$a_k(\lambda) = \frac{\ell_k(u_k - c_k) + u_k(c_k - \ell_k)\exp(A_k x_k'\lambda)}{(u_k - c_k) + (c_k - \ell_k)\exp(A_k x_k'\lambda)},$$

where ck are pre specified centering constants, such that Rk < ck < uk and Ak = (uk - Rk) / (uk - ck)(ck - Rk). The variables Rk, ck, and uk are user-specified bounds, and X is the column vector of p model parameters corresponding to the p covariates x. The X-parameters are estimated by solving

$$\sum_s x_k d_k a_k(\lambda) - \tilde{T}_x = 0.$$

where T%x denotes control totals that could be either nonrandom, as is generally the case with poststratification, or random, as is generally the case for nonresponse adjustment.

$$\Delta(w,d) = \sum_{k \in s} \frac{d_k}{A_k}\left\{(a_k - \ell_k)\log\frac{a_k - \ell_k}{c_k - \ell_k} + (u_k - a_k)\log\frac{u_k - a_k}{u_k - c_k}\right\}.$$

This general approach was used at several stages of the weight adjustment process, including (1) adjustment of household weights for nonresponse at the screener level, (2) poststratification of household weights to meet population controls for various demographic groups by State, (3) adjustment of household weights for extremes, (4) poststratification of selected person weights, (5) adjustment of responding person weights for nonresponse at the questionnaire level, (6) poststratification of responding person weights, and (7) adjustment of responding person weights for extremes.

Every effort was made to include as many relevant State-specific covariates (typically defined by demographic domains within States) as possible in the multivariate models used to calibrate the weights (nonresponse adjustment and poststratification steps). Because further subdivision of State samples by demographic covariates often produced small cell sample sizes, it was not possible to retain all State-specific covariates (even after meaningful collapsing of covariate categories) and still estimate the necessary model parameters with reasonable precision. Therefore, a hierarchical structure was used in grouping States with covariates defined at the national level, at the census division level within the Nation, at the State group within the census division, and, whenever possible, at the State level. In every case, the controls for the total population within a State and the five age groups (12 to 17, 18 to 25, 26 to 34, 35 to 49, 50 or older) within a State were maintained except that, in the last step of poststratification of person weights, six age groups (12 to 17, 18 to 25, 26 to 34, 35 to 49, 50 to 64, 65 or older) were used. Census control totals by age, race, gender, and Hispanicity were required for the civilian, noninstitutionalized population of each State. Beginning with the 2002 NSDUH, the Population Estimates Branch of the U.S. Census Bureau has produced the necessary population estimates in response to a special request based on the 2000 census.

Consistent with the surveys from 1999 onward, control of extreme weights through separate bounds for adjustment factors was incorporated into the GEM calibration processes for both nonresponse and poststratification. This is unlike the traditional method of winsorization in which extreme weights are truncated at prespecified levels and the trimmed portions of weights are distributed to the nontruncated cases. In GEM, it is possible to set bounds around the prespecified levels for extreme weights, and then the calibration process provides an objective way of deciding the extent of adjustment (or truncation) within the specified bounds. A step was added to poststratify the household-level weights to obtain census-consistent estimates based on the household rosters from all screened households; these household roster-based estimates then provided the control totals needed to calibrate the respondent pair weights for subsequent planned analyses. An additional step poststratified the selected person sample to conform to the adjusted roster estimates. This additional step takes advantage of the inherent two-phase nature of the NSDUH design. The final step poststratified the respondent person sample to external census data (defined within the State whenever possible, as discussed above). For more detailed information, see the 2006 NSDUH Methodological Resource Book (RTI International, 2008).

In addition to the person-level analysis weights discussed above, person pair–level analysis weights also were calculated. In each year of NSDUH, the person pair–level analysis weights and person-level analysis weights shared the same weight components at the screening dwelling unit (SDU) level. In addition to these common weight components, the person pair– level analysis weights had several specific weight components: (1) inverse of person-pair selection probability, (2) poststratification of selected person-pair weights, (3) adjustment of responding person-pair weights for nonresponse, (4) poststratification of responding person-pair weights, and (5) adjustment of responding person-pair weights for extremes. The person-pair analysis weights were the product of all of the weight components.

For more detailed information, see the 2006 NSDUH Methodological Resource Book (RTI International, 2008).

For many populations of interest in this report, 5 years of NSDUH data were combined to obtain annual averages. The person-level weights and the person-pair weight for estimates based on the annual averages were obtained by dividing the person-level analysis weights and the person-pair analysis weight for the 5 specific years by a factor of 5

APPENDIX B: STATISTICAL METHODS AND MEASUREMENT

B.1. Target Population

An important limitation of estimates of drug use prevalence from the National Survey on Drug Use and Health (NSDUH) is that they are only designed to describe the target population of the survey—the civilian, noninstitutionalized population aged 12 or older. Although this population includes almost 98 percent of the total U.S. population aged 12 or older, it excludes some important and unique subpopulations who may have very different alcohol and drug use patterns. Within the population aged 12 or older, this report focuses on persons between the ages of 12 and 20, that is, those who are below the legal drinking age.

B.2. Sampling Error and Statistical Significance

This report includes tables for national and State estimates, produced using a multiprocedure package called SUDAAN® Software for Statistical Analysis of Correlated Data. SUDAAN was designed for the statistical analysis of data collected using stratified, multistage cluster sampling designs, as well as other observational and experimental studies involving repeated measures or studies subject to cluster correlation effects (RTI International, 2004). The final, nonresponse-adjusted, and poststratified analysis weights were used in SUDAAN to compute unbiased design-based drug use estimates.

The sampling error (i.e., the standard error or SE) of an estimate is the error caused by the selection of a sample instead of conducting a census of the population. The sampling error may be reduced by selecting a large sample and/or by using efficient sample design and estimation strategies, such as stratification, optimal allocation, and ratio estimation.

With the use of probability sampling methods in NSDUH, it is possible to develop estimates of sampling error from the survey data. These estimates have been calculated using SUDAAN for all estimates presented in this report using a Taylor series linearization approach that takes into account the effects of NSDUH's complex design features. The sampling errors are used to identify unreliable estimates and to test for the statistical significance of differences between estimates.

B.2.1. Variance Estimation for Totals

Estimates of means or proportions, pˆd, such as drug use prevalence estimates for a domain d, can be expressed as a ratio estimate:

$$\hat{p}_d = \frac{\hat{Y}_d}{\hat{N}_d},$$

where Yd is a linear statistic estimating number of substance users in the domain, and Nd is a linear statistic estimating the total number of persons in domain d (both users and nonusers). The SUDAAN software used to develop estimates and their SEs produces direct estimates Y d and ˆNd and their SEs. The SUDAAN application also uses a Taylor series approximation method toestimate the SEs of the ratio estimate pˆd .

When the domain size, Nd , is free of sampling error, an appropriate estimate of the SE for the total number of substance users is

$$SE(\hat{Y}_d) = \hat{N}_d SE(\hat{p}_d).$$

This approach is theoretically correct when the domain size estimates, Nd , are among those forced to match their respective U.S. Census Bureau population projections through the weight calibration process (Chen et al., 2005). In these cases, Nd is not subject to sampling error. For a more detailed explanation of the weight calibration process, see Section A.3.2 in Appendix A.

For estimated domain totals, Yd , where Nd is not fixed (i.e., where domain size estimates are not forced to match the U.S. Census Bureau population projections), this formulation may still provide a good approximation if it can be assumed that the sampling variation in Nd is negligible relative to the sampling variation in pˆ d. This is a reasonable assumption for most cases in this study.

For a subset of the estimates produced from the 2002 to 2006 data, the above approach yielded an underestimate of the variance of a total because Nd was subject to considerable variation. In these cases, the SEs for the total estimates calculated directly within SUDAAN are reported. Using the SEs from the total estimates directly from SUDAAN does not affect the SE estimates for the corresponding proportions presented in the same sets of tables.

B.2.2. Suppression Criteria for Unreliable Estimates

As has been done in other NSDUH reports, direct survey estimates produced for this study that are considered to be unreliable due to unacceptably large sampling errors are not shown in this report and are noted by asterisks (*) in the tables containing such estimates. The criteria used for suppressing all direct survey estimates were based on the relative standard error (RSE) (defined as the ratio of the SE over the estimate), nominal (actual) sample size, and effective sample size for each estimate.

Proportion estimates (ˆ p) within the range [0 < pˆ < 1], rates, and the corresponding estimated number of users were suppressed if

$$RSE[-\ln(\hat{p})] > .175 \text{ when } \hat{p} \leq .5$$

or

$$RSE[-\ln(1 - \hat{p})] > .175 \text{ when } \hat{p} > .5.$$

Using a first-order Taylor series approximation to estimate RSE[-ln (^p)] and RSE[-ln(1 - p^)], the following equation was derived and used for computational purposes:

$$\frac{SE(\hat{p})/\hat{p}}{-\ln(\hat{p})} > .175 \text{ when } \hat{p} \leq .5$$

or

$$\frac{SE(\hat{p})/(1-\hat{p})}{-\ln(1-\hat{p})} > .175 \text{ when } \hat{p} > .5.$$

The separate formulas for p^ ≤.5 and p^ > .5 produce a symmetric suppression rule; that is, if p^ is suppressed, 1−p^ will be suppressed as well. This ad hoc rule requires an effective sample size in excess of 50. When .05 <p^< .95, the symmetric property of the rule produces a local maximum effective sample size of 68 at p^ = .5. Thus, estimates with these values of p along with effective sample sizes falling below 68 are suppressed. See Figure B. 1 for a representation of the required minimum effective sample sizes as a function of the proportion estimated.

A minimum nominal sample size suppression criterion (n = 100) that protects against unreliable estimates caused by small design effects and small nominal sample sizes was employed. Prevalence estimates also were suppressed if they were close to 0 or 100 percent (i.e., if p^ < .00005 or if p^≥ .99995).

Estimates of other totals along with means and rates that are not bounded between 0 and 1 (e.g., mean age at first use and incidence rates) were suppressed if the RSEs of the estimates were larger than .5. Additionally, estimates of the mean age at first use were suppressed if the sample size was smaller than 10 respondents. Also, the estimated incidence rate and number of initiates were suppressed if they rounded to 0.

The suppression criteria for various NSDUH estimates are summarized in Table B. 1 at the end of this appendix.

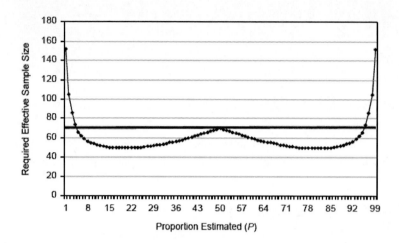

Figure B.1. Required Effective Sample as a Function of the Proportion Estimated Current Rule: NSDUH 2006.

B.2.3. Statistical Significance of Differences

This section describes the methods used to compare prevalence estimates in this report. Customarily, the observed difference between estimates is evaluated in terms of its statistical significance. Statistical significance is based on the p value of the test statistic and refers to the probability that a difference as large as that observed would occur due to random variability in the estimates if there were no difference in the prevalence estimates for the population groups being compared. The significance of observed differences in this report is reported at the .05 level. When comparing prevalence estimates, the null hypothesis (no difference between prevalence estimates) was tested against the alternative hypothesis (there is a difference in prevalence estimates) using the standard difference in proportions test expressed as

$$Z = \frac{\hat{p}_1 - \hat{p}_2}{\sqrt{\mathrm{var}(\hat{p}_1) + \mathrm{var}(\hat{p}_2) - 2\mathrm{cov}(\hat{p}_1, \hat{p}_2)}} \, ,$$

where p^ 1 = first prevalence estimate, p^ 2 = second prevalence estimate, var (p ^ 1) = variance of first prevalence estimate, var (p^2) = variance of second prevalence estimate, and cov (p^ 1 , p ^ 2) = covariance between p^ 1 and p^ 2 . In cases where significance tests between years were performed,

the prevalence estimate from the earlier year (2002, 2003, 2004, or 2005) becomes the first prevalence estimate, and the prevalence estimate from the later year (2006) becomes the second prevalence estimate.

Under the null hypothesis, Z is asymptotically distributed as a normal random variable. Therefore, calculated values of Z can be referred to the unit normal distribution to determine the corresponding probability level (i.e., p value). Because the covariance term between the two estimates is not necessarily zero, SUDAAN was used to compute estimates of Z along with the associated p values using the analysis weights and accounting for the sample design as described in Appendix A. A similar procedure and formula for Z were used for estimated totals; however, it should be noted that because it was necessary to calculate the SE outside of SUDAAN for domains forced by the weighting process to match their respective U.S. Census Bureau population estimates, the corresponding test statistics also were computed outside of SUDAAN.

When comparing population subgroups across three or more levels of a categorical variable, log-linear chi-square tests of independence of the subgroups and the prevalence variables were conducted first to control the error level for multiple comparisons. If the chi-square test indicated overall significant differences, the significance of each particular pairwise comparison of interest was tested using SUDAAN analytic procedures to properly account for the sample design. Using the published estimates and SEs to perform independent t tests for the difference of proportions usually will provide the same results as tests performed in SUDAAN. However, where the significance level is borderline, results may differ for two reasons: (1) the covariance term is included in SUDAAN tests, whereas it is not included in independent t tests; and (2) the reduced number of significant digits shown in the published estimates may cause rounding errors in the independent t tests.

B.3. Other Information on Data Accuracy

The accuracy of survey estimates can be affected by nonresponse, coding errors, computer processing errors, errors in the sampling frame, reporting errors, and other errors not due to sampling. They are sometimes referred to as "nonsampling errors." These types of errors and their impact are reduced through data editing, statistical adjustments for nonresponse, close monitoring and periodic retraining of interviewers, and improvement in various quality control procedures.

Although these types of errors often can be much larger than sampling errors, measurement of most of these errors is difficult. However, some indication of the effects of some types of these errors can be obtained through proxy measures, such as response rates and from other research studies.

B.3.1. Screening and Interview Response Rate Patterns

Beginning in 2002 and continuing through 2006, respondents received a $30 incentive in an effort to maximize response rates. Of the 151,288 eligible households sampled for the 2006 NSDUH, 137,057 were screened successfully, for a weighted screening response rate of 90.6 percent. In these screened households, a total of 85,034 sample persons were selected, and completed interviews were obtained from 67,802 of these sample persons, for a weighted interview response rate of 74.2 percent. The overall weighted response rate, defined as the product of the weighted screening response rate and weighted interview response rate, was 67.2 percent in 2006. The interview response rate for persons aged 12 to 20 was 84.9 percent.

The weighted screening rates for the 2002 to 2005 NSDUHs ranged from 90.7 to 91.3 percent, the interviewer response rates ranged from 76.2 to 78.6 percent, and the overall response rates ranged from 71.3 percent in 2002 to 69.2 percent in 2005. For the sample aged 12 to 20, the interview response rates ranged from 84.9 to 89.2 percent.

Nonresponse bias can be expressed as the product of the nonresponse rate (1 - R) and the difference between the characteristic of interest between respondents and nonrespondents in the population (Pr - Pnr). By maximizing NSDUH response rates, it is hoped that the bias due to the difference between the estimates from respondents and nonrespondents is minimized. Alcohol and drug use surveys are particularly vulnerable to nonresponse due to the difficult nature of accessing heavy alcohol and drug users.

B.3.2. Inconsistent Responses and Item Nonresponse

Among survey participants, item response rates were above 99 percent for most drug use items. However, inconsistent responses for some items were common. Estimates of substance use from NSDUH are based on responses to multiple questions by respondents, so that the maximum amount of information is used in determining whether a respondent is classified as a drug user. Inconsistencies in responses are resolved through a logical editing process that involves some judgment on the part of survey analysts. Additionally, missing or inconsistent responses are imputed using statistical methodology. Editing and imputation of missing responses are potential sources of error.

Respondents were asked the dependence and abuse questions if they reported alcohol use on more than 5 days in the past year, or if they reported any alcohol use in the past year but did not report their frequency of past year use. Therefore, inconsistencies could have occurred where the imputed frequency of use response indicated less frequent use than required for respondents to be asked the dependence and abuse questions originally.

Respondents might have provided ambiguous information about past year use of alcohol, in which case these respondents were not asked the dependence and abuse questions for alcohol. Subsequently, these respondents could have been imputed to be past year users of alcohol. In this situation, the dependence and abuse data were unknown; thus, these respondents were classified as not dependent on or abusing alcohol. However, such a respondent never actually was asked the dependence and abuse questions.

B.3.3. Validity of Self-Reported Substance Use

Most drug use prevalence estimates, including those produced for NSDUH, are based on self-reports of use. Although studies have generally supported the validity of self-report data, it is well documented that these data often are biased (underreported or overreported) by several factors, including the mode of administration, the population under investigation, and the type of drug (Bradburn & Sudman, 1983; Hser & Anglin, 1993). Higher levels of bias also are observed among younger respondents and those with higher levels of drug use (Biglan, Gilpin, Rohrbach, & Pierce, 2004). Methodological procedures, such as biological specimens (e.g., urine, hair, saliva), proxy reports (e.g., family member, peer), and repeated measures (e.g., recanting), have been used to validate self-report data (Fendrich, Johnson, Sudman, Wislar, & Spiehler, 1999).

However, these procedures often are impractical or too costly for community-based epidemiological studies (SRNT Subcommittee on Biochemical Verification, 2002). NSDUH utilizes widely accepted methodological practices for ensuring validity, such as encouraging privacy through audio computer-assisted self-interviewing (ACASI). Comparisons using these methods within NSDUH have been shown to reduce reporting bias (Aquilino, 1994; Turner, Lessler, & Gfroerer, 1992).

B.4. Measurement Issues and Additional Findings for Alcohol Items Added in 2006

As noted in Section 1.4 of Chapter 1, NSDUH in 2006 incorporated a new consumption of alcohol module that collected additional information about respondents' last use of alcohol for those who indicated that they had consumed alcohol at least once in the past month. The module included some items that were administered only to persons aged 12 to 20. Among the items in the new module were two related to binge drinking among females based on consumption of four or more drinks on an occasion, rather than the usual NSDUH criterion of five or more drinks. Other items in the consumption of alcohol module included the source of alcohol, location, and social context of the last drinking episode among past month alcohol users aged 12 to 20; the number of drinks consumed on the last drinking occasion; and the use of illicit drugs in combination with alcohol or within 2 hours of consuming alcohol on the last drinking occasion. Findings for many of these items are covered in the tables in Appendix C and discussed in Chapter 4. This section provides further information on some of the items in the new module, including a discussion of data collection issues with the new four-drink binge drinking measure for females and additional findings for this and selected other variables.

B.4.1. Data Issues Involving the Measurement of Binge Alcohol Use for Females

In 2006, new items were added within the consumption of alcohol module to investigate whether the current binge drinking definition based on drinking five or more drinks on the same occasion should be changed to a lower threshold of four or more drinks on the same occasion for females. The four or more drinks definition corresponds to that used by the National Institute on Alcohol Abuse and Alcoholism (NIAAA, 2004). Although all persons aged 12 or older were asked the new items regarding lifetime binge use and age of initiation of binge use based on the five or more drinks definition, the question pertaining to binge use based on four or more drinks and related follow-up questions were asked only of females. The intent was to route all female respondents who were lifetime drinkers into the questions regarding their history of having four or more drinks on the same occasion.

During the editing process, it was discovered that females who had some history of consuming five or more drinks on the same occasion were skipped out of the questions regarding their history of having four or more drinks. The sole exception to this was that females who had a history of having five or more drinks on the same occasion and who also indicated that they had four or more drinks when they last used alcohol were properly routed into the questions about their history of having five or more drinks on the same occasion. As a result of this error, 1,235 females aged 12 to 20 who were lifetime alcohol users (8.0 percent of all females in this group) were not asked the questions regarding their history of having four or more drinks on the same occasion.

In most cases, females who were incorrectly skipped out of the four or more drinks questions could be assigned a four or more drinks status for both past month and lifetime use either from previous responses to questions about the number of drinks on the last occasion or questions about binge use based on five or more drinks earlier in the same module. In cases where there was unknown data, the information from the core computer-assisted interviewing (CAI) module about binge use status, an imputed revised measure, was used to determine whether the female should be recoded to be a binge drinker based on the four or more drinks definition. Data on initiation of binge alcohol use based on the four or more drinks definition were not available for those females incorrectly skipped from these questions. Because of the large number of females who were improperly skipped, estimates of the age of initiation of binge drinking based on four or more drinks definition are not presented in this report.

B.4.2. Results from Selected Alcohol Use Items Added in 2006

The results based on many of the new items in the consumption of alcohol module are presented in Chapter 4. This section presents supplementary tables on the number of drinks consumed when persons aged 12 to 20 last consumed alcohol, as well as comparisons of binge drinking rates using the criterion of five more drinks on the same occasion for males and females and the criterion of four or more drinks on the same occasion for females.

Table B.2AB presents the number of drinks consumed the last time past month drinkers aged 12 to 20 drank alcohol, both for the full sample and by gender and age group. The majority of underage drinkers in each age and gender group reported drinking four or fewer drinks the last time they used alcohol. Current drinkers aged 12 to 14 were more likely to have had only one drink on their last drinking occasion (43.7 percent) compared with those aged 15 to 17 (23.7 percent) or those aged 18 to 20 (17.0 percent). The 18 to 20 year olds had the highest percentage of persons who reported drinking nine or more drinks at the last occasion (14.6 percent) compared with the other age groups (5.9 percent for those aged 12 to 14, 10.8 percent for those aged 15 to 17). Females were more likely than males to have had one drink (22.8 percent for females, 19.2 percent for males), two drinks (20.2 percent for females, 15.3 percent for males), or three or four drinks (27.1 percent for females, 19.8 percent for males) when they last drank alcohol. In contrast, underage males were more likely than underage females to have had five to eight drinks (26.6 percent for males, 24.1 percent for females) or nine or more drinks (19.1 percent for males, 5.8 percent for females) when they last drank alcohol.

Information on the mean number of drinks for these groups is also included in Table B.2AB. Overall, current drinkers aged 12 to 20 averaged 4.5 drinks when they last used alcohol. The mean number of drinks reported increased with age. Persons aged 12 to 14 had the lowest mean number of drinks (2.8 drinks), those aged 15 to 17 reported a higher amount at 4.3 drinks on average, and the 18 to 20 age group reported the highest average number at 4.8 drinks on the last occasion. Among current drinkers, underage males consumed more drinks on their last drinking occasion (mean of 5.3 drinks) than underage females (mean of 3.7 drinks).

Tables B.3A and B.3B present information from 2006 on binge alcohol use as defined by drinking five or more drinks on one occasion for both males and females, and an alternative definition based on five or more drinks for males but four or more drinks for females. Using the definition of five or more drinks on one occasion for both males and females, the rate of lifetime binge drinking was higher for underage males (32.0 percent) than for underage females (28.0 percent). This difference was principally found for those aged 18 to 20, where males had a higher rate of lifetime binge use (59.0 percent) compared with females (49.5 percent). A similar pattern was found for past month binge use using the five or more drinks criterion, with males having a higher rate than females (21.8 to 16.9 percent, respectively). Among both 15 to 17 year olds and 18 to 20 year olds, males had higher rates of past month binge drinking compared with females when binge drinking was defined as five or more drinks for both males and females.

Although a statistical comparison cannot be drawn between the binge drinking rates based on the two different definitions, it can be seen that using the less stringent definition for lifetime binge use increased the rate of lifetime binge alcohol use for females from 28.0 to 31.0 percent, and it increased the rate of past month binge alcohol use for females from 16.9 to 18.5 percent. This higher rate of binge drinking for females using the four or more drinks criterion also can be seen in the overall rate of binge drinking including both males and females; lifetime binge drinking increased from 30.1 to 31.5 percent, and past month binge drinking increased from 19.4 to 20.2 percent. The increase in the prevalence of binge drinking among females using the four or more drinks criterion was primarily found for females aged 18 to 20.

Regarding initiation of binge drinking, 10.2 percent of all those aged 12 to 20 reported that they first had five or more drinks on the same occasion during the past year. Information on the measurement of initiation can be found in Section B.4.1 of the 2006 NSDUH national findings report (Office of Applied Studies [OAS], 2007a). The past year initiation rate of binge drinking was higher for those aged 15 to 17 and those aged 18 to 20 (13.9 and 13.1 percent, respectively) than for those aged 12 to 14 (3.5 percent). In addition, a higher percentage of males (10.9 percent) than females (9.5 percent) reported that they engaged in binge drinking for the first time in the past year. However, this pattern of gender differences varied by age group. Among those aged 12 to 14, the rate for past year initiation of binge drinking was higher among females (3.9 percent) than among males (3.0 percent). Among those aged 15 to 17, there was no statistically significant difference between males and females in past year initiation of binge drinking. Among those aged 18 to 20, however, males had a higher rate for past year initiation (15.2 percent) than females (10.9 percent).

Table B.1. Summary of NSDUH Suppression Rules

Estimate	Suppress if:
Prevalence Rate, $\hat{p}$, with Nominal Sample Size, n, and Design Effect, $deff$	(1) The estimated prevalence rate, $\hat{p}$, is $< .00005$ or $\geq .99995$, or (2) $\dfrac{SE(\hat{p})\,/\,\hat{p}}{-\ln(\hat{p})} > .175$ when $\hat{p} \leq .5$, or $\dfrac{SE(\hat{p})\,/\,(1-\hat{p})}{-\ln(1-\hat{p})} > .175$ when $\hat{p} \leq .5$, or (3) Effective $n < 68$, where Effective $n = \dfrac{n}{deff}$ or (4) $n < 100$. Note: The rounding portion of this suppression rule for prevalence rates will produce some estimates that round at one decimal place to 0.0 or 100.0 percent but are not suppressed from the tables.
Estimated Number (Numerator of $\hat{p}$)	The estimated prevalence rate, $\hat{p}$, is suppressed. Note: In some instances when $\hat{p}$ is not suppressed, the estimated number may appear as a 0 in the tables. This means that the estimate is greater than 0 but less than 500 (estimated numbers are shown in thousands).
Mean Age at First Use, $\bar{x}$, with Nominal Sample Size, n	(1) $RSE(\bar{x}) > .5$, or (2) $n < 10$.

SE = standard error; RSE = relative standard error; deff = design effect.
Source: SAMHSA, Office of Applied Studies, National Survey on Drug Use and Health, 2006.

Table B.2. AB Number of Drinks Consumed on Last Occasion of Alcohol Use in the Past Month among Past Month Alcohol Users Aged 12 to 20, by Gender and Age Group: Numbers in Thousands, Percentage Distribution and Mean, 2006

| | TOTAL | AGE GROUP | | | | GENDER | |
		12 to 14	15 to 17	18 to 20		Male	Female
Number of Drinks Consumed on Last Occasion of Alcohol Use	Numbers in Thousands, by Number of Drinks Consumed						
1 Drink	2,166	318	754	1,094		1,056	1,111
2 Drinks	1,821	177	565	1,078		839	982
3 or 4 Drinks	2,403	116	721	1,566		1,087	1,316
5 to 8 Drinks	2,633	74	799	1,760		1,461	1,172
9 or More Drinks	1,330	43	345	942		1,046	284
Number of Drinks Consumed on Last Occasion of Alcohol Use	Percentage Distribution, by Number of Drinks Consumed						
1 Drink	20.9	43.7	23.7	17.0		19.2	22.8
2 Drinks	17.6	24.4	17.8	16.7		15.3	20.2
3 or 4 Drinks	23.2	15.9	22.6	24.3		19.8	27.1
5 to 8 Drinks	25.4	10.1	25.1	27.3		26.6	24.1
9 or More Drinks	12.8	5.9	10.8	14.6		19.1	5.8
	Number of Drinks Consumed						
Mean Number of Drinks Consumed	4.5	2.8	4.3	4.8		5.3	3.7

*Low precision; no estimate reported.

NOTE: Respondents with unknown responses to number of drinks consumed on last occasion of alcohol use were excluded.

Source: SAMHSA, Office of Applied Studies, National Survey on Drug Use and Health, 2006.

Table B.3A. Binge Alcohol Use in the Lifetime and Past Month and Binge Alcohol Use Initiates among Persons Aged 12 to 20, by Binge Drinking Definition, Age Group, and Gender: Numbers in Thousands, 2006

	Binge Alcohol Use Defined as Five or More Drinks on One Occasion			Binge Alcohol Use Defined as Four or More Drinks on One Occasion–Females Only[1]	Binge Alcohol Use Defined as Five Drinks for Males and Four Drinks for Females[1]
	TOTAL	Male	Female		
Age Group	Engaged in Binge Alcohol Use in Lifetime				
12 to 20 Years	11,488	6,310	5,178	5,723	12,034
12 to 14 Years	689	339	350	380	719
15 to 17 Years	3,832	2,003	1,829	2,007	4,010
18 to 20 Years	6,967	3,968	2,999	3,336	7,305
Age Group	Engaged in Binge Alcohol Use in Past Month				
12 to 20 Years	7,421	4,293	3,128	3,421	7,719
12 to 14 Years	409	196	213	222	418
15 to 17 Years	2,298	1,239	1,059	1,148	2,387
18 to 20 Years	4,713	2,858	1,855	2,057	4,915
Age Group	Initiated Binge Alcohol Use in Past 12 Months[2,3]				
12 to 20 Years	3,798	2,087	1,712	†	†
12 to 14 Years	423	191	231	†	†
15 to 17 Years	1,761	921	840	†	†
18 to 20 Years	1,615	975	640	†	†

*Low precision; no estimate reported.

† Estimate is available but has not been reported because of an invalid anomaly in the data collection.

[1] The Four or More Drinks definition corresponds to that used by the National Institute on Alcohol Abuse and Alcoholism (NIAAA, 2004).

[2] Respondents with unknown responses were excluded.

[3] Binge Alcohol Use Initiates are defined as persons who binged on alcohol for the first time in the 12 months prior to the date of the interview.

Source: SAMHSA, Office of Applied Studies, National Survey on Drug Use and Health, 2006.

Table B.3B. Binge Alcohol Use in the Lifetime and Past Month and Binge Alcohol Use Initiates among Persons Aged 12 to 20, by Binge Drinking Definition, Age Group, and Gender: Percentages, 2006

	Binge Alcohol Use Defined as Five or More Drinks on One Occasion			Binge Alcohol Use Defined as Four or More Drinks on One Occasion–Females Only[1]	Binge Alcohol Use Defined as Five Drinks for Males and Four Drinks for Females[1]
	TOTAL	Male	Female		
Age Group	*Engaged in Binge Alcohol Use in Lifetime*				
12 to 20 Years	30.1	32.0	28.0	31.0	31.5
12 to 14 Years	5.6	5.3	5.9	6.4	5.8
15 to 17 Years	29.3	30.4	28.3	31.0	30.7
18 to 20 Years	54.5	59.0	49.5	55.0	57.1
Age Group	*Engaged in Binge Alcohol Use in Past Month*				
12 to 20 Years	19.4	21.8	16.9	18.5	20.2
12 to 14 Years	3.3	3.1	3.6	3.7	3.4
15 to 17 Years	17.6	18.8	16.4	17.8	18.3
18 to 20 Years	36.8	42.5	30.6	33.9	38.4
Age Group	*Initiated Binge Alcohol Use in Past 12 Months*[2,3]				
12 to 20 Years	10.2	10.9	9.5	†	†
12 to 14 Years	3.5	3.0	3.9	†	†
15 to 17 Years	13.9	14.4	13.3	†	†
18 to 20 Years	13.1	15.2	10.9	†	†

*Low precision; no estimate reported.

† Estimate is available but has not been reported because of an invalid anomaly in the data collection. See Section B.4.1 in this appendix.

[1] The Four or More Drinks definition corresponds to that used by the National Institute on Alcohol Abuse and Alcoholism (NIAAA, 2004).

[2] Respondents with unknown responses were excluded.

[3] Binge Alcohol Use Initiates are defined as persons who binged on alcohol for the first time in the 12 months prior to the date of the interview.

Source: SAMHSA, Office of Applied Studies, National Survey on Drug Use and Health, 2006.

APPENDIX C: PREVALENCE TABLES

Table 2.1A. Alcohol Use in the Lifetime, Past Year, and Past Month; Binge and Heavy Alcohol Use in the Past Month; and Alcohol Dependence or Abuse in the Past Year among Persons Aged 12 to 20, by Gender: Numbers in Thousands, 2002–2006

Gender/Alcohol Measure	2002	2003	2004	2005	2006
TOTAL					
Lifetime Use	20,911	20,936	20,709	20,671	20,574
Past Year Use	17,492	17,554	17,568	17,729	17,598
Past Month Use	10,713	10,876	10,838	10,819	10,823
Binge Alcohol Use[1]	7,175	7,190	7,397	7,197	7,239
Heavy Alcohol Use[1]	2,301	2,297	2,375	2,296	2,359
Past Year Dependence or Abuse[2]	3,570	3,468	3,616	3,592	3,475
MALE					
Lifetime Use	10,719	10,537	10,624	10,500	10,647
Past Year Use	8,847	8,735	8,946	8,927	9,064
Past Month Use	5,619	5,720	5,723	5,658	5,752
Binge Alcohol Use[1]	4,140	4,162	4,271	4,175	4,192
Heavy Alcohol Use[1]	1,544	1,506	1,582	1,492	1,561
Past Year Dependence or Abuse[2]	2,079	1,905	2,092	1,958	1,893
FEMALE					
Lifetime Use	10,192	10,399[a]	10,085	10,171	9,927
Past Year Use	8,645	8,819	8,622	8,802	8,534
Past Month Use	5,094	5,156	5,115	5,160	5,072
Binge Alcohol Use[1]	3,035	3,027	3,127	3,022	3,047
Heavy Alcohol Use[1]	756	791	793	803	798
Past Year Dependence or Abuse[2]	1,491	1,563	1,524	1,634	1,582

*Low precision; no estimate reported. [a] Difference between estimate and 2006 estimate is statistically significant at the 0.05 level. [b] Difference between estimate and 2006 estimate is statistically significant at the 0.01 level. [1] Binge Alcohol Use is defined as drinking five or more drinks on the same occasion (i.e., at the same time or within a couple of hours of each other) on at least 1 day in the past 30 days. Heavy Alcohol Use is defined as drinking five or more drinks on the same occasion on each of 5 or more days in the past 30 days; all heavy alcohol users are also binge alcohol users. [2] Dependence or abuse is based on definitions found in the 4th edition of the *Diagnostic and Statistical Manual of Mental Disorders* (DSM-IV).

Source: SAMHSA, Office of Applied Studies, National Survey on Drug Use and Health, 2002, 2003, 2004, 2005, and 2006.

Table 2.1B. Alcohol Use in the Lifetime, Past Year, and Past Month; Binge and Heavy Alcohol Use in the Past Month; and Alcohol Dependence or Abuse in the Past Year among Persons Aged 12 to 20, by Gender: Percentages, 2002–2006

Gender/Alcohol Measure	2002	2003	2004	2005	2006
TOTAL					
Lifetime Use	56.2[b]	55.8[b]	54.9	53.9	53.9
Past Year Use	47.0	46.8	46.6	46.3	46.1
Past Month Use	28.8	29.0	28.7	28.2	28.3
Binge Alcohol Use[1]	19.3	19.2	19.6	18.8	19.0
Heavy Alcohol Use[1]	6.2	6.1	6.3	6.0	6.2
Past Year Dependence or Abuse[2]	9.6	9.2	9.6	9.4	9.1
MALE					
Lifetime Use	56.5[b]	55.0	54.9	53.7	54.0
Past Year Use	46.6	45.6	46.3	45.6	46.0
Past Month Use	29.6	29.9	29.6	28.9	29.2
Binge Alcohol Use[1]	21.8	21.7	22.1	21.3	21.3
Heavy Alcohol Use[1]	8.1	7.9	8.2	7.6	7.9
Past Year Dependence or Abuse[2]	10.9[b]	9.9	10.8[a]	10.0	9.6
FEMALE					
Lifetime Use	56.0[b]	56.6[b]	54.8	54.2	53.7
Past Year Use	47.5	48.0[a]	46.9	46.9	46.2
Past Month Use	28.0	28.1	27.8	27.5	27.4
Binge Alcohol Use[1]	16.7	16.5	17.0	16.1	16.5
Heavy Alcohol Use[1]	4.2	4.3	4.3	4.3	4.3
Past Year Dependence or Abuse[2]	8.2	8.5	8.3	8.7	8.6

*Low precision; no estimate reported. [a] Difference between estimate and 2006 estimate is statistically significant at the 0.01 level. [b] Difference between estimate and 2006 estimate is statistically significant at the 0.05 level. [1] Binge Alcohol Use is defined as drinking five or more drinks on the same occasion (i.e., at the same time or within a couple of hours of each other) on at least 1 day in the past 30 days. Heavy Alcohol Use is defined as drinking five or more drinks on the same occasion on each of 5 or more days in the past 30 days; all heavy alcohol users are also binge alcohol users. [2] Dependence or abuse is based on definitions found in the 4th edition of the *Diagnostic and Statistical Manual of Mental Disorders* (DSM-IV).

Source: SAMHSA, Office of Applied Studies, National Survey on Drug Use and Health, 2002, 2003, 2004, 2005, and 2006.

Table 2.2A. Alcohol Use in the Lifetime, Past Year, and Past Month; Binge and Heavy Alcohol Use in the Past Month; and Alcohol Dependence or Abuse in the Past Year among Persons Aged 12 to 20, by Age Group: Numbers in Thousands, 2002-2006

Age Group/Alcohol Measure	2002	2003	2004	2005	2006
AGE 12 TO 14					
Lifetime Use	3,149[b]	3,001[b]	3,008[b]	2,739	2,723
Past Year Use	2,231[b]	2,154	2,193[a]	2,074	2,002
Past Month Use	940[a]	924[a]	902	805	815
Binge Alcohol Use[1]	455	423	415	386	381
Heavy Alcohol Use[1]	81	64	64	61	49
Past Year Dependence or Abuse[2]	247	267[a]	252	213	211
AGE 15 TO 17					
Lifetime Use	7,598	7,713	7,587	7,567	7,532
Past Year Use	6,333	6,409	6,344	6,380	6,359
Past Month Use	3,424	3,501	3,534	3,387	3,406
Binge Alcohol Use[1]	2,186	2,235	2,379	2,127	2,232
Heavy Alcohol Use[1]	549	588	607	550	554
Past Year Dependence or Abuse[2]	1,206	1,204	1,265	1,194	1,149
AGE 18 TO 20					
Lifetime Use	10,164	10,223	10,113	10,365	10,319
Past Year Use	8,928	8,991	9,031	9,275	9,236
Past Month Use	6,348	6,451	6,402	6,628	6,602
Binge Alcohol Use[1]	4,534	4,531	4,604	4,684	4,625
Heavy Alcohol Use[1]	1,671	1,645	1,704	1,685	1,756
Past Year Dependence or Abuse[2]	2,117	1,997	2,099	2,185	2,115

*Low precision; no estimate reported. [a] Difference between estimate and 2006 estimate is statistically significant at the 0.05 level [b] Difference between estimate and 2006 estimate is statistically significant at the 0.01 level. [1] Binge Alcohol Use is defined as drinking five or more drinks on the same occasion (i.e., at the same time or within a couple of hours of each other) on at least 1 day in the past 30 days. Heavy Alcohol Use is defined as drinking five or more drinks on the same occasion on each of 5 or more days in the past 30 days; all heavy alcohol users are also binge alcohol users [2] Dependence or abuse is based on definitions found in the 4th edition of the *Diagnostic and Statistical Manual of Mental Disorders* (DSM-IV).

Source: SAMHSA, Office of Applied Studies, National Survey on Drug Use and Health, 2002, 2003, 2004, 2005, and 2006.

Table 2.2B. Alcohol Use in the Lifetime, Past Year, and Past Month; Binge and Heavy Alcohol Use in the Past Month; and Alcohol Dependence or Abuse in the Past Year among Persons Aged 12 to 20, by Age Group: Percentages, 2002-2006

Age Group/Alcohol Measure	2002	2003	2004	2005	2006
AGE 12 TO 14					
Lifetime Use	24.9[b]	23.9[a]	23.6[a]	21.8	22.1
Past Year Use	17.6[a]	17.1	17.2	16.5	16.2
Past Month Use	7.4	7.3	7.1	6.4	6.6
Binge Alcohol Use[1]	3.6	3.4	3.3	3.1	3.1
Heavy Alcohol Use[1]	0.6	0.5	0.5	0.5	0.4
Past Year Dependence or Abuse[2]	2.0	2.1	2.0	1.7	1.7
AGE 15 TO 17					
Lifetime Use	62.7[b]	62.1[b]	60.8[b]	59.2	57.7
Past Year Use	52.3[b]	51.6[b]	50.9[a]	49.9	48.7
Past Month Use	28.3[b]	28.2[b]	28.3[b]	26.5	26.1
Binge Alcohol Use[1]	18.1	18.0	19.1[b]	16.6	17.1
Heavy Alcohol Use[1]	4.5	4.7	4.9	4.3	4.2
Past Year Dependence or Abuse[2]	10.0[a]	9.7	10.1[b]	9.3	8.8
AGE 18 TO 20					
Lifetime Use	81.7	81.6	80.8	79.9	80.7
Past Year Use	71.7	71.8	72.1	71.5	72.2
Past Month Use	51.0	51.5	51.1	51.1	51.6
Binge Alcohol Use[1]	36.4	36.2	36.8	36.1	36.2
Heavy Alcohol Use[1]	13.4	13.1	13.6	13.0	13.7
Past Year Dependence or Abuse[2]	17.0	16.0	16.8	16.9	16.5

*Low precision; no estimate reported. [a] Difference between estimate and 2006 estimate is statistically significant at the 0.05 level. [b] Difference between estimate and 2006 estimate is statistically significant at the 0.01 level. [1] Binge Alcohol Use is defined as drinking five or more drinks on the same occasion (i.e., at the same time or within a couple of hours of each other) on at least 1 day in the past 30 days. Heavy Alcohol Use is defined as drinking five or more drinks on the same occasion on each of 5 or more days in the past 30 days; all heavy alcohol users are also binge alcohol users. [2] Dependence or abuse is based on definitions found in the 4th edition of the *Diagnostic and Statistical Manual of Mental Disorders* (DSM-IV).

Source: SAMHSA, Office of Applied Studies, National Survey on Drug Use and Health, 2002, 2003, 2004, 2005, and 2006.

Table 3.1A. Alcohol Use in the Lifetime, Past Year, and Past Month; Binge and Heavy Alcohol Use in the Past Month; and Alcohol Dependence or Abuse in the Past Year among Persons Aged 12 to 20, by Demographic Characteristics: Numbers in Thousands, Annual Averages Based on 2002-2006

Demographic Characteristic	Lifetime Use	Past Year Use	Past Month Use	Binge Use in Past Month[1]	Heavy Use in Past Month[1]	Dependence or Abuse in Past Year[2]
TOTAL	20,760	17,588	10,814	7,240	2,325	3,544
GENDER						
Male	10,605	8,904	5,694	4,188	1,537	1,985
Female	10,155	8,684	5,119	3,052	788	1,559
AGE						
12	441	263	94	38	3	20
13	954	682	257	109	16	67
14	1,530	1,185	526	266	45	151
15	2,178	1,765	858	499	100	280
16	2,577	2,174	1,171	749	181	420
17	2,845	2,427	1,422	984	288	504
18	3,478	3,082	2,062	1,461	507	671
19	3,313	2,930	2,119	1,527	572	719
20	3,445	3,081	2,305	1,607	612	712
GENDER/RACE/HISPANIC ORIGIN						
Male, White, Not Hispanic	6,851	5,938	3,967	3,013	1,214	1,381
Female, White, Not Hispanic	6,673	5,899	3,640	2,269	654	1,157
Male, Black, Not Hispanic	1,326	1,005	561	310	71	159
Female, Black, Not Hispanic	1,259	974	485	207	25	95
Male, Hispanic	1,849	1,494	911	684	201	334
Female, Hispanic	1,635	1,323	732	434	82	222

*Low precision; no estimate reported. [1] Binge Alcohol Use is defined as drinking five or more drinks on the same occasion (i.e., at the same time or within a couple of hours of each other) on at least 1 day in the past 30 days. Heavy Alcohol Use is defined as drinking five or more drinks on the same occasion on each of 5 or more days in the past 30 days; all heavy alcohol users are also binge alcohol users. [2] Dependence or abuse is based on definitions found in the 4th edition of the *Diagnostic and Statistical Manual of Mental Disorders* (DSM-IV).

Source: SAMHSA, Office of Applied Studies, National Survey on Drug Use and Health, 2002, 2003, 2004, 2005, and 2006.

Table 3.1B. Alcohol Use in the Lifetime, Past Year, and Past Month; Binge and Heavy Alcohol Use in the Past Month; and Alcohol Dependence or Abuse in the Past Year among Persons Aged 12 to 20, by Demographic Characteristics: Percentages, Annual Averages Based on 2002-2006

Demographic Characteristic	Lifetime Use	Past Year Use	Past Month Use	Binge Use in Past Month[1]	Heavy Use in Past Month[1]	Dependence or Abuse in Past Year[2]
TOTAL	54.9	46.5	28.6	19.2	6.2	9.4
GENDER						
Male	54.8	46.0	29.4	21.6	7.9	10.3
Female	55.1	47.1	27.8	16.5	4.3	8.5
AGE						
12	11.0	6.5	2.3	0.9	0.1	0.5
13	22.4	16.0	6.0	2.6	0.4	1.6
14	35.6	27.6	12.3	6.2	1.0	3.5
15	50.8	41.2	20.0	11.6	2.3	6.5
16	61.4	51.8	27.9	17.8	4.3	10.0
17	69.7	59.4	34.8	24.1	7.1	12.3
18	76.5	67.8	45.4	32.2	11.2	14.8
19	81.3	71.9	52.0	37.5	14.0	17.7
20	85.5	76.4	57.2	39.9	15.2	17.7
GENDER/RACE/HISPANIC ORIGIN						
Male, White, Not Hispanic	57.5	49.8	33.3	25.3	10.2	11.6
Female, White, Not Hispanic	58.5	51.7	31.9	19.9	5.7	10.1
Male, Black, Not Hispanic	46.8	35.5	19.8	11.0	2.5	5.6
Female, Black, Not Hispanic	46.2	35.8	17.8	7.6	0.9	3.5
Male, Hispanic	55.4	44.7	27.3	20.5	6.0	10.0
Female, Hispanic	53.5	43.3	23.9	14.2	2.7	7.3

*Low precision; no estimate reported. [1] Binge Alcohol Use is defined as drinking five or more drinks on the same occasion (i.e., at the same time or within a couple of hours of each other) on at least 1 day in the past 30 days. Heavy Alcohol Use is defined as drinking five or more drinks on the same occasion on each of 5 or more days in the past 30 days; all heavy alcohol users are also binge alcohol users. [2] Dependence or abuse is based on definitions found in the 4th edition of the *Diagnostic and Statistical Manual of Mental Disorders* (DSM-IV).

Source: SAMHSA, Office of Applied Studies, National Survey on Drug Use and Health, 2002, 2003, 2004, 2005, and 2006.

Table 3.2A. Alcohol Use in the Lifetime, Past Year, and Past Month; Binge and Heavy Alcohol Use in the Past Month; and Alcohol Dependence or Abuse in the Past Year among Persons Aged 12 to 20, by Racial/Ethnic Subgroups: Numbers in Thousands, Annual Averages Based on 2002-2006

Racial/Ethnic Subgroup	Lifetime Use	Past Year Use	Past Month Use	Binge Use in Past Month[1]	Heavy Use in Past Month[1]	Dependence or Abuse in Past Year[2]
TOTAL[3]	20,760	17,588	10,814	7,240	2,325	3,544
NOT HISPANIC OR LATINO[3]	17,276	14,771	9,171	6,122	2,043	2,988
White	13,523	11,837	7,607	5,282	1,868	2,538
Black or African American	2,585	1,979	1,046	517	96	255
American Indian or Alaska Native	139	112	67	51	11	37
Native Hawaiian or Other Pacific Islander	75	60	34	26	6	18
Asian	654	529	268	143	28	77
Chinese	131	106	48	22	6	12
Filipino	137	106	56	33	5	17
Japanese	34	30	17	9	2	2
Indian	89	79	44	24	3	11
Korean	83	70	40	22	4	16
Vietnamese	77	59	25	9	1	6
HISPANIC OR LATINO[3]	3,484	2,817	1,643	1,118	283	556
Mexican	2,420	1,938	1,113	780	201	396
Puerto Rican	391	321	176	114	28	48
Central or South American	374	301	182	123	23	60
Cuban	107	94	62	33	10	16

* Low precision; no estimate reported. [1] Binge Alcohol Use is defined as drinking five or more drinks on the same occasion (i.e., at the same time or within a couple of hours of each other) on at least 1 day in the past 30 days. Heavy Alcohol Use is defined as drinking five or more drinks on the same occasion on each of 5 or more days in the past 30 days; all heavy alcohol users are also binge alcohol users. [2] Dependence or abuse is based on definitions found in the 4th edition of the *Diagnostic and Statistical Manual of Mental Disorders* (DSM-IV). [3] Totals include data from respondents reporting racial/ethnic subgroups not shown, as well as respondents reporting more than one subgroup.

Source: SAMHSA, Office of Applied Studies, National Survey on Drug Use and Health, 2002, 2003, 2004, 2005, and 2006.

Table 3.2B. Alcohol Use in the Lifetime, Past Year, and Past Month; Binge and Heavy Alcohol Use in the Past Month; and Alcohol Dependence or Abuse in the Past Year among Persons Aged 12 to 20, by Racial/Ethnic Subgroups: Percentages, Annual Averages Based on 2002-2006

Racial/Ethnic Subgroup	Lifetime Use	Past Year Use	Past Month Use	Binge Use in Past Month[1]	Heavy Use in Past Month[1]	Dependence or Abuse in Past Year[2]
TOTAL[3]	54.9	46.5	28.6	19.2	6.2	9.4
NOT HISPANIC OR LATINO[3]	55.0	47.0	29.2	19.5	6.5	9.5
White	58.0	50.8	32.6	22.6	8.0	10.9
Black or African American	46.5	35.6	18.8	9.3	1.7	4.6
American Indian or Alaska Native	56.7	45.5	27.2	20.8	4.5	14.9
Native Hawaiian or Other Pacific Islander	53.4	42.6	24.3	18.8	4.0	12.7
Asian	41.7	33.7	17.1	9.1	1.8	4.9
Chinese	41.9	33.9	15.2	7.2	1.9	3.9
Filipino	49.0	37.9	20.0	12.0	1.9	6.1
Japanese	47.7	42.6	24.0	12.9	2.7	3.0
Indian	26.7	23.6	13.1	7.1	1.0	3.4
Korean	48.3	40.6	23.4	12.9	2.2	9.3
Vietnamese	46.6	36.1	14.9	5.2	0.9	3.9
HISPANIC OR LATINO[3]	54.4	44.0	25.7	17.5	4.4	8.7
Mexican	54.1	43.3	24.9	17.4	4.5	8.9
Puerto Rican	55.5	45.6	25.0	16.2	4.1	6.8
Central or South American	53.3	42.9	26.0	17.6	3.4	8.5
Cuban	55.9	48.8	32.0	17.4	5.3	8.1

* Low precision; no estimate reported. [1] Binge Alcohol Use is defined as drinking five or more drinks on the same occasion (i.e., at the same time or within a couple of hours of each other) on at least 1 day in the past 30 days. Heavy Alcohol Use is defined as drinking five or more drinks on the same occasion on each of 5 or more days in the past 30 days; all heavy alcohol users are also binge alcohol users. [2] Dependence or abuse is based on definitions found in the 4th edition of the *Diagnostic and Statistical Manual of Mental Disorders* (DSM-IV). [3] Totals include data from respondents reporting racial/ethnic subgroups not shown, as well as respondents reporting more than one subgroup.

Source: SAMHSA, Office of Applied Studies, National Survey on Drug Use and Health, 2002, 2003, 2004, 2005, and 2006.

Table 3.3A. Alcohol Use in the Lifetime, Past Year, and Past Month; Binge and Heavy Alcohol Use in the Past Month; and Alcohol Dependence or Abuse in the Past Year among Persons Aged 12 to 14, by Demographic Characteristics: Numbers in Thousands, Annual Averages Based on 2002-2006

Demographic Characteristic	Lifetime Use	Past Year Use	Past Month Use	Binge Use in Past Month[1]	Heavy Use in Past Month[1]	Dependence or Abuse in Past Year[2]
TOTAL	2,924	2,131	877	412	64	238
GENDER						
Male	1,506	1,025	403	200	32	103
Female	1,418	1,106	474	212	32	135
HISPANIC ORIGIN AND RACE						
Not Hispanic or Latino	2,377	1,732	705	318	47	190
White	1,829	1,379	571	255	40	157
Black or African American	399	245	91	40	3	20
American Indian or Alaska Native	24	19	9	7	1	4
Native Hawaiian or Other Pacific Islander	6	6	3	2	0	1
Asian	62	41	15	7	1	3
Two or More Races	57	42	16	7	2	5
Hispanic or Latino	548	398	172	94	17	48
GENDER/RACE/HISPANIC ORIGIN						
Male, White, Not Hispanic	943	663	260	121	17	64
Female, White, Not Hispanic	886	716	311	133	23	93
Male, Black, Not Hispanic	198	113	42	19	2	9
Female, Black, Not Hispanic	201	132	49	22	1	12
Male, Hispanic	286	195	83	50	11	25
Female, Hispanic	262	204	89	44	6	23

*Low precision; no estimate reported. [1] Binge Alcohol Use is defined as drinking five or more drinks on the same occasion (i.e., at the same time or within a couple of hours of each other) on at least 1 day in the past 30 days. Heavy Alcohol Use is defined as drinking five or more drinks on the same occasion on each of 5 or more days in the past 30 days; all heavy alcohol users are also binge alcohol users. [2] Dependence or abuse is based on definitions found in the 4th edition of the *Diagnostic and Statistical Manual of Mental Disorders* (DSM-IV).

Source: SAMHSA, Office of Applied Studies, National Survey on Drug Use and Health, 2002, 2003, 2004, 2005, and 2006.

Table 3.3B. Alcohol Use in the Lifetime, Past Year, and Past Month; Binge and Heavy Alcohol Use in the Past Month; and Alcohol Dependence or Abuse in the Past Year among Persons Aged 12 to 14, by Demographic Characteristics: Percentages, Annual Averages Based on 2002-2006

Demographic Characteristic	Lifetime Use	Past Year Use	Past Month Use	Binge Use in Past Month[1]	Heavy Use in Past Month[1]	Dependence or Abuse in Past Year[2]
TOTAL	23.3	16.9	7.0	3.3	0.5	1.9
GENDER						
Male	23.4	15.9	6.3	3.1	0.5	1.6
Female	23.1	18.0	7.7	3.5	0.5	2.2
HISPANIC ORIGIN AND RACE						
Not Hispanic or Latino	22.9	16.7	6.8	3.1	0.5	1.8
White	24.1	18.2	7.5	3.4	0.5	2.1
Black or African American	20.6	12.7	4.7	2.1	0.2	1.0
American Indian or Alaska Native	27.7	22.0	10.3	8.1	1.0	4.2
Native Hawaiian or Other Pacific Islander	15.1	14.4	6.4	4.6	0.1	1.8
Asian	12.8	8.5	3.2	1.5	0.1	0.7
Two or More Races	25.2	18.3	7.2	3.1	0.8	2.3
Hispanic or Latino	24.8	18.1	7.8	4.3	0.8	2.2
GENDER/RACE/HISPANIC ORIGIN						
Male, White, Not Hispanic	24.3	17.1	6.7	3.1	0.4	1.6
Female, White, Not Hispanic	23.8	19.2	8.3	3.6	0.6	2.5
Male, Black, Not Hispanic	20.1	11.5	4.2	1.9	0.2	0.9
Female, Black, Not Hispanic	21.2	14.0	5.2	2.3	0.1	1.2
Male, Hispanic	24.9	17.0	7.2	4.4	1.0	2.2
Female, Hispanic	24.7	19.2	8.4	4.1	0.6	2.2

*Low precision; no estimate reported. [1] Binge Alcohol Use is defined as drinking five or more drinks on the same occasion (i.e., at the same time or within a couple of hours of each other) on at least 1 day in the past 30 days. Heavy Alcohol Use is defined as drinking five or more drinks on the same occasion on each of 5 or more days in the past 30 days; all heavy alcohol users are also binge alcohol users.[2] Dependence or abuse is based on definitions found in the 4th edition of the *Diagnostic and Statistical Manual of Mental Disorders* (DSM-IV).

Source: SAMHSA, Office of Applied Studies, National Survey on Drug Use and Health, 2002, 2003, 2004, 2005, and 2006.

Table 3.4A. Alcohol Use in the Lifetime, Past Year, and Past Month; Binge and Heavy Alcohol Use in the Past Month; and Alcohol Dependence or Abuse in the Past Year among Persons Aged 15 to 17, by Demographic Characteristics: Numbers in Thousands, Annual Averages Based on 2002-2006

Demographic Characteristic	Lifetime Use	Past Year Use	Past Month Use	Binge Use in Past Month[1]	Heavy Use in Past Month[1]	Dependence or Abuse in Past Year[2]
TOTAL	7,599	6,365	3,451	2,232	569	1,204
GENDER						
Male	3,819	3,142	1,751	1,217	354	604
Female	3,780	3,223	1,700	1,014	216	600
HISPANIC ORIGIN AND RACE						
Not Hispanic or Latino	6,334	5,340	2,922	1,885	495	1,009
White	4,999	4,339	2,468	1,650	458	873
Black or African American	932	679	310	147	20	71
American Indian or Alaska Native	52	40	21	16	4	15
Native Hawaiian or Other Pacific Islander	26	20	8	4	1	3
Asian	213	168	66	33	4	21
Two or More Races	112	93	49	34	8	25
Hispanic or Latino	1,265	1,025	529	347	75	195
GENDER/RACE/HISPANIC ORIGIN						
Male, White, Not Hispanic	2,516	2,149	1,260	905	281	434
Female, White, Not Hispanic	2,483	2,190	1,209	745	176	439
Male, Black, Not Hispanic	472	337	160	84	14	42
Female, Black, Not Hispanic	460	342	150	63	5	30
Male, Hispanic	627	503	263	184	48	97
Female, Hispanic	638	522	265	163	27	97

*Low precision; no estimate reported. [1] Binge Alcohol Use is defined as drinking five or more drinks on the same occasion (i.e., at the same time or within a couple of hours of each other) on at least 1 day in the past 30 days. Heavy Alcohol Use is defined as drinking five or more drinks on the same occasion on each of 5 or more days in the past 30 days; all heavy alcohol users are also binge alcohol users. [2] Dependence or abuse is based on definitions found in the 4th edition of the *Diagnostic and Statistical Manual of Mental Disorders* (DSM-IV).

Source: SAMHSA, Office of Applied Studies, National Survey on Drug Use and Health, 2002, 2003, 2004, 2005, and 2006.

Table 3.4B. Alcohol Use in the Lifetime, Past Year, and Past Month; Binge and Heavy Alcohol Use in the Past Month; and Alcohol Dependence or Abuse in the Past Year among Persons Aged 15 to 17, by Demographic Characteristics: Percentages, Annual Averages Based on 2002–2006

Demographic Characteristic	Lifetime Use	Past Year Use	Past Month Use	Binge Use in Past Month[1]	Heavy Use in Past Month[1]	Dependence or Abuse in Past Year[2]
TOTAL	60.5	50.6	27.5	17.8	4.5	9.6
GENDER						
Male	59.6	49.0	27.3	19.0	5.5	9.4
Female	61.4	52.3	27.6	16.5	3.5	9.7
HISPANIC ORIGIN AND RACE						
Not Hispanic or Latino	60.1	50.7	27.7	17.9	4.7	9.6
White	63.7	55.3	31.4	21.0	5.8	11.1
Black or African American	50.3	36.6	16.7	7.9	1.1	3.8
American Indian or Alaska Native	65.2	50.3	26.3	20.0	4.7	19.0
Native Hawaiian or Other Pacific Islander	58.5	46.7	17.4	9.1	3.0	7.3
Asian	40.3	31.7	12.4	6.3	0.8	3.9
Two or More Races	62.0	51.6	27.0	18.8	4.7	13.8
Hispanic or Latino	62.3	50.5	26.0	17.1	3.7	9.6
GENDER/RACE/HISPANIC ORIGIN						
Male, White, Not Hispanic	62.4	53.3	31.2	22.4	7.0	10.8
Female, White, Not Hispanic	65.0	57.4	31.7	19.5	4.6	11.5
Male, Black, Not Hispanic	50.2	35.9	17.0	8.9	1.5	4.4
Female, Black, Not Hispanic	50.3	37.4	16.5	6.9	0.6	3.2
Male, Hispanic	61.6	49.5	25.9	18.1	4.7	9.6
Female, Hispanic	63.0	51.6	26.2	16.1	2.7	9.6

*Low precision; no estimate reported. [1] Binge Alcohol Use is defined as drinking five or more drinks on the same occasion (i.e., at the same time or within a couple of hours of each other) on at least 1 day in the past 30 days. Heavy Alcohol Use is defined as drinking five or more drinks on the same occasion on each of 5 or more days in the past 30 days; all heavy alcohol users are also binge alcohol users. [2] Dependence or abuse is based on definitions found in the 4th edition of the *Diagnostic and Statistical Manual of Mental Disorders* (DSM-IV).

Source: SAMHSA, Office of Applied Studies, National Survey on Drug Use and Health, 2002, 2003, 2004, 2005, and 2006.

Table 3.5A. Alcohol Use in the Lifetime, Past Year, and Past Month; Binge and Heavy Alcohol Use in the Past Month; and Alcohol Dependence or Abuse in the Past Year among Persons Aged 18 to 20, by Demographic Characteristics: Numbers in Thousands, Annual Averages Based on 2002-2006

Demographic Characteristic	Lifetime Use	Past Year Use	Past Month Use	Binge Use in Past Month[1]	Heavy Use in Past Month[1]	Dependence or Abuse in Past Year[2]
TOTAL	10,237	9,092	6,486	4,596	1,692	2,103
GENDER						
Male	5,280	4,736	3,541	2,770	1,152	1,278
Female	4,957	4,356	2,945	1,825	540	824
HISPANIC ORIGIN AND RACE						
Not Hispanic or Latino	8,566	7,698	5,544	3,919	1,501	1,789
White	6,696	6,119	4,567	3,377	1,370	1,508
Black or African American	1,254	1,054	645	330	73	163
American Indian or Alaska Native	63	52	37	28	6	18
Native Hawaiian or Other Pacific Islander	44	34	24	21	4	14
Asian	379	320	187	102	24	53
Two or More Races	131	119	85	62	24	34
Hispanic or Latino	1,671	1,394	942	677	191	313
GENDER/RACE/HISPANIC ORIGIN						
Male, White, Not Hispanic	3,392	3,126	2,447	1,986	915	883
Female, White, Not Hispanic	3,304	2,993	2,121	1,390	455	625
Male, Black, Not Hispanic	656	555	359	208	54	109
Female, Black, Not Hispanic	598	499	285	122	18	54
Male, Hispanic	937	797	565	450	142	212
Female, Hispanic	734	597	377	227	49	101

*Low precision; no estimate reported. [1] Binge Alcohol Use is defined as drinking five or more drinks on the same occasion (i.e., at the same time or within a couple of hours of each other) on at least 1 day in the past 30 days. Heavy Alcohol Use is defined as drinking five or more drinks on the same occasion on each of 5 or more days in the past 30 days; all heavy alcohol users are also binge alcohol users. [2] Dependence or abuse is based on definitions found in the 4th edition of the *Diagnostic and Statistical Manual of Mental Disorders* (DSM-IV).

Source: SAMHSA, Office of Applied Studies, National Survey on Drug Use and Health, 2002, 2003, 2004, 2005, and 2006.

Table 3.5B. Alcohol Use in the Lifetime, Past Year, and Past Month; Binge and Heavy Alcohol Use in the Past Month; and Alcohol Dependence or Abuse in the Past Year among Persons Aged 18 to 20, by Demographic Characteristics: Percentages, Annual Averages Based on 2002–2006

Demographic Characteristic	Lifetime Use	Past Year Use	Past Month Use	Binge Use in Past Month[1]	Heavy Use in Past Month[1]	Dependence or Abuse in Past Year[2]
TOTAL	80.9	71.9	51.3	36.3	13.4	16.6
GENDER						
Male	81.2	72.8	54.4	42.6	17.7	19.6
Female	80.7	70.9	47.9	29.7	8.8	13.4
HISPANIC ORIGIN AND RACE						
Not Hispanic or Latino	81.7	73.4	52.9	37.4	14.3	17.1
White	85.1	77.7	58.0	42.9	17.4	19.2
Black or African American	70.7	59.5	36.4	18.6	4.1	9.2
American Indian or Alaska Native	79.1	65.9	46.3	35.4	7.9	22.1
Native Hawaiian or Other Pacific Islander	75.9	58.8	41.9	35.9	7.4	24.5
Asian	68.5	57.8	33.7	18.4	4.3	9.6
Two or More Races	86.0	78.2	55.6	40.5	15.9	22.4
Hispanic or Latino	77.3	64.5	43.5	31.3	8.8	14.5
GENDER/RACE/HISPANIC ORIGIN						
Male, White, Not Hispanic	84.5	77.9	61.0	49.5	22.8	22.0
Female, White, Not Hispanic	85.6	77.6	55.0	36.0	11.8	16.2
Male, Black, Not Hispanic	71.9	60.9	39.4	22.8	5.9	12.0
Female, Black, Not Hispanic	69.4	58.0	33.1	14.1	2.1	6.3
Male, Hispanic	79.6	67.7	48.0	38.2	12.1	18.0
Female, Hispanic	74.5	60.6	38.2	23.0	5.0	10.2

*Low precision; no estimate reported. [1] Binge Alcohol Use is defined as drinking five or more drinks on the same occasion (i.e., at the same time or within a couple of hours of each other) on at least 1 day in the past 30 days. Heavy Alcohol Use is defined as drinking five or more drinks on the same occasion on each of 5 or more days in the past 30 days; all heavy alcohol users are also binge alcohol users. [2] Dependence or abuse is based on definitions found in the 4th edition of the *Diagnostic and Statistical Manual of Mental Disorders* (DSM-IV).

Source: SAMHSA, Office of Applied Studies, National Survey on Drug Use and Health, 2002, 2003, 2004, 2005, and 2006.

Table 3.6A. Alcohol Use in the Lifetime, Past Year, and Past Month; Binge and Heavy Alcohol Use in the Past Month; and Alcohol Dependence or Abuse in the Past Year among Persons Aged 12 to 20, by Family Income and Geographic Characteristics: Numbers in Thousands, Annual Averages Based on 2002-2006

Family Income/ Geographic Characteristic	Lifetime Use	Past Year Use	Past Month Use	Binge Use in Past Month[1]	Heavy Use in Past Month[1]	Dependence or Abuse in Past Year[2]
TOTAL	20,760	17,588	10,814	7,240	2,325	3,544
FAMILY INCOME						
Less Than $20,000	5,365	4,504	3,002	2,102	767	1,030
$20,000 - $49,999	6,817	5,619	3,274	2,136	602	1,056
$50,000 - $74,999	3,408	2,911	1,726	1,132	326	555
$75,000 or More	5,171	4,555	2,812	1,870	631	903
GEOGRAPHIC REGION						
Northeast	3,890	3,401	2,156	1,445	481	645
Midwest	4,881	4,225	2,664	1,875	635	917
South	7,246	6,014	3,584	2,330	743	1,135
West	4,743	3,949	2,410	1,589	467	847
COUNTY TYPE						
Metropolitan	17,120	14,527	8,942	5,914	1,888	2,872
Large Metropolitan	10,680	9,066	5,465	3,518	1,048	1,686
Small Metropolitan	6,440	5,461	3,477	2,396	840	1,187
250K - 1 Mil. Pop.	4,171	3,522	2,213	1,513	519	749
< 250K Pop.	2,268	1,939	1,264	883	321	437
Nonmetropolitan	3,640	3,061	1,872	1,326	437	672
Urbanized (Urban Pop. ≥ 20K)	1,552	1,323	830	589	218	309
Rural (Urban Pop. < 20K)	2,089	1,739	1,042	737	219	363
Urban Pop. 2,500-19,999	1,730	1,449	874	613	180	296
Urban Pop. < 2,500	359	289	168	123	39	67

*Low precision; no estimate reported. [1] Binge Alcohol Use is defined as drinking five or more drinks on the same occasion (i.e., at the same time or within a couple of hours of each other) on at least 1 day in the past 30 days. Heavy Alcohol Use is defined as drinking five or more drinks on the same occasion on each of 5 or more days in the past 30 days; all heavy alcohol users are also binge alcohol users. [2] Dependence or abuse is based on definitions found in the 4th edition of the *Diagnostic and Statistical Manual of Mental Disorders* (DSM-IV).

Source: SAMHSA, Office of Applied Studies, National Survey on Drug Use and Health, 2002, 2003, 2004, 2005, and 2006.

Table 3.6B. Alcohol Use in the Lifetime, Past Year, and Past Month; Binge and Heavy Alcohol Use in the Past Month; and Alcohol Dependence or Abuse in the Past Year among Persons Aged 12 to 20, by Family Income and Geographic Characteristics: Percentages, Annual Averages Based on 2002-2006

Family Income/ Geographic Characteristic	Lifetime Use	Past Year Use	Past Month Use	Binge Use in Past Month[1]	Heavy Use in Past Month[1]	Dependence or Abuse in Past Year[2]
TOTAL	54.9	46.5	28.6	19.2	6.2	9.4
FAMILY INCOME						
Less Than $20,000	60.6	50.9	33.9	23.7	8.7	11.6
$20,000 - $49,999	54.2	44.7	26.0	17.0	4.8	8.4
$50,000 - $74,999	52.2	44.6	26.4	17.3	5.0	8.5
$75,000 or More	52.6	46.3	28.6	19.0	6.4	9.2
GEOGRAPHIC REGION						
Northeast	57.5	50.3	31.9	21.4	7.1	9.5
Midwest	56.8	49.2	31.0	21.8	7.4	10.7
South	53.7	44.6	26.6	17.3	5.5	8.4
West	53.0	44.2	26.9	17.8	5.2	9.5
COUNTY TYPE						
Metropolitan	54.5	46.2	28.5	18.8	6.0	9.1
Large Metropolitan	53.7	45.6	27.5	17.7	5.3	8.5
Small Metropolitan	55.8	47.3	30.1	20.8	7.3	10.3
250K - 1 Mil. Pop.	54.6	46.1	29.0	19.8	6.8	9.8
<250K Pop.	58.1	49.6	32.4	22.6	8.2	11.2
Nonmetropolitan	57.2	48.1	29.4	20.8	6.9	10.6
Urbanized (Urban Pop. ≥ 20K)	58.4	49.8	31.3	22.2	8.2	11.7
Rural (Urban Pop. < 20K)	56.2	46.8	28.1	19.8	5.9	9.8
Urban Pop. 2,500-19,999	56.3	47.2	28.5	20.0	5.9	9.6
Urban Pop. < 2,500	55.8	45.0	26.1	19.2	6.0	10.5

*Low precision; no estimate reported. [1] Binge Alcohol Use is defined as drinking five or more drinks on the same occasion (i.e., at the same time or within a couple of hours of each other) on at least 1 day in the past 30 days. Heavy Alcohol Use is defined as drinking five or more drinks on the same occasion on each of 5 or more days in the past 30 days; all heavy alcohol users are also binge alcohol users. [2] Dependence or abuse is based on definitions found in the 4th edition of the *Diagnostic and Statistical Manual of Mental Disorders* (DSM-IV).

Source: SAMHSA, Office of Applied Studies, National Survey on Drug Use and Health, 2002, 2003, 2004, 2005, and 2006.

Table 3.7A. Alcohol Use in the Lifetime, Past Year, and Past Month; Binge and Heavy Alcohol Use in the Past Month; and Alcohol Dependence or Abuse in the Past Year among Persons Aged 12 to 20 Residing in Metropolitan Counties, by Demographic Characteristics: Numbers in Thousands, Annual Averages Based on 2002-2006

Demographic Characteristic	Lifetime Use	Past Year Use	Past Month Use	Binge Use in Past Month[1]	Heavy Use in Past Month[1]	Dependence or Abuse in Past Year[2]
TOTAL	17,120	14,527	8,942	5,914	1,888	2,872
AGE						
12 to 14	2,375	1,728	700	320	47	183
15 to 17	6,251	5,244	2,824	1,802	461	967
18 to 20	8,494	7,555	5,417	3,792	1,381	1,722
GENDER						
Male	8,729	7,329	4,673	3,396	1,240	1,611
Female	8,391	7,198	4,269	2,517	648	1,261
HISPANIC ORIGIN AND RACE						
Not Hispanic or Latino	13,909	11,933	7,438	4,900	1,643	2,370
White	10,637	9,380	6,081	4,191	1,495	1,995
Black or African American	2,266	1,731	911	441	83	216
American Indian or Alaska Native	65	52	31	23	5	16
Native Hawaiian or Other Pacific Islander	65	52	30	23	5	15
Asian	625	505	257	136	27	74
Two or More Races	251	213	128	87	29	54
Hispanic or Latino	3,211	2,594	1,503	1,014	245	502

*Low precision; no estimate reported. *NOTE*: Metropolitan Counties include both large metropolitan areas (≥1 million population) and small metropolitan areas (<1 million population). For more detailed definitions of county types, see Section 1.5 in Chapter 1. [1] Binge Alcohol Use is defined as drinking five or more drinks on the same occasion (i.e., at the same time or within a couple of hours of each other) on at least 1 day in the past 30 days. Heavy Alcohol Use is defined as drinking five or more drinks on the same occasion on each of 5 or more days in the past 30 days; all heavy alcohol users are also binge alcohol users. [2] Dependence or abuse is based on definitions found in the 4th edition of the *Diagnostic and Statistical Manual of Mental Disorders* (DSM-IV).

Source: SAMHSA, Office of Applied Studies, National Survey on Drug Use and Health, 2002, 2003, 2004, 2005, and 2006.

Table 3.7B. Alcohol Use in the Lifetime, Past Year, and Past Month; Binge and Heavy Alcohol Use in the Past Month; and Alcohol Dependence or Abuse in the Past Year among Persons Aged 12 to 20 Residing in Metropolitan Counties, by Demographic Characteristics: Percentages, Annual Averages Based on 2002–2006

Demographic Characteristic	Lifetime Use	Past Year Use	Past Month Use	Binge Use in Past Month[1]	Heavy Use in Past Month[1]	Dependence or Abuse in Past Year[2]
TOTAL	54.5	46.2	28.5	18.8	6.0	9.1
AGE						
12 to 14	22.7	16.5	6.7	3.1	0.4	1.7
15 to 17	60.0	50.3	27.1	17.3	4.4	9.3
18 to 20	80.8	71.9	51.5	36.1	13.1	16.4
GENDER						
Male	54.3	45.6	29.1	21.1	7.7	10.0
Female	54.7	46.9	27.8	16.4	4.2	8.2
HISPANIC ORIGIN AND RACE						
Not Hispanic or Latino	54.6	46.8	29.2	19.2	6.4	9.3
White	58.0	51.2	33.2	22.9	8.2	10.9
Black or African American	46.1	35.2	18.5	9.0	1.7	4.4
American Indian or Alaska Native	54.9	44.0	26.5	19.1	4.1	13.3
Native Hawaiian or Other Pacific Islander	52.2	41.5	23.8	18.3	3.7	12.1
Asian	41.3	33.3	17.0	9.0	1.8	4.9
Two or More Races	53.5	45.4	27.4	18.5	6.3	11.6
Hispanic or Latino	54.0	43.6	25.3	17.0	4.1	8.4

*Low precision; no estimate reported. *NOTE*: Metropolitan Counties include both large metropolitan areas (≥1 million population) and small metropolitan areas (<1 million population). For more detailed definitions of county types, see Section 1.5 in Chapter 1. [1] Binge Alcohol Use is defined as drinking five or more drinks on the same occasion (i.e., at the same time or within a couple of hours of each other) on at least 1 day in the past 30 days. Heavy Alcohol Use is defined as drinking five or more drinks on the same occasion on each of 5 or more days in the past 30 days; all heavy alcohol users are also binge alcohol users. [2] Dependence or abuse is based on definitions found in the 4th edition of the *Diagnostic and Statistical Manual of Mental Disorders* (DSM-IV).

Source: SAMHSA, Office of Applied Studies, National Survey on Drug Use and Health, 2002, 2003, 2004, 2005, and 2006.

Table 3.8A. Alcohol Use in the Lifetime, Past Year, and Past Month; Binge and Heavy Alcohol Use in the Past Month; and Alcohol Dependence or Abuse in the Past Year among Persons Aged 12 to 20 Residing in Urbanized Nonmetropolitan Counties, by Demographic Characteristics: Numbers in Thousands, Annual Averages Based on 2002-2006

Demographic Characteristic	Lifetime Use	Past Year Use	Past Month Use	Binge Use in Past Month[1]	Heavy Use in Past Month[1]	Dependence or Abuse in Past Year[2]
TOTAL	1,552	1,323	830	589	218	309
AGE						
12 to 14	217	159	69	32	6	22
15 to 17	537	445	240	165	44	94
18 to 20	798	719	521	392	168	193
GENDER						
Male	799	677	449	350	147	170
Female	753	646	381	239	71	139
HISPANIC ORIGIN AND RACE						
Not Hispanic or Latino	1,427	1,221	768	544	200	285
White	1,211	1,049	673	481	186	247
Black or African American	142	111	62	39	7	21
American Indian or Alaska Native	21	16	9	8	2	7
Native Hawaiian or Other Pacific Islander	*	*	*	*	*	*
Asian	15	13	8	5	*	3
Two or More Races	31	26	13	9	3	5
Hispanic or Latino	125	101	62	45	19	24

*Low precision; no estimate reported. *NOTE*: Urbanized Nonmetropolitan Counties include counties containing populations of 20,000 or more in urbanized areas. For more detailed definitions of county types, see Section 1.5 in Chapter 1. [1] Binge Alcohol Use is defined as drinking five or more drinks on the same occasion (i.e., at the same time or within a couple of hours of each other) on at least 1 day in the past 30 days. Heavy Alcohol Use is defined as drinking five or more drinks on the same occasion on each of 5 or more days in the past 30 days; all heavy alcohol users are also binge alcohol users. [2] Dependence or abuse is based on definitions found in the 4th edition of the *Diagnostic and Statistical Manual of Mental Disorders* (DSM-IV).

Source: SAMHSA, Office of Applied Studies, National Survey on Drug Use and Health, 2002, 2003, 2004, 2005, and 2006.

Table 3.8B. Alcohol Use in the Lifetime, Past Year, and Past Month; Binge and Heavy Alcohol Use in the Past Month; and Alcohol Dependence or Abuse in the Past Year among Persons Aged 12 to 20 Residing in Urbanized Nonmetropolitan Counties, by Demographic Characteristics: Percentages, Annual Averages Based on 2002-2006

Demographic Characteristic	Lifetime Use	Past Year Use	Past Month Use	Binge Use in Past Month[1]	Heavy Use in Past Month[1]	Dependence or Abuse in Past Year[2]
TOTAL	58.4	49.8	31.3	22.2	8.2	11.7
AGE						
12 to 14	25.5	18.7	8.1	3.7	0.7	2.5
15 to 17	62.9	52.1	28.1	19.3	5.2	11.1
18 to 20	83.8	75.5	54.8	41.2	17.7	20.3
GENDER						
Male	58.7	49.7	33.0	25.7	10.8	12.5
Female	58.2	49.9	29.4	18.5	5.5	10.7
HISPANIC ORIGIN AND RACE						
Not Hispanic or Latino	58.4	50.0	31.5	22.3	8.2	11.7
White	59.4	51.4	33.0	23.6	9.1	12.1
Black or African American	52.3	41.1	23.0	14.2	2.4	7.8
American Indian or Alaska Native	58.2	46.0	24.8	21.3	5.2	19.6
Native Hawaiian or Other Pacific Islander	*	*	*	*	*	*
Asian	49.2	41.6	25.5	15.6	*	9.7
Two or More Races	57.0	47.5	23.9	17.3	5.3	9.4
Hispanic or Latino	58.7	47.7	29.1	21.1	8.7	11.3

*Low precision; no estimate reported. *NOTE*: Urbanized Nonmetropolitan Counties include counties containing populations of 20,000 or more in urbanized areas. For more detailed definitions of county types, see Section 1.5 in Chapter 1. [1] Binge Alcohol Use is defined as drinking five or more drinks on the same occasion (i.e., at the same time or within a couple of hours of each other) on at least 1 day in the past 30 days. Heavy Alcohol Use is defined as drinking five or more drinks on the same occasion on each of 5 or more days in the past 30 days; all heavy alcohol users are also binge alcohol users. [2] Dependence or abuse is based on definitions found in the 4th edition of the *Diagnostic and Statistical Manual of Mental Disorders* (DSM-IV).

Source: SAMHSA, Office of Applied Studies, National Survey on Drug Use and Health, 2002, 2003, 2004, 2005, and 2006.

Table 3.9A. Alcohol Use in the Lifetime, Past Year, and Past Month; Binge and Heavy Alcohol Use in the Past Month; and Alcohol Dependence or Abuse in the Past Year among Persons Aged 12 to 20 Residing in Rural Counties, by Demographic Characteristics: Numbers in Thousands, Annual Averages Based on 2002–2006

Demographic Characteristic	Lifetime Use	Past Year Use	Past Month Use	Binge Use in Past Month[1]	Heavy Use in Past Month[1]	Dependence or Abuse in Past Year[2]
TOTAL	2,089	1,739	1,042	737	219	363
AGE						
12 to 14	332	243	108	60	11	33
15 to 17	812	676	386	265	65	143
18 to 20	945	819	548	411	143	187
GENDER						
Male	1,077	898	573	442	150	204
Female	1,011	840	469	295	69	159
HISPANIC ORIGIN AND RACE						
Not Hispanic or Latino	1,941	1,616	964	678	200	333
White	1,676	1,407	853	610	186	295
Black or African American	177	137	73	38	7	18
American Indian or Alaska Native	54	44	27	21	4	14
Native Hawaiian or Other Pacific Islander	*	*	*	*	*	*
Asian	*	*	*	*	*	*
Two or More Races	19	15	8	6	2	5
Hispanic or Latino	148	123	78	59	19	30

*Low precision; no estimate reported. *NOTE*: Rural Counties include nonmetropolitan counties containing populations of fewer than 20,000 in urbanized areas. For more detailed definitions of county types, see Section 1.5 in Chapter 1. [1] Binge Alcohol Use is defined as drinking five or more drinks on the same occasion (i.e., at the same time or within a couple of hours of each other) on at least 1 day in the past 30 days. Heavy Alcohol Use is defined as drinking five or more drinks on the same occasion on each of 5 or more days in the past 30 days; all heavy alcohol users are also binge alcohol users. [2] Dependence or abuse is based on definitions found in the 4th edition of the *Diagnostic and Statistical Manual of Mental Disorders* (DSM-IV).

Source: SAMHSA, Office of Applied Studies, National Survey on Drug Use and Health, 2002, 2003, 2004, 2005, and 2006.

Table 3.9B. Alcohol Use in the Lifetime, Past Year, and Past Month; Binge and Heavy Alcohol Use in the Past Month; and Alcohol Dependence or Abuse in the Past Year among Persons Aged 12 to 20 Residing in Rural Counties, by Demographic Characteristics: Percentages, Annual Averages Based on 2002-2006

Demographic Characteristic	Lifetime Use	Past Year Use	Past Month Use	Binge Use in Past Month[1]	Heavy Use in Past Month[1]	Dependence or Abuse in Past Year[2]
TOTAL	56.2	46.8	28.1	19.8	5.9	9.8
AGE						
12 to 14	26.8	19.7	8.7	4.9	0.9	2.7
15 to 17	62.9	52.4	30.0	20.6	5.0	11.1
18 to 20	79.6	68.9	46.1	34.6	12.0	15.7
GENDER						
Male	56.3	47.0	30.0	23.1	7.8	10.7
Female	56.1	46.6	26.0	16.4	3.8	8.8
HISPANIC ORIGIN AND RACE						
Not Hispanic or Latino	55.9	46.5	27.8	19.5	5.8	9.6
White	56.8	47.7	28.9	20.7	6.3	10.0
Black or African American	48.0	37.0	19.6	10.4	1.8	4.9
American Indian or Alaska Native	58.4	47.2	29.0	22.9	4.7	15.1
Native Hawaiian or Other Pacific Islander	*	*	*	*	*	*
Asian	*	*	*	*	*	*
Two or More Races	49.0	40.8	22.3	16.8	5.9	12.3
Hispanic or Latino	61.7	51.2	32.4	24.7	7.9	12.5

*Low precision; no estimate reported. *NOTE*: Rural Counties include nonmetropolitan counties containing populations of fewer than 20,000 in urbanized areas. For more detailed definitions of county types, see Section 1.5 in Chapter 1. [1] Binge Alcohol Use is defined as drinking five or more drinks on the same occasion (i.e., at the same time or within a couple of hours of each other) on at least 1 day in the past 30 days. Heavy Alcohol Use is defined as drinking five or more drinks on the same occasion on each of 5 or more days in the past 30 days; all heavy alcohol users are also binge alcohol users. [2] Dependence or abuse is based on definitions found in the 4th edition of the *Diagnostic and Statistical Manual of Mental Disorders* (DSM-IV).

Source: SAMHSA, Office of Applied Studies, National Survey on Drug Use and Health, 2002, 2003, 2004, 2005, and 2006.

Table 3.10A. Alcohol Use in the Lifetime, Past Year, and Past Month; Binge and Heavy Alcohol Use in the Past Month; and Alcohol Dependence or Abuse in the Past Year among Persons Aged 12 to 20, by State: Numbers in Thousands, Annual Averages Based on 2002-2006

State	Lifetime Use	Past Year Use	Past Month Use	Binge Use in Past Month[1]	Heavy Use in Past Month[1]	Dependence or Abuse in Past Year[2]
Total United States	20,760	17,588	10,814	7,240	2,325	3,544
Alabama	315	254	154	102	32	48
Alaska	51	43	26	18	5	9
Arizona	401	328	208	142	45	71
Arkansas	200	161	97	71	25	38
California	2,484	2,054	1,222	782	205	414
Colorado	344	302	191	123	34	65
Connecticut	243	215	141	94	28	41
Delaware	59	50	31	20	6	9
District of Columbia	32	26	18	11	4	5
Florida	1,140	975	573	361	124	188
Georgia	582	469	271	173	48	84
Hawaii	81	66	40	28	8	15
Idaho	94	79	49	35	14	23
Illinois	899	776	485	335	109	166
Indiana	448	374	220	156	56	77
Iowa	222	199	128	95	38	50
Kansas	215	184	121	89	28	44
Kentucky	291	240	145	100	25	39
Louisiana	360	306	185	116	36	58
Maine	94	81	51	35	11	16
Maryland	377	323	194	114	41	57
Massachusetts	447	396	259	186	67	77
Michigan	746	645	403	276	90	128
Minnesota	366	323	207	147	48	71
Mississippi	208	162	96	64	22	29
Missouri	440	374	239	165	56	82
Montana	77	68	47	35	12	21

State	Lifetime Use	Past Year Use	Past Month Use	Binge Use in Past Month[1]	Heavy Use in Past Month[1]	Dependence or Abuse in Past Year[2]
Nebraska	131	115	78	54	18	31
Nevada	156	128	76	49	15	26
New Hampshire	100	90	59	42	19	21
New Jersey	599	526	323	195	53	92
New Mexico	162	134	83	57	18	34
New York	1,366	1,196	763	504	168	225
North Carolina	539	443	262	176	49	81
North Dakota	59	53	37	28	12	16
Ohio	835	718	440	310	104	141
Oklahoma	255	213	124	87	27	47
Oregon	250	210	127	85	30	43
Pennsylvania	904	777	477	331	114	146
Rhode Island	85	76	52	36	14	17
South Carolina	272	212	126	84	28	40
South Dakota	67	60	39	29	9	17
Tennessee	368	304	167	106	37	57
Texas	1,644	1,361	816	522	166	249
Utah	137	111	71	52	17	30
Vermont	51	45	31	22	8	10
Virginia	480	409	260	177	58	86
Washington	463	391	248	166	58	85
West Virginia	125	105	63	47	15	23
Wisconsin	453	404	268	191	67	94
Wyoming	43	36	23	17	6	10

*Low precision; no estimate reported. [1] Binge Alcohol Use is defined as drinking five or more drinks on the same occasion (i.e., at the same time or within a couple of hours of each other) on at least 1 day in the past 30 days. Heavy Alcohol Use is defined as drinking five or more drinks on the same occasion on each of 5 or more days in the past 30 days; all heavy alcohol users are also binge alcohol users. [2] Dependence or abuse is based on definitions found in the 4th edition of the *Diagnostic and Statistical Manual of Mental Disorders* (DSM-IV).

Source: SAMHSA, Office of Applied Studies, National Survey on Drug Use and Health, 2002, 2003, 2004, 2005, and 2006.

Table 3.10B. Alcohol Use in the Lifetime, Past Year, and Past Month; Binge and Heavy Alcohol Use in the Past Month; and Alcohol Dependence or Abuse in the Past Year among Persons Aged 12 to 20, by State: Percentages, Annual Averages Based on 2002–2006

State	Lifetime Use	Past Year Use	Past Month Use	Binge Use in Past Month[1]	Heavy Use in Past Month[1]	Dependence or Abuse in Past Year[2]
Total United States	54.9	46.5	28.6	19.2	6.2	9.4
Alabama	52.5	42.4	25.7	17.0	5.4	7.9
Alaska	53.0	44.0	26.8	18.2	5.4	9.8
Arizona	54.9	44.8	28.5	19.4	6.1	9.7
Arkansas	55.6	44.6	27.0	19.8	7.1	10.4
California	51.5	42.5	25.3	16.2	4.2	8.6
Colorado	59.7	52.4	33.1	21.4	5.8	11.2
Connecticut	57.3	50.6	33.1	22.0	6.6	9.7
Delaware	57.2	47.9	29.5	19.2	5.7	8.2
District of Columbia	53.6	44.7	30.2	19.0	6.3	8.1
Florida	55.1	47.1	27.7	17.4	6.0	9.1
Georgia	50.5	40.7	23.5	15.0	4.1	7.3
Hawaii	53.7	43.9	26.7	18.9	5.2	9.9
Idaho	47.8	40.2	24.9	18.0	7.2	11.7
Illinois	54.9	47.4	29.7	20.5	6.6	10.2
Indiana	53.8	44.9	26.4	18.7	6.7	9.2
Iowa	58.0	51.8	33.4	24.8	9.9	13.2
Kansas	58.4	50.1	32.9	24.2	7.7	11.9
Kentucky	57.9	47.9	29.0	19.9	4.9	7.9
Louisiana	59.0	50.2	30.4	19.0	5.9	9.4
Maine	57.0	48.8	30.7	21.4	6.5	9.7
Maryland	53.8	46.1	27.6	16.3	5.9	8.1
Massachusetts	58.5	51.8	33.9	24.3	8.7	10.1
Michigan	55.6	48.1	30.0	20.5	6.7	9.6
Minnesota	56.1	49.5	31.7	22.6	7.3	10.9
Mississippi	51.9	40.4	24.1	15.9	5.6	7.1
Missouri	59.1	50.2	32.1	22.2	7.5	11.0
Montana	64.0	56.7	38.5	29.3	10.2	17.8

State	Lifetime Use	Past Year Use	Past Month Use	Binge Use in Past Month[1]	Heavy Use in Past Month[1]	Dependence or Abuse in Past Year[2]
Nebraska	57.4	50.3	34.0	23.6	8.1	13.5
Nevada	56.0	45.8	27.1	17.4	5.5	9.3
New Hampshire	59.0	53.2	34.9	24.6	11.5	12.6
New Jersey	57.3	50.3	30.9	18.7	5.0	8.7
New Mexico	61.3	50.8	31.3	21.4	6.8	13.0
New York	57.3	50.2	32.0	21.2	7.1	9.4
North Carolina	51.5	42.3	25.1	16.8	4.6	7.7
North Dakota	66.2	59.1	41.2	31.7	12.9	17.7
Ohio	56.6	48.7	29.8	21.0	7.0	9.5
Oklahoma	55.3	46.3	26.9	18.9	5.9	10.2
Oregon	56.3	47.4	28.6	19.2	6.8	9.7
Pennsylvania	56.9	48.8	30.0	20.8	7.1	9.2
Rhode Island	61.0	54.8	37.8	26.2	9.9	12.2
South Carolina	52.0	40.6	24.2	16.0	5.3	7.7
South Dakota	63.6	56.8	37.2	27.9	8.9	15.9
Tennessee	50.1	41.3	22.7	14.4	5.0	7.7
Texas	54.0	44.7	26.8	17.2	5.5	8.2
Utah	37.1	30.0	19.3	14.1	4.6	8.0
Vermont	61.8	54.9	37.2	26.5	9.2	12.4
Virginia	52.8	45.0	28.6	19.5	6.4	9.4
Washington	56.4	47.6	30.3	20.3	7.1	10.4
West Virginia	57.1	48.0	29.0	21.6	6.7	10.6
Wisconsin	61.9	55.2	36.6	26.1	9.2	12.9
Wyoming	62.6	53.2	33.8	24.4	8.2	14.8

*Low precision; no estimate reported. [1] Binge Alcohol Use is defined as drinking five or more drinks on the same occasion (i.e., at the same time or within a couple of hours of each other) on at least 1 day in the past 30 days. Heavy Alcohol Use is defined as drinking five or more drinks on the same occasion on each of 5 or more days in the past 30 days; all heavy alcohol users are also binge alcohol users. [2] Dependence or abuse is based on definitions found in the 4th edition of the *Diagnostic and Statistical Manual of Mental Disorders* (DSM-IV).

Source: SAMHSA, Office of Applied Studies, National Survey on Drug Use and Health, 2002, 2003, 2004, 2005, and 2006.

Table 3.11A. Alcohol Use in the Lifetime, Past Year, and Past Month; Binge and Heavy Alcohol Use in the Past Month; and Alcohol Dependence or Abuse in the Past Year among Persons Aged 12 to 20, by Parental Alcohol Use: Numbers in Thousands, Annual Averages Based on 2002-2006

Parental Alcohol Use[1]	Lifetime Use	Past Year Use	Past Month Use	Binge Use in Past Month[2]	Heavy Use in Past Month[2]	Dependence or Abuse in Past Year[3]
Mother's Alcohol Use						
No Use in Past Year	4,067	3,025	1,465	966	260	537
Used in Past Year	11,593	9,956	5,916	3,820	1,128	1,712
Used in Past Month But No Binge Use[2]	5,759	5,083	3,043	1,908	557	841
Binge Use at Least Once in Past Month[2]	2,778	2,395	1,536	1,039	368	440
Father's Alcohol Use						
No Use in Past Year	2,607	1,979	999	665	147	341
Used in Past Year	9,594	8,132	4,798	3,083	944	1,493
Used in Past Month But No Binge Use[2]	3,799	3,321	1,865	1,203	313	551
Binge Use at Least Once in Past Month[2]	4,274	3,693	2,319	1,482	570	773

*Low precision; no estimate reported. *NOTE*: Estimates were created from mother-child and father-child pair data. For further details, see Section A.2 in Appendix A. [1] Parent was female in 60 percent of the cases [2] Binge Alcohol Use is defined as drinking five or more drinks on the same occasion (i.e., at the same time or within a couple of hours of each other) on at least 1 day in the past 30 days. Heavy Alcohol Use is defined as drinking five or more drinks on the same occasion on each of 5 or more days in the past 30 days; all heavy alcohol users are also binge alcohol users. [3] Dependence or abuse is based on definitions found in the 4th edition of the *Diagnostic and Statistical Manual of Mental Disorders* (DSM-IV).

Source: SAMHSA, Office of Applied Studies, National Survey on Drug Use and Health, 2002, 2003, 2004, 2005, and 2006.

Table 3.11B. Alcohol Use in the Lifetime, Past Year, and Past Month; Binge and Heavy Alcohol Use in the Past Month; and Alcohol Dependence or Abuse in the Past Year among Persons Aged 12 to 20, by Parental Alcohol Use: Percentages, Annual Averages Based on 2002-2006

Parental Alcohol Use[1]	Lifetime Use	Past Year Use	Past Month Use	Binge Use in Past Month[2]	Heavy Use in Past Month[2]	Dependence or Abuse in Past Year[3]
Mother's Alcohol Use						
No Use in Past Year	39.1	29.1	14.1	9.3	2.5	5.2
Used in Past Year	53.5	46.0	27.3	17.6	5.2	7.9
Used in Past Month But No Binge Use[2]	52.7	46.5	27.9	17.5	5.1	7.7
Binge Use at Least Once in Past Month[2]	57.0	49.1	31.5	21.3	7.5	9.0
Father's Alcohol Use						
No Use in Past Year	39.9	30.3	15.3	10.2	2.2	5.2
Used in Past Year	51.5	43.6	25.7	16.5	5.1	8.0
Used in Past Month But No Binge Use[2]	48.6	42.5	23.9	15.4	4.0	7.1
Binge Use at Least Once in Past Month[2]	56.1	48.5	30.5	19.5	7.5	10.2

*Low precision; no estimate reported. *NOTE:* Estimates were created from mother-child and father-child pair data. For further details, see Section A.2 in Appendix A. [1] Parent was female in 60 percent of the cases. [2] Binge Alcohol Use is defined as drinking five or more drinks on the same occasion (i.e., at the same time or within a couple of hours of each other) on at least 1 day in the past 30 days. Heavy Alcohol Use is defined as drinking five or more drinks on the same occasion on each of 5 or more days in the past 30 days; all heavy alcohol users are also binge alcohol users. [3] Dependence or abuse is based on definitions found in the 4th edition of the *Diagnostic and Statistical Manual of Mental Disorders* (DSM-IV).

Source: SAMHSA, Office of Applied Studies, National Survey on Drug Use and Health, 2002, 2003, 2004, 2005, and 2006.

Table 3.12A. Alcohol Use in the Lifetime, Past Year, and Past Month; Binge and Heavy Alcohol Use in the Past Month; and Alcohol Dependence or Abuse in the Past Year among Persons Aged 12 to 20, by Parental Alcohol Use and Household Structure: Numbers in Thousands, Annual Averages Based on 2002–2006

Parental Alcohol Use/ Household Structure[1]	Lifetime Use	Past Year Use	Past Month Use	Binge Use in Past Month[2]	Heavy Use in Past Month[2]	Dependence or Abuse in Past Year[3]
MOTHER'S ALCOHOL USE						
One-Parent Household						
No Use in Past Year	1,066	752	295	184	19	151
Used in Past Year	2,482	2,097	1,239	761	242	427
Used in Past Month But No Binge Use[2]	1,004	883	572	322	80	147
Binge Use at Least Once in Past Month[2]	798	678	422	272	101	145
Two-Parent Household[4]						
No Use in Past Year	3,001	2,273	1,170	782	241	386
Used in Past Year	9,111	7,859	4,676	3,059	886	1,285
Used in Past Month But No Binge Use[2]	4,755	4,200	2,471	1,586	477	694
Binge Use at Least Once in Past Month[2]	1,981	1,716	1,113	767	267	295
FATHER'S ALCOHOL USE						
One-Parent Household[4]						
No Use in Past Year	*	*	*	18	3	*
Used in Past Year	580	514	278	190	53	108
Used in Past Month But No Binge Use[2]	*	*	*	50	*	*
Binge Use at Least Once in Past Month[2]	*	*	154	112	22	63
Two-Parent Household[4]						
No Use in Past Year	2,494	1,887	967	647	144	334
Used in Past Year	9,014	7,619	4,519	2,894	891	1,385
Used in Past Month But No Binge Use[2]	3,613	3,158	1,793	1,153	284	518
Binge Use at Least Once in Past Month[2]	3,985	3,437	2,165	1,370	548	711

*Low precision; no estimate reported. *NOTE*: Estimates were created from mother-child and father-child pair data. For further details, see Section A.2 in Appendix A. [1] Parent was female in 60 percent of the cases. [2] Binge Alcohol Use is defined as drinking five or more drinks on the same occasion (i.e., at the same time or within a couple of hours of each other) on at least 1 day in the past 30 days. Heavy Alcohol Use is defined as drinking five or more drinks on the same occasion on each of 5 or more days in the past 30 days; all heavy alcohol users are also binge alcohol users. [3] Dependence or abuse is based on definitions found in the 4th edition of the *Diagnostic and Statistical Manual of Mental Disorders* (DSM-IV). [4] Includes parent-child pairs reporting more than two parents in the household, which may occur because the definition of parent includes all biological, adoptive, step-, and foster relationships.

Source: SAMHSA, Office of Applied Studies, National Survey on Drug Use and Health, 2002, 2003, 2004, 2005, and 2006.

Table 3.12B. Alcohol Use in the Lifetime, Past Year, and Past Month; Binge and Heavy Alcohol Use in the Past Month; and Alcohol Dependence or Abuse in the Past Year among Persons Aged 12 to 20, by Parental Alcohol Use and Household Structure: Percentages, Annual Averages Based on 2002-2006

Parental Alcohol Use/ Household Structure[1]	Lifetime Use	Past Year Use	Past Month Use	Binge Use in Past Month[2]	Heavy Use in Past Month[2]	Dependence or Abuse in Past Year[3]
MOTHER'S ALCOHOL USE						
One-Parent Household						
No Use in Past Year	45.3	31.9	12.5	7.8	0.8	6.4
Used in Past Year	51.7	43.7	25.8	15.9	5.0	8.9
Used in Past Month But No Binge Use[2]	53.1	46.7	30.3	17.0	4.2	7.8
Binge Use at Least Once in Past Month[2]	52.6	44.7	27.8	17.9	6.6	9.6
Two-Parent Household[4]						
No Use in Past Year	37.4	28.3	14.6	9.7	3.0	4.8
Used in Past Year	54.0	46.6	27.7	18.1	5.3	7.6
Used in Past Month But No Binge Use[2]	52.7	46.5	27.4	17.6	5.3	7.7
Binge Use at Least Once in Past Month[2]	59.0	51.1	33.2	22.9	8.0	8.8
FATHER'S ALCOHOL USE						
One-Parent Household[4]						
No Use in Past Year	*	*	*	5.6	0.9	*
Used in Past Year	57.5	50.9	27.5	18.8	5.2	10.7
Used in Past Month But No Binge Use[2]	*	*	*	15.0	*	*
Binge Use at Least Once in Past Month[2]	*	*	33.0	23.8	4.7	13.4
Two-Parent Household[4]						
No Use in Past Year	40.2	30.4	15.6	10.4	2.3	5.4
Used in Past Year	51.1	43.2	25.6	16.4	5.1	7.9
Used in Past Month But No Binge Use[2]	48.3	42.2	24.0	15.4	3.8	6.9
Binge Use at Least Once in Past Month[2]	55.8	48.1	30.3	19.2	7.7	9.9

*Low precision; no estimate reported. *NOTE*: Estimates were created from mother-child and father-child pair data. For further details, see Section A.2 in Appendix A. [1] Parent was female in 60 percent of the cases. [2] Binge Alcohol Use is defined as drinking five or more drinks on the same occasion (i.e., at the same time or within a couple of hours of each other) on at least 1 day in the past 30 days. Heavy Alcohol Use is defined as drinking five or more drinks on the same occasion on each of 5 or more days in the past 30 days; all heavy alcohol users are also binge alcohol users. [3] Dependence or abuse is based on definitions found in the 4th edition of the *Diagnostic and Statistical Manual of Mental Disorders* (DSM-IV). [4] Includes parent-child pairs reporting more than two parents in the household, which may occur because the definition of parent includes all biological, adoptive, step-, and foster relationships.

Source: SAMHSA, Office of Applied Studies, National Survey on Drug Use and Health, 2002, 2003, 2004, 2005, and 2006.

Table 4.1A. Social Context and Location of Last Alcohol Use in the Past Month among Past Month Alcohol Users Aged 12 to 20, by Age Group and Gender: Numbers in Thousands, 2006

Social Context and Location of Last Alcohol Use	TOTAL	AGE GROUP			GENDER	
		12-14	15-17	18-20	Male	Female
SOCIAL CONTEXT OF LAST ALCOHOL USE[1]						
Alone	514	68	171	275	351	164
With One Other Person	1,506	167	481	858	859	647
With Two or More Other People	8,540	525	2,645	5,371	4,398	4,143
LOCATION OF LAST ALCOHOL USE[1,2]						
In a Car or Other Vehicle	580	39	251	290	295	285
At Home	3,174	290	846	2,038	1,790	1,383
At Someone Else's Home	5,606	335	1,985	3,287	2,910	2,696
At a Park, on a Beach, or in a Parking Lot	500	62	250	188	255	245
At a Restaurant, Bar, or Club	990	35	120	836	400	590
At a Concert or Sports Game	172	8	69	96	89	83
At School	240	21	60	158	117	123
At Some Other Place[3]	686	53	238	395	381	304
Party, Wedding, or Celebration	199	18	70	112	87	112
Outside; location not specified	98	12	46	40	66	32
Hotel, Motel, or Resort	80	4	21	55	30	50
Camping, Hunting, or Fishing	40	3	20	18	18	23
Cabin, Cottage, Vacation Home, etc.	35	3	13	18	28	6
Dorm Room	19	*	2	18	9	11

*Low precision; no estimate reported. [1] Respondents with unknown responses were excluded. [2] Respondents could indicate multiple locations for the last time they used alcohol; thus, these response categories are not mutually exclusive. [3] Some Other Place includes only valid responses from the other-specify questions, including these six most commonly reported locations.

Source: SAMHSA, Office of Applied Studies, National Survey on Drug Use and Health, 2006.

Table 4.1B. Social Context and Location of Last Alcohol Use in the Past Month among Past Month Alcohol Users Aged 12 to 20, by Age Group and Gender: Percentages, 2006

Social Context and Location of Last Alcohol Use[1]	TOTAL	AGE GROUP			GENDER	
		12-14	15-17	18-20	Male	Female
SOCIAL CONTEXT OF LAST ALCOHOL USE[1]						
Alone	4.9	9.0	5.2	4.2	6.3	3.3
With One Other Person	14.3	21.9	14.6	13.2	15.3	13.1
With Two or More Other People	80.9	69.1	80.2	82.6	78.4	83.6
LOCATION OF LAST ALCOHOL USE[1,2]						
In a Car or Other Vehicle	5.5	5.2	7.7	4.5	5.3	5.8
At Home	30.3	38.8	26.0	31.4	32.2	28.1
At Someone Else's Home	53.4	45.0	60.9	50.7	52.3	54.7
At a Park, on a Beach, or in a Parking Lot	4.8	8.3	7.7	2.9	4.6	5.0
At a Restaurant, Bar, or Club	9.4	4.6	3.7	12.9	7.2	12.0
At a Concert or Sports Game	1.6	1.0	2.1	1.5	1.6	1.7
At School	2.3	2.8	1.9	2.4	2.1	2.5
At Some Other Place[3]	6.6	7.2	7.5	6.2	7.0	6.3
Party, Wedding, or Celebration	1.9	2.4	2.2	1.7	1.6	2.3
Outside; location not specified	0.9	1.6	1.4	0.6	1.2	0.7
Hotel, Motel, or Resort	0.8	0.6	0.7	0.9	0.5	1.0
Camping, Hunting, or Fishing	0.4	0.4	0.6	0.3	0.3	0.5
Cabin, Cottage, Vacation Home, etc.	0.3	0.4	0.4	0.3	0.5	0.1
Dorm Room	0.2	*	0.1	0.3	0.2	0.2

*Low precision; no estimate reported. [1] Respondents with unknown responses were excluded. [2] Respondents could indicate multiple locations for the last time they used alcohol; thus, these response categories are not mutually exclusive. [3] Some Other Place includes only valid responses from the other-specify questions, including these six most commonly reported locations.

Source: SAMHSA, Office of Applied Studies, National Survey on Drug Use and Health, 2006.

Table 4.2. Mean Number of Drinks Consumed on Last Occasion of Alcohol Use in the Past Month among Past Month Alcohol Users Aged 12 to 20, by Social Context and Location of Last Alcohol Use, Age Group, and Gender: 2006

Social Context and Location of Last Alcohol Use	TOTAL	AGE GROUP			GENDER	
		12-14	15-17	18-20	Male	Female
TOTAL	4.5	2.8	4.3	4.8	5.3	3.7
SOCIAL CONTEXT OF LAST ALCOHOL USE[1]						
Alone	2.9	2.4	2.8	3.1	3.1	2.6
With One Other Person	3.1	2.0	3.1	3.3	3.5	2.5
With Two or More Other People	4.9	3.1	4.6	5.2	5.8	3.9
LOCATION OF LAST ALCOHOL USE[1,2]						
In a Car or Other Vehicle	5.1	3.2	4.9	5.5	5.7	4.4
At Home	4.0	2.2	3.6	4.4	4.6	3.3
At Someone Else's Home	4.9	3.4	4.7	5.2	5.8	4.0
At a Park, on a Beach, or in a Parking Lot	5.1	4.6	4.9	5.7	5.7	4.6
At a Restaurant, Bar, or Club	4.6	2.1	4.4	4.7	5.5	4.0
At a Concert or Sports Game	6.0	*	5.4	6.6	7.7	4.1
At School	5.1	2.0	5.6	5.3	6.4	3.8
At Some Other Place[3]	5.8	3.1	5.0	6.6	6.9	4.4
Party, Wedding, or Celebration	5.3	2.8	4.5	6.1	6.2	4.6
Outside; location not specified	6.1	4.0	5.0	8.0	7.5	3.4
Hotel, Motel, or Resort	5.7	*	4.9	6.3	7.0	4.9
Camping, Hunting, or Fishing	3.5	*	2.9	4.5	4.2	3.0
Cabin, Cottage, Vacation Home, etc.	5.7	*	5.7	6.4	6.5	*
Dorm Room	4.3	*	*	4.4	5.5	3.2

*Low precision; no estimate reported. *NOTE*: Respondents with unknown responses to number of drinks consumed on last occasion of alcohol use were excluded. [1] Respondents with unknown responses were excluded. [2] Respondents could indicate multiple locations for the last time they used alcohol; thus, these response categories are not mutually exclusive [3] Some Other Place includes only valid responses from the other-specify questions, including these six most commonly reported locations.

Source: SAMHSA, Office of Applied Studies, National Survey on Drug Use and Health, 2006.

Table 4.3A. Source of Last Alcohol Use in the Past Month among Past Month Alcohol Users Aged 12 to 20, by Age Group and Gender: Numbers in Thousands, 2006

Source of Last Alcohol Use in the Past Month[1]	TOTAL	AGE GROUP			GENDER	
		12-14	15-17	18-20	Male	Female
UNDERAGE DRINKER PAID	3,269	50	772	2,448	2,052	1,217
Purchased It Himself or Herself	983	9	178	796	640	343
From Store, Restaurant, Bar, Club, or Event	763	7	119	636	508	255
Liquor, Convenience, or Grocery Store	497	7	84	406	356	141
Restaurant, Bar, or Club	254	*	29	225	141	113
Concert, Sports, or Other Event	10	*	5	5	10	0
From Another Person	94	1	35	58	63	30
From Person under Age 21	30	*	18	12	18	12
From Person Aged 21 or Older	63	1	17	45	46	17
Purchased by Someone Else	2,271	40	589	1,642	1,404	868
Parent or Guardian	71	3	16	52	48	22
Another Family Member Aged 21 or Older	254	2	44	208	145	109
Someone Not Related Aged 21 or Older	1,577	22	384	1,170	943	634
Someone under Age 21	310	11	121	178	225	85
UNDERAGE DRINKER DID NOT PAY	7,284	705	2,519	4,061	3,542	3,742
Got It from Parent or Guardian	652	121	253	277	316	336
Got It from Another Family Member Aged 21 or Older	854	93	282	478	465	389
Got It from Someone Not Related Aged 21 or Older	2,637	97	632	1,908	1,200	1,437
Got It from Someone under Age 21	1,449	124	626	698	677	772
Took It from Own Home	396	106	157	132	202	193
Took It from Someone Else's Home	296	47	148	102	157	139
Got It Some Other Way	675	71	278	326	343	332
From Friend or Acquaintance, Unspecified Age and Method	313	35	156	122	140	173

*Low precision; no estimate reported.

NOTE: Respondents with unknown responses to number of drinks consumed on last occasion of alcohol use were excluded.

Source: SAMHSA, Office of Applied Studies, National Survey on Drug Use and Health, 2006.

Table 4.3B. Source of Last Alcohol Use in the Past Month among Past Month Alcohol Users Aged 12 to 20, by Age Group and Gender: Percentages, 2006

Source of Last Alcohol Use in the Past Month[1]	TOTAL	AGE GROUP			GENDER	
		12-14	15-17	18-20	Male	Female
UNDERAGE DRINKER PAID	31.0	6.6	23.5	37.6	36.7	24.5
Purchased It Himself or Herself	9.3	1.2	5.4	12.2	11.5	6.9
From Store, Restaurant, Bar, Club, or Event	7.3	1.0	3.7	9.9	9.2	5.2
Liquor, Convenience, or Grocery Store	4.8	1.0	2.6	6.3	6.5	2.9
Restaurant, Bar, or Club	2.4	*	0.9	3.5	2.5	2.3
Concert, Sports, or Other Event	0.1	*	0.2	0.1	0.2	0.0
From Another Person	0.9	0.1	1.1	0.9	1.1	0.6
From Person under Age 21	0.3	*	0.6	0.2	0.3	0.2
From Person Aged 21 or Older	0.6	0.1	0.5	0.7	0.8	0.3
Purchased by Someone Else	21.6	5.3	17.9	25.3	25.1	17.5
Parent or Guardian	0.7	0.4	0.5	0.8	0.9	0.5
Another Family Member Aged 21 or Older	2.4	0.2	1.4	3.2	2.6	2.2
Someone Not Related Aged 21 or Older	15.0	3.0	11.8	18.1	17.0	12.8
Someone under Age 21	3.0	1.5	3.7	2.8	4.1	1.7
UNDERAGE DRINKER DID NOT PAY	69.0	93.4	76.5	62.4	63.3	75.5
Got It from Parent or Guardian	6.4	17.1	8.0	4.4	5.8	7.0
Got It from Another Family Member Aged 21 or Older	8.3	13.1	9.0	7.5	8.6	8.1
Got It from Someone Not Related Aged 21 or Older	25.8	13.7	20.1	30.0	22.2	29.8
Got It from Someone under Age 21	14.2	17.5	19.9	11.0	12.5	16.0
Took It from Own Home	3.9	15.0	5.0	2.1	3.7	4.0
Took It from Someone Else's Home	2.9	6.6	4.7	1.6	2.9	2.9
Got It Some Other Way	6.6	10.0	8.8	5.1	6.3	6.9
From Friend or Acquaintance, Unspecified Age and Method	3.1	4.9	5.0	1.9	2.6	3.6

*Low precision; no estimate reported.

NOTE: Respondents with unknown responses to number of drinks consumed on last occasion of alcohol use were excluded.

Source: SAMHSA, Office of Applied Studies, National Survey on Drug Use and Health, 2006.

Table 4.4. Mean Number of Drinks Consumed on Last Occasion of Alcohol Use in the Past Month among Past Month Alcohol Users Aged 12 to 20, by Source of Last Alcohol Used in the Past Month, Age Group, and Gender: 2006

Source of Last Alcohol Use in the Past Month[1]	TOTAL	AGE GROUP			GENDER	
		12-14	15-17	18-20	Male	Female
TOTAL	4.5	2.8	4.3	4.8	5.3	3.7
UNDERAGE DRINKER PAID	5.9	4.8	6.1	5.9	6.8	4.5
Purchased It Himself or Herself	5.7	*	6.0	5.7	6.5	4.2
From Store, Restaurant, Bar, Club, or Event	5.7	*	6.1	5.6	6.5	4.2
Liquor, Convenience, or Grocery Store	6.0	*	6.5	6.0	6.7	4.3
Restaurant, Bar, or Club	4.8	*	5.0	4.8	5.5	4.0
Concert, Sports, or Other Event	9.8	*	*	*	*	*
From Another Person	6.6	*	6.0	7.0	7.2	5.4
From Person under Age 21	8.0	*	5.7	11.5	9.3	6.0
From Person Aged 21 or Older	6.0	*	6.3	5.8	6.4	4.9
Purchased by Someone Else	6.0	4.9	6.1	6.0	6.8	4.6
Parent or Guardian	4.9	*	5.3	4.8	5.5	3.6
Another Family Member Aged 21 or Older	5.2	*	5.4	5.1	6.3	3.8
Someone Not Related Aged 21 or Older	6.1	4.4	6.3	6.1	7.0	4.8
Someone under Age 21	6.1	*	5.7	6.5	6.7	4.6
UNDERAGE DRINKER DID NOT PAY	3.9	2.7	3.7	4.2	4.4	3.4
Got It from Parent or Guardian	2.5	1.7	2.1	3.2	2.8	2.2
Got It from Another Family Member Aged 21 or Older	3.8	2.4	3.6	4.3	4.2	3.3
Got It from Someone Not Related Aged 21 or Older	4.1	3.5	4.1	4.2	4.9	3.6
Got It from Someone under Age 21	4.2	3.1	3.9	4.7	4.7	3.8
Took It from Own Home	2.9	2.5	3.5	2.6	3.3	2.5
Took It from Someone Else's Home	3.8	2.2	4.0	4.3	3.7	4.0
Got It Some Other Way	4.4	3.4	4.3	4.7	4.9	3.9
From Friend or Acquaintance, Unspecified Age and Method	3.9	3.6	4.1	3.7	4.2	3.7

*Low precision; no estimate reported. NOTE: Respondents with unknown responses to number of drinks consumed on last occasion of alcohol use were excluded.

[1] Respondents with unknown responses to the questions on source of last alcohol use were excluded.

Source: SAMHSA, Office of Applied Studies, National Survey on Drug Use and Health, 2006.

Table 4.5A. Illicit Drug Use in the Past Month and Illicit Drugs Used in the Past Month with Alcohol or within 2 Hours of Alcohol Use on Last Occasion of Alcohol Use among Past Month Alcohol Users Aged 12 to 20, by Age Group and Gender: Numbers in Thousands, 2006

Drug	TOTAL	AGE GROUP			GENDER	
		12-14	15-17	18-20	Male	Female
		Used Specified Drug Anytime in the Past Month				
ILLICIT DRUGS[1]	3,871	205	1,261	2,404	2,145	1,726
Marijuana or Hashish	3,244	126	1,056	2,062	1,823	1,421
Cocaine (Including Crack)	416	14	77	325	236	181
Heroin	37	5	7	25	24	12
Hallucinogens	423	22	105	295	224	198
Inhalants	234	46	118	70	121	113
Pain Relievers[2]	957	68	280	609	522	435
Tranquilizers[2]	329	9	84	237	160	169
Stimulants[2]	264	15	69	181	123	141
Methamphetamine[3]	101	1	23	77	45	56
Sedatives[2]	39	4	13	23	16	23
ILLICIT DRUGS OTHER THAN MARIJUANA[1]	1,812	124	521	1,167	964	849
Drug[4]		Used Specified Drug with Alcohol or within 2 Hours of Alcohol Use on Last Occasion of Alcohol Use in the Past Month				
ILLICIT DRUGS[1]	1,701	42	523	1,135	1,035	666
Marijuana or Hashish	1,594	37	500	1,058	967	627
Cocaine (Including Crack)	70	2	16	52	42	28
Heroin	2	*	1	1	2	0
Hallucinogens	21	*	10	11	13	8
Inhalants	13	2	10	1	6	7
Pain Relievers[2]	128	4	28	95	70	58
Tranquilizers[2]	26	*	7	20	17	9
Stimulants[2]	15	*	4	11	8	7
Methamphetamine[3]	22	*	4	18	14	8
Sedatives[2]	1	*	1	*	*	1
ILLICIT DRUGS OTHER THAN MARIJUANA[1]	267	9	67	191	157	109

*Low precision; no estimate reported. [1] Illicit Drugs include marijuana/hashish, cocaine (including crack), heroin, hallucinogens, inhalants, or prescription-type psychotherapeutics used nonmedically. Illicit Drugs Other Than Marijuana include cocaine (including crack), heroin, hallucinogens, inhalants, or prescription-type psychotherapeutics used nonmedically. [2] Refers to nonmedical use; does not include over-the-counter drugs. [3] Estimate includes responses to the core Stimulants module with imputations for unknown responses, as well as additional questions in the noncore Special Drugs module for respondents who initially did not report methamphetamine use in the core module because they did not consider methamphetamine to be a prescription drug. [4] Respondents could indicate multiple other drugs used with alcohol; thus, these response categories are not mutually exclusive. Respondents with unknown responses to questions about other drugs used with alcohol were excluded. [5] Estimate is based responses to the core Stimulants module *without* imputations for unknown responses, as well as additional questions in the noncore Special Drugs module for respondents who initially did not report methamphetamine use in the core module, as described in footnote 3. *Source:* SAMHSA, Office of Applied Studies, National Survey on Drug Use and Health, 2006.

Table 4.5B. Illicit Drug Use in the Past Month and Illicit Drugs Used in the Past Month with Alcohol or within 2 Hours of Alcohol Use on Last Occasion of Alcohol Use among Past Month Alcohol Users Aged 12 to 20, by Age Group and Gender: Percentages, 2006

Drug	TOTAL	AGE GROUP			GENDER	
		12-14	15-17	18-20	Male	Female
Used Specified Drug Anytime in the Past Month						
ILLICIT DRUGS[1]	35.8	25.2	37.0	36.4	37.3	34.0
Marijuana or Hashish	30.0	15.5	31.0	31.2	31.7	28.0
Cocaine (Including Crack)	3.8	1.7	2.3	4.9	4.1	3.6
Heroin	0.3	0.6	0.2	0.4	0.4	0.2
Hallucinogens	3.9	2.7	3.1	4.5	3.9	3.9
Inhalants	2.2	5.7	3.5	1.1	2.1	2.2
Pain Relievers[2]	8.8	8.4	8.2	9.2	9.1	8.6
Tranquilizers[2]	3.0	1.1	2.5	3.6	2.8	3.3
Stimulants[2]	2.4	1.8	2.0	2.7	2.1	2.8
Methamphetamine[3]	0.9	0.1	0.7	1.2	0.8	1.1
Sedatives[2]	0.4	0.5	0.4	0.3	0.3	0.5
ILLICIT DRUGS OTHER THAN MARIJUANA[1]	16.74	15.2	15.3	17.7	16.8	16.7
Used Specified Drug with Alcohol or within 2 Hours of Alcohol Use on Last Occasion of Alcohol Use in the Past Month						
Drug[4]						
ILLICIT DRUGS[1]	16.0	5.4	15.7	17.4	18.3	13.4
Marijuana or Hashish	15.0	4.6	15.1	16.3	17.2	12.6
Cocaine (Including Crack)	0.7	0.3	0.5	0.8	0.7	0.6
Heroin	0.0	*	0.0	0.0	0.0	0.0
Hallucinogens	0.2	*	0.3	0.2	0.2	0.2
Inhalants	0.1	0.2	0.3	0.0	0.1	0.1
Pain Relievers[2]	1.2	0.6	0.8	1.5	1.2	1.2
Tranquilizers[2]	0.2	*	0.2	0.3	0.3	0.2
Stimulants[2]	0.1	*	0.1	0.2	0.1	0.1
Methamphetamine[5]	0.2	*	0.1	0.3	0.2	0.2
Sedatives[2]	0.0	*	0.0	*	*	0.0
ILLICIT DRUGS OTHER THAN MARIJUANA[1]	2.5	1.1	2.0	2.9	2.8	2.2

*Low precision; no estimate reported. [1] Illicit Drugs include marijuana/hashish, cocaine (including crack), heroin, hallucinogens, inhalants, or prescription-type psychotherapeutics used nonmedically. Illicit Drugs Other Than Marijuana include cocaine (including crack), heroin, hallucinogens, inhalants, or prescription-type psychotherapeutics used nonmedically. [2] Refers to nonmedical use; does not include over-the-counter drugs. [3] Estimate includes responses to the core Stimulants module with imputations for unknown responses, as well as additional questions in the noncore Special Drugs module for respondents who initially did not report methamphetamine use in the core module because they did not consider methamphetamine to be a prescription drug. [4] Respondents could indicate multiple other drugs used with alcohol; thus, these response categories are not mutually exclusive. Respondents with unknown responses to questions about other drugs used with alcohol were excluded. [5] Estimate is based responses to the core Stimulants module *without* imputations for unknown responses, as well as additional questions in the noncore Special Drugs module for respondents who initially did not report methamphetamine use in the core module, as described in footnote 3. *Source:* SAMHSA, Office of Applied Studies, National Survey on Drug Use and Health, 2006.

REFERENCES

American Psychiatric Association. (1994). *Diagnostic and statistical manual of mental disorders* (DSM-IV) (4th ed.). Washington, DC: American Psychiatric Association.

Aquilino, W. S. (1994). Interview mode effects in surveys of drug and alcohol use: A field experiment. *Public Opinion Quarterly*, 58, 2 10-240.

Biglan, M., Gilpin, E. A., Rohrbach, L. A., & Pierce, J. P. (2004). Is there a simple correction factor for comparing adolescent tobacco-use estimates from school- and home-based surveys? *Nicotine & Tobacco Research*, 6, 427-437.

Bradburn, N. M., & Sudman, S. (1983). *Improving interview method and questionnaire design*. Washington, DC: Jossey-Bass.

Butler, M. A., & Beale, C. L. (1994, September). Rural–urban continuum codes for metro and non-metro counties, 1993 (Staff Report No. AGES 9425). Washington, DC: U.S. Department of Agriculture, Economic Research Service. [Current codes available at http://ers.usda.gov/Briefing/Rurality/ruralurbcon]

Chen, P., Dai, L., Gordek, H., Shi, W., Singh, A., & Westlake, M. (2005, January). Person-level sampling weight calibration for the 2003 NSDUH. In 2003 National Survey on Drug Use and Health: Methodological resource book (Section 3, prepared for the Substance Abuse and Mental Health Services Administration, Office of Applied Studies, under Contract No. 283-98-9008, Deliverable No. 28, RTI/07190.574.100). Research Triangle Park, NC: RTI International. [Available as a PDF at http://oas.samhsa.gov/nhsda/methods.cfm]

Deville, J. C., & Särndal, C. E. (1992). Calibration estimators in survey sampling. *Journal of the American Statistical Association,* 87, 376-382.

Fendrich, M., Johnson, T. P., Sudman, S., Wislar, J. S., & Spiehler, V. (1999). Validity of drug use reporting in a high-risk community sample: A comparison of cocaine and heroin survey reports with hair tests. *American Journal of Epidemiology*, 149, 955-962.

Folsom, R. E., & Singh, A. C. (2000). The generalized exponential model for sampling weight calibration for extreme values, nonresponse, and poststratification. In Proceedings of the 2000 Joint Statistical Meetings, American Statistical Association, Survey Research Methods Section, Indianapolis, IN (pp. 598-603). Alexandria, VA: American Statistical Association. [Available as a PDF at http://www.amstat.org/sections/SRMS/proceedings/]

Grant, B. F., & Dawson, D. A. (1997). Age at onset of alcohol use and its association with DSMIV alcohol abuse and dependence: Results from the National Longitudinal Alcohol Epidemiologic Survey. *Journal of Substance Abuse*, 9, 103-110.

Hingson, R., & Kenkel, D. (2004). Social, health, and economic consequences of underage drinking. In R. J. Bonnie & M. E. O'Connell (Eds.), *Reducing underage drinking: A collective responsibility* (pp. 351-382). Washington, DC: National Academies Press. [Available at http://www.nap.edu/books/0309089352/html]

Hser, Y. I., & Anglin, M. D. (Eds.). (1993). Prevalence estimation techniques for drug-using populations [Special issue]. *Journal of Drug Issues*, 23(2), 163-360.

Johnston, L. D., O'Malley, P. M., Bachman, J. G. , & Schulenberg, J. E. (2007a). Monitoring the Future national survey results on drug use, 1975-2006: Secondary school students (NIH Publication No. 07-6205, Vol. I). Bethesda, MD: National Institute on Drug Abuse. [Available as a PDF at http://monitoringthefuture.org/pubs.html#monographs]

Johnston, L. D., O'Malley, P. M., Bachman, J. G. , & Schulenberg, J. E. (2007b). Monitoring the Future national survey results on drug use, 1975-2006: College students and adults ages 19-45 (NIH Publication No. 07-6206, Vol. II). Bethesda, MD: National Institute on Drug Abuse. [Available as a PDF at http://monitoringthefuture.org/pubs.html# monographs]

Manly, B. F. J. (1986). *Multivariate statistical methods*: A primer. London, England: Chapman and Hall.

Morton, K. B., Chromy, J. R., Hunter, S. R., & Martin, P. C. (2007, January; revised February 2008). Sample design report [2006]. In 2006 National Survey on Drug Use and Health: Methodological resource book (Section 2, prepared for the Substance Abuse and Mental Health Services Administration, Office of Applied Studies, under Contract No. 283-2004-00022, Phase II, Deliverable No. 8, RTI/0209009.230.004). Research Triangle Park, NC: RTI International. [Available as a PDF at http://oas.samhsa.gov/ nsduh/methods.cfm]

National Highway Traffic Safety Administration. (2002). Youth fatal crash and alcohol facts 2000 (DOT HS 809 406). Washington, DC: Author.

National Institute on Alcohol Abuse and Alcoholism. (2004, Winter). NIAAA council approves definition of binge drinking. NIAAA Newsletter, 3, 3. [Available as NIH Publication No. 04-5346 at http://pubs.niaaa.nih.gov/publications/Newsletter/winter2004/ Newsletter_Number3.pdf]

National Institute on Alcohol Abuse and Alcoholism. (2006, January). Alcohol Alert No. 67: Underage drinking: Why do adolescents drink, what are the risks, and how can underage drinking be prevented? Retrieved January 28, 2008, from http://pubs.niaaa.nih.gov/ publications/AA67/AA67.htm

Office of Applied Studies. (2007a). Results from the 2006 National Survey on Drug Use and Health: National findings (DHHS Publication No. SMA 07-4293, NSDUH Series H-32). Rockville, MD: Substance Abuse and Mental Health Services Administration. [Available at http://oas.samhsa.gov/p0000016.htm]

Office of Applied Studies. (2007b). Table 7.36A. Alcohol dependence or abuse in the past year among persons aged 21 or older, by age first used alcohol and age group: Numbers in thousands, 2005 and 2006. In *Results from the 2006 National Survey on Drug Use and Health: Detailed tables.* Rockville, MD: Substance Abuse and Mental Health Services Administration. [Available at http://oas.samhsa.gov/WebOnly.htm#NHSDAtabs]

Office of Management and Budget. (2003, June 6). OMB Bulletin No. 03-04: Revised definitions of metropolitan statistical areas, new definitions of micropolitan statistical areas and combined statistical areas, and guidance on uses of the statistical definitions of these areas. Retrieved March 21, 2008, from http://www.whitehouse.gov/omb/ bulletins/b03-04.html

Office of Management and Budget. (1997). Revisions to the standards for the classification of federal data on race and ethnicity. Federal Register, 62(210), 58781-58790. [Available at http://www.whitehouse.gov/omb/fedreg/1997standards.html].

RTI International. (2004). *SUDAAN® language manual*, Release 9.0. Research Triangle Park, NC: Author.

RTI International. (2008). 2006 National Survey on Drug Use and Health: Methodological resource book (RTI 0209009, prepared for the Substance Abuse and Mental Health Services Administration, Office of Applied Studies, under Contract No. 283-2004-00022,

Deliverable No. 39). Research Triangle Park, NC: Author. [Available as PDFs at http://oas.samhsa.gov/nsduh/methods.cfm]

Rubin, D. B. (1986). Statistical matching using file concatenation with adjusted weights and multiple imputations. *Journal of Business and Economic Statistics*, 4(1), 87-94.

Singh, A., Grau, E., & Folsom, R., Jr. (2001). Predictive mean neighborhood imputation with application to the person-pair data of the National Household Survey on Drug Abuse. In Proceedings of the 2001 Joint Statistical Meetings, American Statistical Association, Survey Research Methods Section, Atlanta, GA [CD-ROM] . Alexandria, VA: American Statistical Association. [Available as a PDF at http://www.amstat.org/sections/ SRMS/proceedings/]

Singh, A., Grau, E., & Folsom, R., Jr. (2002). Predictive mean neighborhood imputation for NHSDA substance use data. In J. Gfroerer, J. Eyerman, & J. Chromy (Eds.), Redesigning an ongoing national household survey: Methodological issues (DHHS Publication No. SMA 03- 3768, pp. 111-133). Rockville, MD: Substance Abuse and Mental Health Services Administration, Office of Applied Studies. [Available as a PDF at http://oas.samhsa.gov/nhsda/methods.cfm]

SRNT Subcommittee on Biochemical Verification. (2002). Biochemical verification of tobacco use and cessation. *Nicotine & Tobacco Research*, 4(2), 149-159.

Stueve, A., & O'Donnell, L. N. (2005). Early alcohol initiation and subsequent sexual and alcohol risk behaviors among urban youths. *American Journal of Public Health*, 95, 887-893.

Substance Abuse and Mental Health Data Archive. (2008). Online analysis of data from the 2006 Treatment Episode Data Set. Retrieved on April 1, 2008, from http://www. icpsr.umich.edu/SAMHDA/

Swahn, M. H., Bossarte, R. M., & Sullivent, E. E. 3rd. (2008). Age of alcohol use initiation, suicidal behavior, and peer and dating violence victimization and perpetration among high-risk, seventh-grade adolescents. *Pediatrics,* 121, 297-305.

Turner, C. F., Lessler, J. T., & Gfroerer, J. C. (Eds.). (1992). Survey measurement of drug use: Methodological studies (DHHS Publication No. ADM 92-1929). Rockville, MD: National Institute on Drug Abuse.

U.S. Department of Health and Human Services. (2006, January). A comprehensive plan for preventing and reducing underage drinking (DHHS Publication No. SMA 01-35 17). Rockville, MD: U.S. Department of Health and Human Services, Substance Abuse and Mental Health Services Administration. [Available as a PDF at http://www. stopalcoholabuse.gov/more.aspx]

U.S. Department of Health and Human Services. (2007). The Surgeon General's call to action to prevent and reduce underage drinking. Rockville, MD: Office of the Surgeon General. [Available at http://www.surgeongeneral.gov/topics/underagedrinking/]

Wright, D., Sathe, N., & Spagnola, K. (2007). State estimates of substance use from the 2004-2005 National Surveys on Drug Use and Health (DHHS Publication No. SMA 07-423 5, NSDUH Series H-31). Rockville, MD: Substance Abuse and Mental Health Services Administration, Office of Applied Studies. [Available at http://oas.samhsa.gov/ states.htm]

Appendix A

[1] Prior to 2002, the survey was known as the National Household Survey on Drug Abuse (NHSDA).

[2] SAE is a hierarchical Bayes modeling technique used to make State-level estimates for approximately 20 substance-use-related measures. For more details, see the *State Estimates of Substance Use from the 2004- 2005 National Surveys on Drug Use and Health* (Wright, Sathe, & Spagnola, 2007).

[3] Areas were defined using 2000 census geography. Dwelling units (DUs) and population counts were obtained from the 2000 census data supplemented with revised population counts from Claritas (http://cluster1 .claritas.com/claritas/Default.jsp).

[4] Census tracts are relatively permanent statistical subdivisions of counties and provide a stable set of geographic units across decennial census periods.

[5] Some census tracts had to be aggregated in order to meet the minimum DU requirement of 150 DUs in urban areas and 100 DUs in rural areas.

[6] For more details on the 5-year sample, see the 2006 sample design report in the *2006 NSDUH Methodological Resource Book* (Morton, Chromy, Hunter, & Martin, 2007).

In: Alcohol and Drug Use among Youth
Editor: Agatha M. Pichler

ISSN: 978-1-61209-084-9
© 2012 Nova Science Publishers, Inc.

Chapter 4

UNDERAGE ALCOHOL USE: WHERE DO YOUNG PEOPLE DRINK?*

National Survey on Drug Use and Health

IN BRIEF

- A majority (53.4 percent) of current alcohol users aged 12 to 20 drank at someone else's home the last time they used alcohol, and another 30.3 percent drank in their own home
- The percentage of underage alcohol users who had their most recent drink in a car or other vehicle peaked at 10.1 percent at age 16 (12.8 percent of females and 7.3 percent of males)
- Among 20-year-old current drinkers, 20.0 percent of females drank in a restaurant, bar, or club the last time they used alcohol compared with 10.2 percent of males

In 2006, more than one in four persons aged 12 to 20 in the United States, or about 10.8 million persons, drank alcohol in the past month (i.e., were current drinkers) [1]. Nearly one in five persons aged 18 to 20 drove under the influence of alcohol in the past 12 months in 2006,1 and each year approximately 1,900 people under the age of 21 die as a result of alcohol-involved motor vehicle crashes [2]. In addition, early initiation of alcohol use is associated with increased likelihood of unprotected sexual intercourse and multiple sex partners [3,4]. The 2006 National Survey on Drug Use and Health (NSDUH) asked past month alcohol users aged 12 to 20 how they obtained the last alcohol they drank and where they were when they consumed it. This issue of The NSDUH Report examines age-related changes in the locations where male and female underage drinkers use alcohol. It also examines differences by college enrollment and living situation for those aged 18 to 20. Findings presented in this report are based on 2006 NSDUH data.

---

* This is an edited, reformatted and augmented version of a National Survey on Drug Use and Health Report, dated August 28, 2008.

How Do Drinking Locations Change with Age?

In 2006, a majority (53.4 percent) of current alcohol users aged 12 to 20 drank at someone else's home the last time they used alcohol, and another 30.3 percent drank in their own home. This overall pattern of last using alcohol in their own home or at someone else's home held for drinkers at each age from 13 to 20 (Figure 1) [5].

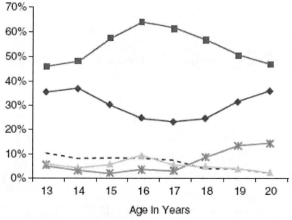

Source: SAMHSA, 2006 NSDUH.

• Respondents could indicate multiple locations for the most recent time they used alcohol; thus, these response categories are not mutually exclusive.

•• Respondents with unknown responses were excluded.

Figure 1. Location of the Most Recent Alcohol Use in the Past Month* among Past Month Alcohol Users Aged 13 to 20, by Individual Years of Age: 2006**.

More than 60 percent of drinkers aged 16 or 17 used alcohol in someone else's home the last time they drank. About 36 percent or more of drinkers aged 13, 14, and 20 last used alcohol in their own homes. In addition, 10.0 percent of 13-year-old drinkers last consumed alcohol in public places (such as a park, a beach, or a parking lot). The percentage of underage alcohol users who had their most recent drink in a car or other vehicle peaked at 10.1 percent at age 16. An estimated 15.0 percent of those aged 20 last drank in a restaurant, bar, or club. Approximately 7 to 10 percent of alcohol users aged 13 to 17 last drank in public places, with the percentages decreasing to fewer than 4 percent of drinkers aged 18 to older. In contrast, most recent use of alcohol in a restaurant, bar, or club started to increase at age 18 and was at its highest point at age 20.

DO AGE-RELATED CHANGES IN DRINKING LOCATIONS DIFFER FOR MALES AND FEMALES?

Among male alcohol users, the percentage reporting that they drank most recently in a car or other vehicle did not differ significantly by age between ages 15 and 20,6 but it did differ for females (Figure 2). An estimated 12.8 percent of female alcohol users who were aged 16 last drank alcohol in a car or other motor vehicle, a rate that was 8 times greater than the rate for female drinkers who were aged 20 (1.6 percent). At age 16, 7.3 percent of male current drinkers had their last drink in a car or other vehicle.

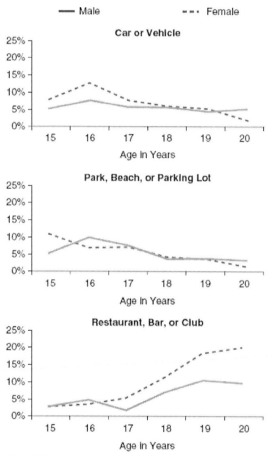

Source: SAMHSA, 2006 NSDUH.
· Respondents could indicate multiple locations for the most recent time they used alcohol; thus, these response categories are not mutually exclusive.
·· Respondents with unknown responses were excluded.

Figure 2. Location of the Most Recent Alcohol Use in the Past Month* among Past Month Alcohol Users Aged 15 to 20, by gender within Individual Years of Age: 2006**.

Among 15-year-old drinkers, females were twice as likely as males to have last used alcohol in a public place, such as a park, beach, or parking lot (10.6 vs. 5.0 percent). Among males, alcohol consumption in public places peaked at age 16 and then declined. Among females, alcohol consumption in public places declined after age 15. The proportion of underage current drinkers who consumed their last alcohol in a restaurant, bar, or club generally increased with age. Starting at age 17, female drinkers were more likely than their male counterparts to have consumed alcohol in one of these locations. Among 20-year-old current drinkers, 20.0 percent of females drank in a restaurant, bar, or club the last time they used alcohol compared with 10.2 percent of males.

WHERE DO PERSONS AGED 18 TO 20 DRINK?

Among drinkers aged 18 to 20, those who were living with a parent or similar relative were more likely than those who were not living with a parental relative to have most recently used alcohol in someone else's home (55.4 and 43.1 percent, respectively) (Table 1).

Table 1. Most Recent Alcohol Use in the Past Month at Home or at Someone Else's Home* among Past Month Alcohol Users Aged 18 to 20, by College Enrollment Status and Parental Living Situation***: 2006**

| College Enrollment Status/Parental Living Situation | Location of Most Recent Alcohol Use | | | |
| | Home | | Someone Else's Home | |
	%	SE[+]	%	SE[+]
Total Aged 18 to 20[++]				
Living with a Parental Relative	24.3	1.07	55.4	1.29
Not Living with a Parental Relative	42.9	1.90	43.1	1.92
Full-Time College Student				
Living with a Parental Relative	21.2	1.49	56.8	2.03
Not Living with a Parental Relative	33.5	2.28	50.7	2.33
Other[++]				
Living with a Parental Relative	26.6	1.54	54.4	1.72
Not Living with a Parental Relative	56.9	2.55	31.7	2.47

Source: SAMHSA, 2006 NSDUH.

*** Persons with unknown parental living situations were excluded. Parental relatives include a parent, grandparent, or parent-in-law.

+ Standard error (SE) is a measure of the sampling variability or precision of an estimate, where smaller values represent greater precision and larger values represent less precision.

++ Estimates for persons aged 18 to 20 include those with unknown enrollment status. Other persons include those aged 18 to 20 not enrolled in college, enrolled in college part time, enrolled in other grades either full or part time, or enrolled with no other information available.

This pattern was more pronounced for drinkers in this age group who were not full-time college students (54.4 percent of those living with a parental relative vs. 31.7 percent of those who were not). However, more than half of underage drinkers who were full-time college students last drank alcohol in someone else's home regardless of whether they were living with a parental relative.

DISCUSSION

Underage alcohol use poses important public health and public safety risks. Knowing the locations where this behavior is most likely to occur can help parents talk with their teenagers more effectively about the dangers of alcohol use and alert parents to times when they need to exercise greater monitoring and supervision. These data also provide prevention specialists with new information to help guide program development or modify existing prevention activities in their communities.

SUGGESTED CITATION

Substance Abuse and Mental Health Services Administration, Office of Applied Studies. (August 28, 2008). The NSDUH Report: Underage Alcohol Use: Where Do Young People Drink? Rockville, MD.

The National Survey on Drug Use and Health (NSDUH) is an annual survey sponsored by the Substance Abuse and Mental Health Services Administration (SAMHSA). The 2006 data used in this report are based on information obtained from 31,320 persons aged 12 to 20. The survey collects data by administering questionnaires to a representative sample of the population through face-to-face interviews at their place of residence.

The NSDUH Report is prepared by the Office of Applied Studies (OAS), SAMHSA, and by RTI International in Research Triangle Park, North Carolina. (RTI International is a trade name of Research Triangle Institute.)

Information on the most recent NSDUH is available in the following publication:

Office of Applied Studies. (2007). Results from the 2006 National Survey on Drug Use and Health: National findings (DHHS Publication No. SMA 07-4293, NSDUH Series H-32). Rockville, MD: Substance Abuse and Mental Health Services Administration.

Also available online: http://oas.samhsa.gov.

Because of improvements and modifications to the 2002 NSDUH, estimates from the 2002 through 2006 surveys should not be compared with estimates from the 2001 or earlier versions of the survey to examine changes over time.

RESEARCH FINDINGS FROM THE SAMHSA 2006 NATIONAL SURVEY ON DRUG USE AND HEALTH (NSDUH)

- A majority (53.4 percent) of current alcohol users aged 12 to 20 drank at someone else's home the last time they used alcohol, and another 30.3 percent drank in their own home.
- The percentage of underage alcohol users who had their most recent drink in a car or other vehicle peaked at 10.1 percent at age 16 (12.8 percent of females and 7.3 percent of males)
- Among 20-year-old current drinkers, 20.0 percent of females drank in a restaurant, bar, or club the last time they used alcohol compared with 10.2 percent of males

END NOTES

[1]   Office of Applied Studies. (2007). *Results from the 2006 National Survey on Drug Use and Health: National findings* (DHHS Publication No. SMA 07-4293, NSDUH Series H-32). Rockville, MD: Substance Abuse and Mental Health Services Administration. [Available at http://oas.samhsa.gov/p0000016.htm]

[2]   Hingson, R., & Kenkel, D. (2004). Social, health, and economic consequences of underage drinking. In R. J. Bonnie & M. E. O'Connell (Eds.), Reducing underage drinking: A collective responsibility (pp. 351-382). Washington, DC: National Academies Press. [Available at http://www.nap.edu/books/0309089352/html]

[3]   Stueve, A., & O'Donnell, L. N. (2005). Early alcohol initiation and subsequent sexual and alcohol risk behaviors among urban youths. *American Journal of Public Health*, 95, 887-893.

[4]   Swahn, M. H., Bossarte, R. M., & Sullivent, E. E. 3rd. (2008). Age of alcohol use initiation, suicidal behavior, and peer and dating violence victimization and perpetration among high-risk, seventh-grade adolescents. *Pediatrics,* 121, 297-305.

[5]   Estimates were unreliable for 12-year-old drinkers and were therefore not used.

[6]   A lower age limit of 15 years was set for estimates regarding locations of the most recent alcohol use among male and female underage drinkers by single years of age because of the larger sample sizes of male and female drinkers aged 15 to 20.

In: Alcohol and Drug Use among Youth
Editor: Agatha M. Pichler

ISSN: 978-1-61209-084-9
© 2012 Nova Science Publishers, Inc.

Chapter 5

UNDERAGE ALCOHOL USE: WHERE DO YOUNG PEOPLE GET ALCOHOL?*

National Survey on Drug Use and Health

IN BRIEF

- More than one quarter (28.1 percent) of persons aged 12 to 20 used alcohol in the past month, including more than half (51.1 percent) of those aged 18 to 20, 25.9 percent of those aged 15 to 17, and 6.1 percent of those aged 12 to 14
- Nearly one third of current alcohol users aged 12 to 20 (30.6 percent) paid for the last alcohol they used, more than one in four (26.4 percent) got it for free from a nonrelative aged 21 or older, 14.6 percent got it for free from another underage person, 5.9 percent got it from a parent or guardian, and 8.5 percent got it from another relative aged 21 or older
- Current alcohol users aged 12 to 20 consumed more drinks on average the last time if they paid for the last alcohol they used (6.0 drinks) compared with those who did not pay for their last alcohol (3.9 drinks)

A lthough the use of alcohol is illegal for persons under the age of 21, its use constitutes one of the principal public health issues for this age group, [1] and reduction of underage alcohol use is a top public health priority of the Federal Government [2]. Many of the efforts to prevent or reduce underage alcohol use attempt to reduce the availability of alcohol to underage drinkers. Data from the 2006 and 2007 National Surveys on Drug Use and Health (NSDUHs) indicate that even with efforts to reduce availability, underage drinkers are still able to obtain alcohol. This issue of The NSDUH Report examines how current (i.e., "past month") drinkers aged 12 to 20 obtain alcohol, by age group and gender. The 2006 and 2007 NSDUHs included items that asked past month alcohol users aged 12 to 20 how they obtained the last alcohol they drank.

---

* This is an edited, reformatted and augmented version of a National Survey on Drug Use and Health Report, dated November 20, 2008.

This report also presents data on the prevalence of current underage alcohol use and findings on the average number of drinks that underage drinkers had on their last occasion of alcohol use, depending on where they obtained alcohol. All findings presented are annual averages based on combined 2006 and 2007 NSDUH data.

WHAT PERCENTAGE OF YOUNG PEOPLE ARE UNDERAGE DRINKERS?

More than one quarter (28.1 percent) of persons aged 12 to 20 (an estimated 10.8 million persons) used alcohol in the past month. More than half (51.1 percent) of those aged 18 to 20 were current alcohol users compared with 25.9 percent of those aged 15 to 17 and 6.1 percent of those aged 12 to 14. Underage males were more likely than their female counterparts to be current alcohol users (28.8 vs. 27.4 percent).

HOW DO CURRENT ALCOHOL USERS AGED 12 TO 20 OBTAIN ALCOHOL?

Nearly one third (30.6 percent) of current alcohol users aged 12 to 20 in 2006 and 2007 (an estimated 3.2 million persons) paid for the last alcohol they used, and 69.4 percent (an estimated 7.3 million persons) got the last alcohol they used for free. More than one in four (26.4 percent) got the last alcohol they used for free from a nonrelative aged 21 or older, 14.6 percent got it for free from another underage person, 5.9 percent got it from a parent or guardian, 8.5 percent got it from another relative aged 21 or older, and 3.9 percent took it from their own home without asking [3]

HOW DO UNDERAGE DRINKERS IN DIFFERENT AGE GROUPS OBTAIN ALCOHOL?

Among underage current alcohol users, over one third (36.5 percent) of persons aged 18 to 20 paid for the last alcohol they drank compared with 23.5 percent of those aged 15 to 17 and 7.5 percent of those aged 12 to 14 (Figure 1).

Current alcohol users aged 18 to 20 also were more likely than their younger counterparts to have gotten alcohol for free from a nonrelative of legal drinking age (30.5 percent compared with 20.3 percent of those aged 15 to 17 and 13.4 percent of those aged 12 to 14) (Figure 2). However, alcohol users aged 18 to 20 were less likely than those aged 12 to 14 to have gotten the last alcohol they used from a parent or guardian (4.2 vs. 16.6 percent), to have taken it from their own home without asking (2.2 vs. 14.0 percent), or to have gotten it from another underage person (11.1 vs. 18.6 percent).

HOW DO UNDERAGE MALES AND FEMALES OBTAIN ALCOHOL?

Underage male alcohol users were more likely than their female counterparts to have paid for the last alcohol they used (36.8 vs. 23.6 percent) (Figure 1). Conversely, more than three fourths of female underage drinkers (76.4 percent) obtained their last alcohol for free compared with 63.2 percent of males. Female underage drinkers were more likely than their male counterparts to have gotten the last alcohol they used for free from a nonrelative of legal drinking age (31.0 vs. 22.1 percent) (Figure 3).

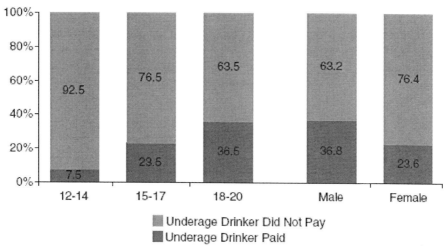

Source: SAMHSA, 2006 and 2007 NSDUHs.
* Respondents with unknown responses were excluded.

Figure 1. Payment or Receipt of Alcohol for Free for the last Use in the Past Month among Alcohol Users Aged 12 to 20, by Age Group and Gender: Annual Averages, 2006 and 2007*.

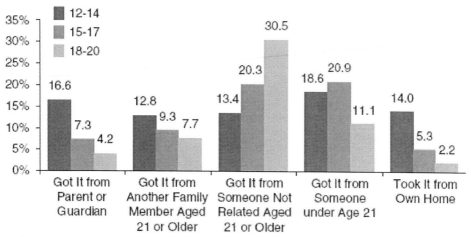

Source: SAMHSA, 2006 and 2007 NSDUHs.
* Respondents with unknown responses were excluded.

Figure 2. Source of Alcohol Obtained for Free for the last Use in the Past Month among Alcohol Users Aged 12 to 20, by Age Group: Annual Averages, 2006 and 2007*.

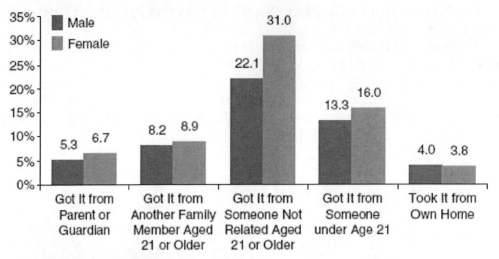

Source: SAMHSA, 2006 and 2007 NSDUHs.
* Respondents with unknown responses were excluded.

Figure 3. Source of Alcohol Obtained for Free for the last Use in the Past Month among Alcohol Users Aged 12 to 20, by Gender: Annual Averages, 2006 and 2007*.

How Many Drinks Do Underage Drinkers Have, Depending on How They Obtain Alcohol?

Current alcohol users aged 12 to 20 consumed more drinks on average the last time if they paid for the last alcohol they used (6.0 drinks) compared with those who did not pay for their last alcohol (3.9 drinks) (Table 1). Underage current drinkers who got alcohol for free from a nonrelative of legal drinking age consumed more drinks on average (4.3 drinks) than those who got the last alcohol they used from a parent or guardian (2.5 drinks).

These patterns also held within individual age groups of underage alcohol users. For example, current alcohol users aged 12 to 14 who paid for the alcohol themselves consumed an average of 4.8 drinks the last time they drank compared with an average of 2.7 drinks if they did not pay for it. These 12 to 14 year olds consumed an average of 3.4 drinks if they got their alcohol from a nonrelative aged 21 or older and 1.7 drinks if they got it from a parent or guardian. Among current alcohol users aged 18 to 20, those who paid for the last alcohol they used averaged 6.0 drinks compared with 4.2 drinks among those who got it for free.

Discussion

Even with increased efforts to reduce the availability of alcohol to young people, data from NSDUH indicate that underage drinkers are able to purchase or obtain alcohol from relatives and friends at an unacceptably high rate. This should be of concern to professionals, policymakers, parents, and others who are attempting to reduce the negative consequences of underage alcohol use.

Table 1. Mean Number of Drinks consumed on last Occasion of Alcohol Use in the Past Month among Past Month Alcohol Users Aged 12 to 20, by Age Group and Source of Alcohol Used: Annual Averages, 2006 and 2007

Source of Last Alcohol Used In the Past Month*	Total		Age Group					
			12-14		15-17		18-20	
	Mean	SE	Mean	SE	Mean	SE	Mean	SE
Total	4.6	0.05	2.8	0.11	4.4	0.07	4.8	0.07
Underage Drinker Paid	6.0	0.11	4.8	0.50	6.3	0.18	6.0	0.13
Underage Drinker Did Not Pay**	3.9	0.04	2.7	0.10	3.8	0.07	4.2	0.06
Got It from Parent or Guardian	2.5	0.10	1.7	0.11	2.1	0.11	3.1	0.19
Got It from Another Family Member Aged 21 or Older	3.6	0.16	2.3	0.18	3.5	0.25	3.9	0.23
Got It from Someone Not Related Aged 21 or Older	4.3	0.07	3.4	0.38	4.3	0.14	4.3	0.09
Got It from Someone under Age 21	4.2	0.09	3.2	0.25	4.0	0.12	4.5	0.13
Took It from Own Home	3.0	0.18	2.3	0.25	3.6	0.32	2.9	0.28

Source: SAMHSA, 2006 and 2007 NSDUHs.

· Respondents with unknown responses were excluded.

·· Underage drinkers who did not pay for the last alcohol they used include those who got alcohol from someone else's house, those who got it some other way, and those whose source was missing, as well as the respondents who reported getting alcohol without paying for it from the other sources shown in the report.

SUGGESTED CITATION

Substance Abuse and Mental Health Services Administration, Office of Applied Studies. (November 20, 2008). The NSDUH Report: Underage Alcohol Use: Where Do Young People Get Alcohol? Rockville, MD.

The National Survey on Drug Use and Health (NSDUH) is an annual survey sponsored by the Substance Abuse and Mental Health Services Administration (SAMHSA). The 2006 and 2007 data used in this report are based on information obtained from 62,495 persons aged 12 to 20. The survey collects data by administering questionnaires to a representative sample of the population through face-to-face interviews at their place of residence.

The NSDUH Report is prepared by the Office of Applied Studies (OAS), SAMHSA, and by RTI International in Research Triangle Park, North Carolina. (RTI International is a trade name of Research Triangle Institute.)

Information on the most recent NSDUH is available in the following publication:

Office of Applied Studies. (2008). Results from the 2007 National Survey on Drug Use and Health: National findings (DHHS Publication No. SMA 08-4343, NSDUH Series H-34). Rockville, MD: Substance Abuse and Mental Health Services Administration.

Information for earlier NSDUHs is available in the following publication:

2006 NSDUH (DHHS Publication No. SMA 07-4293, NSDUH Series H-32)

Also available online: http://oas.samhsa.gov.

Because of improvements and modifications to the 2002 NSDUH, estimates from the 2002 through 2007 surveys should not be compared with estimates from the 2001 or earlier versions of the survey to examine changes over time.

RESEARCH FINDINGS FROM THE SAMHSA 2006 AND 2007 NATIONAL SURVEYS ON DRUG USE AND HEALTH (NSDUHs)

- More than one quarter (28.1 percent) of persons aged 12 to 20 used alcohol in the past month, including more than half (51.1 percent) of those aged 18 to 20, 25.9 percent of those aged 15 to 17, and 6.1 percent of those aged 12 to 14
- Nearly one third of current alcohol users aged 12 to 20 (30.6 percent) paid for the last alcohol they used, more than one in four (26.4 percent) got it for free from a nonrelative aged 21 or older, 14.6 percent got it for free from another underage person, 5.9 percent got it from a parent or guardian, and 8.5 percent got it from another relative aged 21 or older
- Current alcohol users aged 12 to 20 consumed more drinks on average the last time if they paid for the last alcohol they used (6.0 drinks) compared with those who did not pay for their last alcohol (3.9 drinks)

END NOTES

[1] National Institute on Alcohol Abuse and Alcoholism. (2006, January). Alcohol Alert No. 67: Underage drinking: Why do adolescents drink, what are the risks, and how can underage drinking be prevented? [Available at http://pubs.niaaa.nih.gov/publications/ AA67/AA67.htm]

[2] U.S. Department of Health and Human Services. (2007). The Surgeon General's call to action to prevent and reduce underage drinking. Rockville, MD: Office of the Surgeon General. [Available at http://www.surgeongeneral.gov/topics/underagedrinking/]

[3] Other sources of alcohol for which underage drinkers did not pay include alcohol from someone else's house, alcohol that was obtained some other way, and situations in which underage persons did not pay for the last alcohol they used but the specific source was unknown.

In: Alcohol and Drug Use among Youth
Editor: Agatha M. Pichler
ISSN: 978-1-61209-084-9
© 2012 Nova Science Publishers, Inc.

Chapter 6

URBAN, SUBURBAN, AND RURAL MIDDLE SCHOOL COUNSELORS' PERCEIVED COMPETENCY FOR ADDRESSING STUDENT SUBSTANCE ABUSE[#]

Jason J. Burrow-Sanchez[*1], *Nicole T. Cruz*[2] *and Megan E. Call*[1]
[1]University of Utah, US
[2]Brandeis University, US

ABSTRACT

Student substance abuse is a serious concern for middle school personnel. Of all school personnel, counselors are the most likely to deliver mental health services to students which includes substance abuse. There is no research available on the perceived competence of urban, suburban, and rural middle school counselors for addressing student substance abuse concerns. The primary goal of this study was to determine how middle school counselors perceive their training in seven competency areas related to student substance abuse based on urbanicity. This study employed secondary data analysis of a national sample of 274 middle school counselors Findings indicated that urban, suburban and rural school counselors were similar in their perceived competence depending on the specific area of student substance abuse and were clearly able to identify the most important areas for future training. The findings from this study indicate that middle school counselors, regardless of urbanicity, require more training in the area of student substance abuse. Implications for in-service and pre-service training are discussed.

Keywords: middle school, school counselor, substance abuse, professional training.

[#] This research was supported by a grant awarded to the first author from the University Research Committee at the University of Utah

[*] Corresponding Author Information: Jason Burrow-Sanchez, PhD. Dept. of Educational Psychology. University of Utah. 1705 Campus Center Dr., Rm. 327. Salt Lake City, UT 84112. Voice: 801-581-6212. Fax: 801-581-5566. E-mail: sanchez_j@ed.utah.edu

It is clear from the data of national studies that a proportion of middle school students report the use of substances (Johnston, O'Malley, Bachman, and Schulenberg, 2006). In general, the three most commonly used drugs by students is alcohol, cigarettes and marijuana. More specifically, almost 20% of 8th grade students report using alcohol in the past 30 days. For drugs, such as marijuana and inhalants, over 10% of 8th grade students report using one of these illicit substances in the past 30 days (Johnston, O'Malley, Bachman, and Schulenberg, 2006). A small, but significant, proportion of students who use drugs will develop more severe substance abuse problems which will negatively affect their lives (Newcomb, 1995; Shelder and Block, 1990). It is estimated that about 10% of youth in the U.S. between the ages of 12-17 are illicit drug users, and 8% of these youth meet the criteria for a substance abuse or dependence disorder (SAMHSA, 2006). Based on these statistics, middle school personnel are likely to come into contact with students who have substance abuse problems.

The results from a national survey conducted by Foster et al., (2003) indicated that school counselors were the most common staff to deliver mental health services to students in school settings. In their study, mental health services were defined broadly and included substance abuse counseling. Seventy-seven percent of school administrators surveyed indicated that a school counselor was the type of staff who provided mental health services followed by nurses (69%), psychologists (68%) and social workers (44%). One recommendation by Foster et al. is that more research is needed to understand what type of specialized training school personnel have, if any, who deliver mental health services in schools. School counselors are in a unique position to provide assistance to students with substance abuse problems because of their continual contact with students, parents, and other school faculty (Lambie and Rokutani, 2002; Watkins, Ellickson, Vaiana, and Hiromoto, 2006). Substance abuse is a problem that many students have initial difficulty discussing with adults; however, students do report that one of the people they would talk to about a substance use problem is their school counselor (Mason, 1997; Palmer and Ringwalt, 1988). In many cases, school counselors may be the first professional contact for a student suffering from a mental health problem such as substance abuse. However, there is limited research on the competence of school counselors for effectively addressing student substance abuse problems.

A review of the literature revealed three prior studies which surveyed school counselors about their perceived competence and practices related to student substance abuse issues. Goldberg and Governali (1995) surveyed a sample of school counselors (N = 54) in central New York across all grade levels (i.e., elementary, middle, and high school) about their comfort level providing substance abuse related services to students. These researchers found that more than half of their sample (59%) felt adequate and comfortable counseling students about alcohol whereas only a few counselors (11%) felt the same regarding steroids. In general, the counselors in this study felt most prepared and comfortable counseling students when the drugs were alcohol, tobacco, and marijuana and least prepared and comfortable counseling students when the drugs were inhalants, stimulants, hallucinogens, and steroids. In another study, Burrow-Sanchez and Lopez (2009) surveyed a national sample of high school counselors (N = 289) about their perceived competence and training needs for working with students who abuse substances. The counselors in this study perceived themselves as being more confident about their consultation skills, such as with teachers and parents, related to student substance abuse concerns rather than working directly with students. In addition, counselors identified the two most needed training areas for student substance abuse as screening/assessment and individual interventions. Burrow-Sanchez, Lopez, and Slagle

(2008) replicated this study with a national sample of middle school counselors (N = 283) and, in general, found similar results.

The results from the studies reviewed above provide a general understanding of the competence and training needs of school counselors for effectively addressing student substance abuse problems. One area that has not been examined is the potential differences among urban, suburban, and rural school counselors in relation to student substance abuse. Researchers argue that urbanicity affects the delivery of school mental health services and potential training needs of school personnel due to differences found among these three settings (Foster et al., 2005; Slade, 2003; Weist et al., 2000). Such differences include school census, caseload size, and student drug use rates. For example, one could assume that counselors in rural schools have little need for substance abuse training due to working in settings with smaller numbers of students compared to suburban schools. Following this logic, schools with fewer students also have a smaller proportion of students who can potentially develop substance abuse problems compared to larger schools. However, these types of assumptions have not been empirically investigated for school counselors in relation to student substance abuse. To address this gap in the literature, the present study was conducted to answer the following exploratory research questions:

1. "What are the perceived competencies for seven areas, related to student substance abuse, for middle school counselors in urban, suburban, and rural settings?"
2. "What is middle school counselors' perceptions of current and past training related to student substance abuse by urbanicity"?
3. "What do urban, suburban and rural middle school counselors perceive as the most needed training areas for addressing student substance abuse in their schools?"

The present study employed secondary analysis of data from a prior study conducted with a national sample of middle school counselors (Burrow-Sanchez, Lopez, and Slagle, 2008).

METHOD

Participants

A national mailing list of 1,082 middle school counselors was obtained from the American School Counselor Association for a prior study on middle school counselors (see Burrow-Sanchez, Lopez, and Slagle, 2008). From this list, a proportional stratified random sample of 500 middle school counselors were selected and sent survey materials. The proportional, stratified random sampling procedure was used to obtain a geographically representative sample of middle school counselors based on the percentage of middle school-aged children living in each of the nine national divisions identified by the 2000 U. S. Census Report. A total of 285 surveys were returned (57.0% return rate) by participants.

Survey

A 38-item survey was used to obtain information about middle school counselors' perceived competence and training needs for working with students with substance abuse problems (a copy of the survey can be obtained from the first author). The survey was originally developed through a validation process for a study of high school counselors (Burrow-Sanchez and Lopez, 2009) and was modified for use with middle school counselors. The modified middle school survey was piloted with a group of graduate students (n = 15) in a school counseling program and was subsequently refined, prior to mailing, based on results of the pilot testing.

Each item on the survey was categorized into one of the following four sections: (a) background information, (b) assessment and referral, (c) types of substances, and (d) substance abuse training areas. The survey employed a variety of question formats, including forced-choice, rank-order, and checklist (Fink and Kosecoff, 1998). The seven items most relevant to the present study asked respondents to indicate if they felt they had the *training necessary* to work with students with substance abuse problems in particular competence areas. These items were rated on a 5-point Likert type scale that included the following choices: *1-Strongly Disagree, 2-Disagree, 3-Neutral, 4-Agree, 5-Strongly Agree.* Reliability analysis indicated that alpha equals .87 for these seven items. In addition, other items asked respondents to rate and subsequently rank-order the substance abuse training areas they felt were *most important* for school counselors. The total time to complete the survey materials was between 10-15 minutes.

Procedure

A survey study design composed of an initial mailing and two follow up mailings in accordance with the Tailored Design Method was used (Dillman, 2000). The first mailing packet was sent to the pre-selected national sample of 500 middle school counselors. More specific details regarding the mailing procedure can be found elsewhere (Burrow-Sanchez and Lopez, 2009). After the initial mailing, a small number of packets (n = 14) had not been completed or had been returned due to either the participants contacting the principal investigator and stating they did not identify as a middle school counselor (e.g., elementary counselor) or the mailing address on the packet not being deliverable by the postal service. After receiving this information, these participants were immediately replaced from the initial mailing sample with other participants from the original mailing list and were randomly selected from within the same geographical regions.

Data Analysis

Prior to analysis, the data were examined for missing and improbable values and any such values were corrected in the database. Two surveys were eliminated due to significant portions of missing data or the respondent not identifying as a middle school counselor. Surveys from counselors in which urbanicity was missing (n = 2) or which did not come from a public school (n = 7) were eliminated from analyses. The final sample for analysis included survey data from 274 participants who indicated they worked in public schools in either an urban, suburban, or rural setting. Statistical analyses included descriptive statistics, correlation, chi-square, ANOVA, and MANOVA.

RESULTS

Participant Demographics

The distribution of percentages for the 500 participants on the initial mailing list by geographical region was: Pacific (16.3%), Mountain (6.8%), West North Central (7.2%), West South Central (12.0%), East North Central (16.3%), East South Central (5.9%), Middle Atlantic (13.4%), South Atlantic (17.4%), and New England (4.7%). Of the 274 participants comprising the final sample for this study, the following percentages reflect the distribution by geographical region: Pacific (16.8%), Mountain (8.4%), West North Central (9.1%), West South Central (10.9%), East North Central (17.5%), East South Central (5.1%), Middle Atlantic (10.6%), South Atlantic (16.8%), and New England (4.7%). The initial and final geographical distributions were not significantly different, $X^2(8) = 4.95$, $p > .05$. Selected demographic variables and descriptive statistics for the sample are presented in Table 1.

Table 1. Selected Demographic Variables and Descriptive Statistics for Middle School Counselors by Urbanicity

Demographics	Percentages		
	Urban (n = 63)	Suburban (n = 131)	Rural (n = 80)
Highest Education			
Bachelors	---	0.76%	---
Masters	93.65%	93.89%	98.75%
Doctorate	6.35%	5.35%	1.25%
Sex			
Female	87.30%	90.08%	85.00%
Male	12.70%	9.92%	15.00%
Race/Ethnicity			
White	82.54%	91.61%	91.25%
Hispanic	4.76%	0.76%	1.53%
Black	6.35%	3.82%	1.25%
Native American	1.59%	---	---
Asian American	---	0.76%	---
Multi-Racial	3.17%	2.29%	5.00%
Other	1.59%	0.76%	---
	Means (standard deviations and n's)		
	Urban	Suburban	Rural
Years experience as school counselor	8.38 (6.38; n = 63)	9.41 (8.37: n = 131)	8.78 (6.33; n = 80)
School student census	913.94 (455.85; n = 62)	905.05 (370.36; n = 129)	534.53 (244.84; n = 79)
Caseload size	418.44 (173.13; n = 61)	421.60 (173.48; n = 130)	356.86 (153.32; n = 78)
Number of typical students seen for which substance abuse is one issue of concern per academic year[a]	32.38 (54.71; n = 61) Mdn = 15	15.54 (15.95; n = 128) Mdn = 10	35.53 (67.37; n = 75) Mdn = 20
Number of typical students referred (out-of-school) for substance abuse assessment or treatment per academic year[a]	7.13 (9.10; n = 60) Mdn = 4	4.43 (6.32; n = 127) Mdn = 3	5.57 (6.74; n = 76) Mdn = 3

[a]Medians are presented as an additional measure of central tendency because the distribution appears skewed as based on the Mean and Standard Deviation.

As can be seen from this table counselors in the sample were predominantly White, female, and held master's degrees. In addition, rural school counselors had the smallest mean school census compared to the other two groups but reported the highest mean numbers of students seen for a substance abuse concern of all three groups.

Perceived Competence

A multivariate analysis of variance (MANOVA) was conducted to compare mean scores for the seven competency items among the three groups of urban, suburban, and rural counselors (see Table 2). The three groups were not of equivalent sample size; however, Box's Test of equality was not significant, $F(56, 121912.2) = .880$, $p = .72$, indicating that equal variances could be assumed. Results from the MANOVA indicated significant differences among the three groups on the dependent variables, Wilks' $\Lambda = .91$, $F(14, 518) = 1.79$, $p < .05$, multivariate $\eta^2 = .046$. To follow-up on these results, between-subjects analysis of variance (ANOVA) was conducted for each dependent variable. ANOVA results indicated that among the three groups differences were only significant for the curriculum units competency area, $F(2, 265) = 3.54$, $p < .05$, partial $\eta^2 = .026$. Bonferroni post-hoc analysis indicated that suburban and rural counselors significantly differed on their mean competency ratings of curriculum units.

Table 2. Perceived Mean Ratings for Seven Competency Areas Related to Student Substance Abuse by Urbanicity

Competency Area	Mean Ratings (Standard Deviations)		
	Urban (n = 63)	Suburban (n = 127)	Rural (n = 78)
Provide *screening or assessment* to students with substance abuse problems	2.57 (1.06)	2.57 (1.08)	2.63 (1.11)
Provide *group counseling interventions* to students with substance abuse problems	3.08 (1.04)	2.99 (1.07)	2.92 (1.11)
Provide *individual counseling interventions* to students with substance abuse problems	3.22 (0.99)	3.11 (0.98)	3.14 (1.03)
Identify students with substance abuse problems	3.29 (0.99)	3.47 (0.99)	3.49 (0.99)
Effectively work with students with substance abuse problems at my school	3.38 (0.97)	3.35 (0.91)	3.40 (0.97)
Develop and teach curriculum units on substance abuse prevention to students in the classroom	3.48 (1.23)	3.42 (1.22)*	3.86 (1.09)*
Consult with teachers about a student with substance abuse problems	3.63 (0.92)	3.78 (0.89)	3.54 (1.04)

Note. Competency ratings were made on a 5-point Likert-type scale: 1 – Strongly Disagree, 2 – Disagree, 3 – Neutral, 4 – Agree, 5 – Strongly Agree.
*p < .05; significant mean difference between suburban and rural for this competency area.

As can be seen from Table 2, screening and group/individual interventions received the lowest mean scores by counselors in each group whereas curriculum development and consultation were among the highest.

Current and Prior Training

Analyses were conducted to better understand counselors' overall perceptions of their current training as well as past training experiences related to addressing student substance abuse concerns. Correlations were conducted between experience as a school counselor (i.e., years of experience) and perceptions of having the training necessary to effectively work with students with substance abuse problems at their school for each counselor group. Results from these correlations indicated that the two variables were not related for any counselor group: *urban* r(63) = -.148, *p* > .05; *suburban* r(128) = .040, *p* > .05; *rural* r(80) = .090, *p* > .05. This indicates that past experience as a school counselor did not make a difference in perceived ability for addressing student substance abuse concerns. Counselors were also asked about the number of prior trainings their school or district had provided them in the past three years and the following data were reported: *urban* – 37.1% none, 27.4% one, 17.7% two, 17.7% three or more; *suburban* – 42.5% none, 30.7% one, 16.5% two, 10.2% three or more; *rural* – 38.0% none, 32.9% one, 10.1% two, 19.0% three or more. These data indicate that about 40% of counselors in each group did not receive any type of student substance abuse related training by their employer in the past three years. In addition, counselors were asked about the number of substance abuse related courses taken in their graduate degree program. The results from this question were as follows: *urban* – 42.9% none, 34.9% one, 14.3% two, 7.9% three or more; *suburban* – 51.2% none, 34.1% one, 10.1% two, 4.7% three or more; *rural* – 48.8% none, 25.0% one, 20.0% two, 6.3% three or more. In other words, about 40-50% of counselors in the sample did not take a substance abuse related course in their graduate degree program.

Most Important Areas for Training

The rank-ordered data of the *most important* areas for school counselors to receive substance abuse related training are presented in Figure 1. These data indicate that 32.3%, 37.7%, and 33.8% of urban, suburban, and rural counselors, respectively, identified screening or assessment as the most important substance abuse related training area. This was closely followed by individual counseling interventions: urban (38.7%), suburban (25.4%), and rural (28.8%). Smaller numbers of participants indicated that consultation, curriculum development, group or family interventions were the most important types of training for school counselors to receive. In regard to training on the topic of student substance abuse, the examination of mean scores indicated that counselors *agreed* they *should receive* (urban – *M* = 4.38, SD = 0.63; suburban – *M* = 4.45, SD = 0.75; rural – *M* = 4.33, SD = 0.84; same 5-point scale as above) and *would attend* (urban – *M* = 4.35, SD = 0.68; suburban – *M* = 4.30, SD = 0.83; rural – *M* = 4.13, SD = 0.85) training in this area. In addition, there were no correlations between counselors' caseload size (an indicator of workload) and their willingness to attend future substance abuse related training for any group: urban r(61) = -.109, *p* > .05; suburban r(127) = -.012, *p* > .05; rural r(78) = .046, *p* > .05. This suggests that workload did not make a difference in how willing counselors were in attending future training on the topic of student substance abuse.

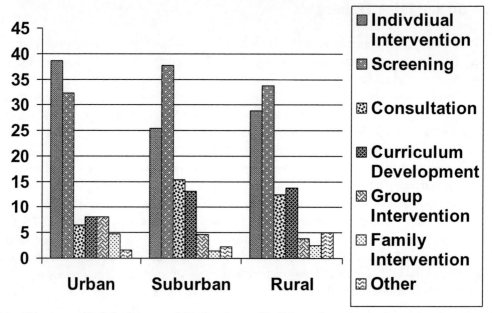

Note. Urban - n = 62, Suburban - n = 130, Rural - n = 80; Other = (e.g., prevention, referral, community resources).

Figure 1. Most Important Areas for Urban, Suburban, and Rural School Counselors to Receive Substance Abuse Related Training.

DISCUSSION

The results of the present study provide information about the perceived competence and training needs of urban, suburban, and rural middle school counselors for addressing student substance abuse problems. Prior research has indicated that differences based on urbanicity can affect the delivery of school mental health services (see Slade, 2003; Weist et al., 2000) as well as the potential training needs of school personal delivering such services (Foster et al., 2005). In addition, counselors are the most likely school personnel to deliver mental health services in schools (Foster et al., 2005). Results from the present study, however, indicate that urban, suburban, and rural middle school counselors are more similar than different in their perceived competencies and training needs related to student substance abuse. Similar to prior research, school counselors in the present study generally perceived themselves as lacking competence in specific areas related to student substance abuse and clearly identified needed areas of future training (see Burrow-Sanchez and Lopez, 2009; Burrow-Sanchez, Lopez, and Slagle, 2008; Goldberg and Governali, 1995).

The three lowest rated competency areas by all counselors in this study were screening/assessment, group and individual counseling interventions, respectively. These findings are not surprising given that approximately half of the total sample indicated not having taken a graduate course in substance abuse and a little less than half reported not having been offered an in-service training on this topic in the past three years. Screening/assessment and individual interventions were clearly the top two areas that counselors, regardless of urbanicity, rated as the most important areas for training. In contrast, consultation with teachers was the most strongly endorsed competency area by counselors and is supported by research that indicates counselors report spending large parts of their time consulting with other school personnel regarding the academic, career, personal, and social needs of their students (Partin, 1993; Tennyson, Miller, Skovholt, and Williams, 1989). These findings have important implications for the training in the area of student substance abuse for pre-service and in-service middle school counselors.

Graduate programs in school counseling could integrate these substance abuse related training areas within the context of required courses or add a substance abuse course to their curriculum. The *Council for Accreditation of Counseling and Related Educational Programs* (2001) does not list substance abuse as a "core curricular experience" (i.e., required course) in the accreditation standards for school counseling graduate programs. Instead, substance abuse is listed as one of many items in the *"knowledge and skill requirements"* section. This could be interpreted to mean that pre-service school counselors should receive some training in substance abuse but the graduate program faculties determine how this will be accomplished. However, data from the present study and prior research (Burrow-Sanchez and Lopez, 2009; Burrow-Sanchez, Lopez, and Slagle, 2008) indicate that approximately half of middle and high school counselors in the nation did not receive substance abuse training in their graduate programs. These data provide good evidence that student substance abuse should be a topic integrated into school counseling graduate curricula.

In terms of in-service training, administrators could make the topic of student substance abuse a training priority for school counselors in their districts. Findings from the present study and prior research indicate that close to half of middle and high school counselors did not receive in-service training on the topic of student substance abuse in the past three years. The two priority areas for in-service training include screening/assessment and individual interventions. However, potential obstacles to providing in-service training on the topic of student substance abuse need to be considered if such training is to be successful. For example, conflicts with existing school policies regarding substance abuse (e.g., zero tolerance), obtaining support from administration, and monetary/personnel costs of training are potential obstacles that can hinder the success of school-based training on this topic. If administrators make training in this area a priority for the schools in their districts then viable solutions to such potential obstacles will likely be achieved (Burrow-Sanchez and Hawken, 2007). Specific strategies for training in the areas of screening/assessment, individual and group interventions are discussed next.

Many screening instruments are available that school counselors can administer with minimal prior training, are low or no-cost and provide valuable information when trying to understand a potential student substance abuse problem. Burrow-Sanchez and Hawken (2007) provide a review of screening instruments that can be utilized by school personnel when addressing student substance abuse concerns. One example of a brief screening measure is Adolescent Alcohol and Drug Involvement Scale (AADIS). The AADIS is a 14-item screening instrument in the public domain and can be administered without any special training (Moberg, 2000). School counselors are also encouraged to choose screening instruments that will help them in determining if referral for a more thorough assessment is needed.

As indicated above, two competency areas rated relatively low by counselors were the use of individual and group interventions for students with substance abuse problems. Counselors also identified individual interventions as one of the two most important areas for future training. The basic interpersonal or micro-counseling skills that counselors were taught in graduate school and regularly use with students could be enhanced for addressing student substance abuse concerns. For example, Lambie (2004) suggests that school counselors can utilize the individual intervention methods employed in motivational enhancement therapy (MET) with students. In particular, school counselors can use MET to assist students in decreasing resistance and increasing motivation to change problem behaviors. As previously mentioned, school counselors are the first line of defense for delivering mental health services to students (see Foster et al., 2005) and thus, are in a good position to develop positive working relationships with students at-risk for substance abuse and other problems. In addition, research findings suggest that students who positively bond with their school and the personnel in it (e.g., school counselors) are at less risk for abusing substances (Hawkins, Catalano, and Miller, 1992).

Group-based interventions are frequently used in school settings (see Greenberg, 2003) and training in this area is a required part of accredited graduate programs in school counseling (CACREP, 2001). However, with some additional knowledge and training middle school counselors can build upon their existing skills and facilitate appropriate school-based substance related groups (e.g., prevention, support) for students. There are many resources available for school counselors on group interventions. These include research-based manuals (see Dennis et al., 2004) that can easily be adapted for group interventions in schools as well as discussion of the most relevant information and skills counselors will need to successfully facilitate groups (see Burrow-Sanchez and Hawken, 2007; Greenberg, 2003) Further, group-based substance abuse interventions are efficient ways to work with many students at one time when considering the typical time constraints and high caseloads of school counselors.

This study provides important findings related to the perceived competence and training needs of urban, suburban, and rural middle school counselors for addressing student substance abuse concerns, however, more research is needed. The majority of participants in this study were White and this is a potential limitation because this sample may not generalize to school counselors from racially and ethnically diverse backgrounds. The perception of school counselors from different racial and ethnic groups on the topic of student substance abuse is an important area for further investigation. A second limitation of this study is that information from nonrespondents to the survey was not obtained. This is important to consider because those who responded could in some way be different from those who did not respond.

CONCLUSION

School counselors are the first line of defense in delivering mental health services to students in school contexts (Foster et al., 2005). Results from this study indicate that urban, suburban, and rural middle school counselors are quite similar in perceived competency and desired training in relation to the topic of student substance abuse. Faculty in graduate training programs should consider including topics of student substance abuse in their curricula for pre-service school counselors. In addition, school administrators could enhance the skills of counselors in their districts by making in-service training on this topic available. The quality of services provided to students with substance abuse problems will likely improve if graduate programs and school administrators make training on this topic a priority for pre-service and in-service school counselors.

REFERENCES

Burrow-Sanchez, J. J., and Hawken, L. S. (2007). Helping Students Overcome Substance Abuse: *Effective Practices for Prevention and Intervention*. New York: Guilford Publications, Inc.

Burrow-Sanchez, J. J., and Lopez, A. L. (2009). Identifying substance abuse issues in high schools: A national survey of high school counselors. *Journal of Counseling and Development*, 87(1), 72-79.

Burrow-Sanchez, J. J., Lopez, A. L., and Slagle, C. P. (2008). Perceived competence in addressing student substance abuse: A national survey of middle school counselors. *Journal of School Health*, 78(5), 280-286.

CACREP. (2001). Accreditation standards of the Council for Accreditation of Counseling and Related Educational Programs. Retrieved January 4, 2007, from http://www. cacrep.org/2001Standards.html

Dennis, M. L., Godley, S. H., Diamond, G., Tims, F. M., Babor, T., Donaldson, J., et al. (2004). The Cannabis Youth Treatment (CYT) study: Main findings from two randomized trials. *Journal of Substance Abuse Treatment*, 27, 197-213.

Dillman, D. A. (2000). *Mail and Internet Surveys: The Tailored Design Method* (2nd ed.). New York: Wiley.

Fink, A., and Kosecoff, J. (1998). *How to Conduct Surveys: A Step-By-Step Guide* (2nd ed.). Thousand Oaks, CA: Sage Publications, Inc.

Foster, S., Rollefson, M., Doksum, T., Noonan, D., Robinson, G., and Teich, J. (2005). *School Mental Health Services in the United States*, 2002-2003 (No. DHHS Pub No. (SMA) 05-4068). Rockville, MD: Substance Abuse and Mental Health Services Administration.

Goldberg, R., and Governali, J. (1995). Substance abuse counseling and the school counselor: A needs assessment. *Wellness Perspectives*, 11(4), 19-29.

Greenberg, K. R. (2003). *Group Counseling in K-12 Schools: A Handbook for School Counselors*. Boston: Allyn and Bacon.

Hawkins, J. D., Catalano, R. F., and Miller, J. Y. (1992). Risk and protective factors for alcohol and other drug problems in adolescence and early adulthood: Implications for substance abuse prevention. *Psychological Bulletin*, 112(1), 64-105.

Johnston, L. D., O'Malley, P. M., Bachman, J. G., and Schulenberg, J. E. (2006). *Monitoring the Future national results on adolescent drug use: Overview of key findings 2005* (No. NIH Publication No. 06-5882). Bethesda, MD: National Institute on Drug Abuse.

Lambie, G. W. (2004). Motivational enhancement therapy: A tool for professional school counselors working with adolescents. *Professional School Counseling*, 7(4), 268-276.

Lambie, G. W., and Rokutani, L. J. (2002). A systems approach to substance abuse identification and intervention for school counselors. *Professional School Counseling*, 5(5), 353-360.

Mason, M. J. (1997). Patterns of service utilization for Mexican American majority students who use alcohol or other drugs. *Journal of Health and Social Policy*, 9(2), 21-27.

Moberg, D. P. (2000). The Adolescent Alcohol and Drug Involvement Scale. Madison, WI: University of Wisconsin, Center for Health Policy and Program Evaluation Retrieved January 4, 2007, from http://www.pophealth.wisc.edu/UWPHI/index.htm

Newcomb, M. D. (1995). Identifying high-risk youth: Prevalence and patterns of adolescent drug abuse. In E. Rahdert and D. Czechowicz (Eds.), *Adolescent drug abuse: Clinical assessment and therapeutic interventions* (NIDA Research Monograph 156) (pp. 7-38). Rockville, MD: US Dept. of Health and Human Services.

Palmer, J. H., and Ringwalt, C. L. (1988). Prevalence of alcohol and drug-use among North Carolina public school students. *Journal of School Health*, 58(7), 288-291.

Partin, R. L. (1993). School counselors' time: Where does it go? *School Counselor*, 40(4), 274-281.

SAMHSA. (2006). Results from the 2005 National Survey on Drug Use and Health: National Findings. (NSDUH Series H-30, DHHS Publication No. SMA 06–4194). Rockville, MD: Substance Abuse and Mental Health Administration, Office of Applied Studies.

Shelder, J., and Block, J. (1990). Adolescent drug use and psychological health: A longitudinal inquiry. *American Psychologist*, 45(5), 612-630.

Slade, E. P. (2003). The relationship between school characteristics and the availability of mental health and related health services in middle and high schools. *The Journal of Behavioral Health Services and Research*, 30(4), 382-392.

Tennyson, W. W., Miller, G. D., Skovholt, T. M., and Williams, R. C. (1989). How they view their role: A survey of counselors in different secondary schools. *Journal of Counseling and Development,* 67(7), 399-403.

Watkins, K. E., Ellickson, P. L., Vaiana, M. E., and Hiromoto, S. (2006). An update on adolescent drug use: What school counselors need to know. *Professional School Counseling,* 10(2).

Weist, M. D., Myers, C. P., Danforth, J., McNeil, D. W., Ollendick, T. H., and Hawkins, R. (2000). Expanded school mental health services: Assessing needs related to school level and geography. *Community Mental Health*, 36(3), 259-273.

In: Alcohol and Drug Use among Youth
Editor: Agatha M. Pichler

ISSN: 978-1-61209-084-9
© 2012 Nova Science Publishers, Inc.

Chapter 7

Teenage Drug Abuse amongst Non School Attending Young People: Messages for Targeted Interventions

*Patrick McCrystal**

Institute of Child Care Research
School of Sociology Social Policy and Social Work
Queens University Belfast, BT7 1LP UK

Abstract

School based drugs education and prevention initiatives should be based upon contemporary empirical evidence. These programmes are traditionally developed with evidence gathered from school surveys which collect data on the prevalence estimates of those receiving mainstream education. As a result most education prevention initiatives which are delivered to school aged young people are not based upon evidence of the drug use experiences of those who do not attend mainstream school during adolescence. This paper will report on the drug use experience of the school exclusion sample of the High Risk Booster Sample of the Belfast Youth Development Study (BYDS) and its value for targeted education and prevention initiatives. The drug use behaviours of these high risk young people from the age of 11-16 will be presented in order to provide insights into the key temporal stages of experimental and onset regular illicit drug use. This analysis over a five year period will highlight the key stages for the development and delivery of drug use education and prevention initiatives for those who stop attending mainstream school before the age of 16 years.

Introduction

Drug education and prevention initiatives should be based upon contemporary empirical evidence. To be most effective this evidence should be obtained from the target population upon which the proposed interventions are to be delivered. For this reason school based

---

* E-mail: P.McCrystal@qub.ac.uk

surveys of drug and alcohol use are an invaluable source upon which to develop drug education interventions to young people whilst attending school. Whilst the information base on young people who remain in school has developed in the UK over the past two decades and over a longer period of time in the USA, for those who have stopped attending school the empirical base upon which to develop such initiatives is much more limited. In this paper the value of empirical drug use behaviours of young people who have stopped attending mainstream school during adolescence will be explored with reference to the existing research base of the High Risk Booster Sample of the Belfast Youth Development Study, a longitudinal study of the onset and development of adolescent drug use that has been ongoing in Northern Ireland over the past decade. Despite their status as being at an increased risk to substance use and abuse in adolescence, comparatively less is known about drug use amongst these young people. This raises questions about the extent to which their needs are being fully addressed by those with responsibility for delivering appropriate drug education and intervention.

The literature has highlighted a range of risk and protective factors associated with the onset of problem drug use during adolescence (Hawkins et al, 1992; 2002). Much of this research is based on empirical findings from school based surveys (Beinart et al. 2002; Dolcini and Adler, 1994; Evertt, et al. 2000; Gottfredson and Gottfredson 2002; Hibell et al. (1997); Johnston et al. 2001; Miler and Plant (1996); Schulenberg et al, 1994; Sussman et al. (1994); Voelkl and Frone, 2000; Willis et al, 1995), many of which are carried out on a longitudinal basis (Botvin et al. (1995); Bryant and Zimmerman, 2002; Ellickson and Bell, 1990; Grant and Dawson, 1997; Griffin et al, 1999; Kandel et al. 1986; Lynam et al. 1999; Newcomb et al. 1986; Park et al. 2000; Werner 1989). These studies, conducted in mainstream educational settings include what Snow et al, 2001 refer to as 'normal' students excluding those no longer attending mainstream school on a regular basis. Generally the study of drug prevention looks at risk and protective factors associated with drug use which Hawkins and his colleagues (2002) have elevated to science status in providing a measure of ecological validity for many of the risk factors identified in the literature. These factors fall into several generic categories corresponding to Oetting and Donnemeyer's (1998a) primary socialistaion factors of the family, school and peer. Other factors, which Oetting and Donnemeyer refer to as secondary socialization factors which mediate primary factors include the area in which the young people live and their social and recreational activities (Oetting and Donnemeyer, 1998b). The literature notes that some young people are more predisposed to certain risk factors than others placing them at a higher level of risk to becoming a problem drug user. This body of literature has been growing recently (Eastwood 2000; Gouden and Sondhi, 2001; Hayden 1997; Hayden and Dunn, 2001; Lloyd, 1998; Melrose, 2000; Olser et al, 2002; Powis et al. 1998; Sloboda, 1999; Ware, 1999). This paper explores the value of one such contribution to this area, the school exclusion sample of the High Risk Booster Sample of the Belfast Youth Development Study.

THE ROLE OF SCHOOL IN THE LIVES OF YOUNG PEOPLE

Society currently assigns schools the responsibility of transmitting certain cultural and behavioural norms. In the same way that there are dysfunctional families, there are also dysfunctional schools which have parallel weaknesses. The typical image of a dysfunctional school, of the resignation to chaos and deviance is only one type. Even in the best schools, there will be an alienated peer group. Poor grades, disciplinary problems etc. tend to erode the bond between an adolescent and school, and thus erode the ability of the school to transmit prosocial norms to its students. These students are forced outside the circle in which other peers may be receiving normative socialisation. Studies of these disaffected groups have shown that students experiencing alienation, lack of success within the school framework, and other problems with deriving rewards from school have a greater tendency toward drug use and deviancy in general. The initial function of schools is to teach intellectual skills and knowledge appropriate to society. School also plays an important role in socializing children to society's social and political values and therefore can have a powerful influence on development. Schools are also social systems in their own right and provide opportunities for peer relationships and student teacher relationships to be generated. Classroom structure, pedagogy, rules, methods of discipline, standards and expectations all play a role in shaping individuals. Birch et al. (1998) state that the quality of the child –teacher relationship can influence several outcomes. Good relationships are associated with linking school and good academic competence. Conflicting relationships are linked with unfavourable school attitudes, classroom disengagement and poor academic functioning. Rutter (1979) states that school is of the utmost importance as it sets in motion pathways for the future. Academic achievement at school will influence career pathways and future socio-economic status. Values learnt at school will also affect future relationships. Sylva (1994) states that there is considerable research to support the claim that schools exert a huge amount of influence on academic achievement, social behaviour and later employment.

WHY DO SOME YOUNG PEOPLE STOP ATTENDING SCHOOL?

Whilst the overwhelming majority of young people complete statutory schooling, a small a number of young people are referred to as being 'out of school' as they are not attending mainstream school. The young people who fall into the following categories identified by Eastwood (2000) describe those who are excluded from school, the main types of young people who stop attending school before the end of compulsory schooling at 16 years:

(a) Young people expelled from school (i.e. have been removed from the school's register and will not be readmitted).
(b) Young people suspended from school awaiting placement in a Guidance Centre or other supportive provision (i.e are retained on the school's register with the aim that they will be re-integrated back into mainstream schooling following therapeutic guidance).
(c) Students who truant (i.e. a voluntary decision by students not to attend school)
(d) Young people who have school-phobia (i.e. a difficulty in attending school due to a separate/school anxiety problem).

School exclusion is associated with educational underachievement, social alienation and criminality which results in serious costs for young people themselves and society as a whole

(Audit Commission, 1996). Various studies have shown that exclusion from school is most common among socially disadvantaged groups and that it reinforces social exclusion as a whole (Harris, 2000). Excluding a young person from school is the most serious sanction available to head teachers, the only individual with such authority (Smith, 1998). The circumstances in which young people can be excluded from school are not set out in law, and guidance provided by education authorities do not have statutory force in the UK.

A number of groups of young people are disproportionately likely to be excluded, for example children with special needs are six times more likely than others to be excluded; children in care are ten times more likely to be excluded and make up 33 per cent of all secondary school exclusions and 66 per cent of all primary school exclusions (SEU, 1998). These destructive patterns benefit no one. They mean that children are relegated to the margins of society while teachers find it difficult to cope, and the public picks up the costs incurred for children who drift onto the streets without qualifications and skills where they can easily gravitate towards crime and prison.

Whilst the reasons for exclusion vary from relatively minor incidents to serious criminal offences almost all school exclusions are due to some form of indiscipline or unacceptable behaviour in school. In many cases school exclusion is the result of repeated displays of such behaviour, which at times is of a trivial nature (Eastwood, 2000; Kilpatrick et al. 1999; SEU, 1998).

THE IMPACT OF NON SCHOOL AT ATTENDANCE

The education system is central to the lives of most young people who get only one chance at school. Once a decision is taken to exclude a young person from school many lose the potential benefits of this experience. The most immediate effect of school exclusion is that the young person falls behind their peers in academic work and they also lose formal contact with one of the three primary socialisation factors (Oetting and Donnemeyer, 1998a). In addition they lose the structure to their day provided by school, and in time will lose the habit of schooling. Warr (1987) claims that having a structure to their day helps maintain psychological well-being.

The SEU (2001) noted that prior to 1997 young people excluded from school received just two to three hours education each week, but that the quality of education is improving for these young people. The longer the young person remains excluded, the greater the difficulty to catch up if they return to school which adds to the difficulty for them to be successfully reintegrated into mainstream schooling. Smith (1998) suggests there is also a risk of reinforcement of problem behaviour through the practice of bringing these young people together to receive alternative education.

School exclusion is rarely found in isolation and is usually associated with other problem behaviours. It is extremely costly to the young person, their family and society at large. These young people do not just disappear from society and should be quickly reintegrated back into mainstream schooling, if possible. However, this happens in only about one third of cases with the others losing their entitlement to full-time education (SEU, 1998). For example, despite the statutory requirement for the education authorities to provide suitable provision for excluded pupils such provision does not have to be full-time. The Social Exclusion Unit

(1998) noted that many excluded pupils receive as little as three or four hours of tuition each week and some get nothing.

Young people excluded from mainstream school are therefore likely to find themselves at a high risk to a number of social disadvantages and at risk to a number of antisocial behaviours including illicit drug use. Catalano et al. (1998) defined high risk as those either exposed to multiple risk factors, or to an elevated level on one particular risk factor, young people excluded from school would fall into this later category. The study of young people categorised as high risk is important for a number of reasons. Firstly, these young people are more likely to use drugs than those considered to be at a lower risk, and may also be more likely to develop problem drug use. Secondly, in times of budgetary constraints it makes good economic sense to target limited resources, if possible at highest risk or where the benefits would be greatest (Catalano et al. 1998; Rutter, 1998). Finally, the study of high risk young people may provide useful insights into the process of resilience, an essential issue in the study of drug use behaviours among young people (Rutter 1990). These factors provide us with some insights into the comparatively smaller information base upon which to design and develop interventions for this group. As a result this questions the extent to which the levels of risk these young people are open to are being appropriately addressed.

NON SCHOOL ATTENDANCE AND ADOLESCENT DRUG TAKING

Research into drug education and prevention relies on empirical evidence from its target population. This evidence is usually obtained from the general public, for those who do not attend mainstream school such evidence is much less limited. As prevention and education programmes are usually developed with reference to such research findings, they often do not take into account the specific needs of vulnerable groups such as those who stop attending school before the age of 16 years. This makes it difficult to gain evidence for informing best practice into the design, prevention and education practices for young people considered to be vulnerable or at risk to drug abuse (Rhodes et al. 2003). Targeting drug prevention strategies towards these vulnerable groups is compatible with the UK Government's emphasis on tackling social exclusion, of which school exclusion has been identified as one are for priority attention.

The assertion that school exclusion is linked to long-term problematic drug use is based upon extrapolation from research undertaken in the USA as Powell et al claimed in 1999 that "no good UK based evidence exists on this topic" (p.2). They claim that as these young people are particularly vulnerable to developing long-term drug problems, the gaps that exist in our understanding of this issue are considerable. A feature of the UK's response to problem drug use is to target the drug prevention initiatives on young people who are particularly vulnerable to future drug problems.

In the USA, Mensch and Kandel (1988) found that high school drop-outs were more likely to abuse drugs and that early onset of drug use was also associated with high school drop out. Wisely et al. (1997) found that in a sample of heroin users, 80% had experienced some form of exclusion from school prior to their heroin use. In Sweden, Holmberg found that those who were registered for drug abuse were more likely to have dropped out of school at an earlier stage. Hawkins et al. (1992) reported an association between 'school failure' among risk factors for drug abuse in young people. However, it has been recognised in the UK that exclusion from school is a strong predictor of problem drug use (Lloyd, 1998; Miller and Plant, 1999). The Health Advisory Service (1996) referred to these young people as a vulnerable group. Furthermore, the Governments anti-drug strategy suggests that "for early to mid-teenagers, there are strong links between drug problems and exclusion from school" (UKADCU, 1998, p.14) Across the UK education authorities are required to offer some education provision for those excluded, but as this is often very limited to a few teaching hours per week, these young people spend most of their time with little organised or structured activities, and few have positive goals to work towards.

Flood-Page et al. (2000) noted that young people excluded from school tended to have significantly higher levels of drug use than those attending school. For example, they found they had taken at least one drug in their lives, which was four times higher than those attending school. In particular, Flood-Page and his colleagues also noted high levels of polydrug use among school excludees with cannabis, solvents and amphetamines featuring strongly. The level of use of Class A drugs was also significantly higher among school excludees than regular school attenders in Flood-Page et al. (2000) analysis. One of the Government's key objectives is to "stifle the availability of illegal drugs on our streets" and specifically, "to reduce access to all drugs among young people" (UKADCU, 1998). One major factor in the level of drug use among vulnerable groups of young people is their exposure to existing drug-using groups (Lloyd, 1998). Young female excludees taking part in the Flood-Page et al's (2000) analysis were generally more likely to report finding it easier to obtain drugs than young males.

INVESTIGATING DRUG USE BY NON SCHOOL ATTENDEES IN THE BELFAST YOUTH DEVELOPMENT STUDY

It is a statutory requirement for all young people to attend full-time education until the age of age of 16 years in the UK. As one of the three primary agents of socialisation, along with the family and peers (Oetting and Donnemyer, 1998a), school can act as a protective factor against drug taking for young people (Hawkins et al.. 1992). More specifically a high level of commitment to school can help protect young people from social disaffection and its resultant problems including delinquency and drug use. Social control theorists (Elliot et al, 1985) and the social development model (Hawkins and Weiss, 1985) posit that among young people who are not committed to school such bonds are weakened and can result in weak attachments to school and its positive role models such as teachers. Young people who are not attending mainstream schooling are more likley to find their bonds to school and its positive models weakened. Petraitis et al. (1995) explain this by saying that these young people will feel they have nothing to lose through attachment to deviant peers that can result in delinquent behaviour which can reinforce deviant actions. Young people who are excluded from school become part of a vulnerable group and are at a high risk of experiencing social disaffection and finding themselves involved in antisocial behaviour. In the Belfast Youth Development Study those selected for inclusion into the High Risk Booster Sample included those who had stopped attending school before the age of 16 years.

Little research has been undertaken in the UK which examines patterns or trends of drug use among young people excluded from school (Goulden and Sondhi, 2001; Powis et al. 1998). The assertion that school exclusion is linked to longterm problematic drug use is based upon extrapolation from research undertaken in the USA as Powell et al. (1999) claim that "no good UK based evidence exists on this topic" (p.2). They claim that as these young people are particularly vulnerable to developing long-term drug problems, the gaps that exist in our understanding of this issue are considerable.

Whist school based surveys of drug and alcohol use have been undertaken for several decades in the UK and even longer in the USA, the comparative information base for school aged young people who are no longer attending school is much more limited. For this reason it is therefore more difficult to design and development appropriate drug use education and prevention initiatives for this group of high risk young people. A repeated cross-sectional design was utilised to research the school exclusion sample of the High Risk Booster Sample of the Belfast Youth Development Study. School excludees are a particularly difficult group to track on a longitudinal basis and limited long-term studies successfully undertaken for this reason. Therefore researching the experience of this group of young people over a five year period was based on identifying a cohort of school excludees each year for inclusion in the research. This enabled the researchers to study their behaviour during this period (aged 11-16 years) by obtaining relevant data which would be comparable with those who continued to attend mainstream school. This research design shares a number of characteristics with what are considered 'traditional' longitudinal single cohort studies. For example at each stage (year of the study) the same criteria were used to identify the cohort for inclusion (i.e. excluded from school) and equivalent age as main school survey (i.e. school year 8, then year 9 the following year and so on until they have reached school year 11) enabling an investigation of the drug use behaviours of school excludees through adolescence to the age of 16 years. This means the data obtained is comparable between years as well as the overall duration of the study similar to the 'traditional' longitudinal designs (Gold and Reimer 1975). Table 1 presents the sample size of school excludees surveyed at each stage of the study. The school survey included approximately 4000 young people attending mainstream school at each stage. The gender composition of each participant is presented in Table 2.

Table 1. Numbers of school young people excluded from school who participated in the Belfast Youth Development Study

Survey Year	Participants	Refusals	Absentees	Total
Year 8 (11/12 years)	12	3	10	25
Year 9 (12/13 years)	29	6	4	39
Year 10 (13/14 years)	48	3	15	66
Year 11 (14/15 years)	51	4	21	76
Year 11 (14/15 years)	77	4	34	115

Data on drug use was obtained from the young people in the alternative education facilities they attended. A passive consent procedure was utilized each year with the parent/guardian of each young person. This involved informing the parent/guardian about the study and requesting their permission for the participation of their son/daughter.

Table 2. Gender of School Excludees who participated in the Belfast Youth Development Study

Survey Year	Male	Female	Total
Year 8 (11/12 years)	11	1	12
Year 9 (12/13 years)	26	3	29
Year 10 (13/14 years)	42	6	48
Year 11 (14/15 years)	35	16	51
Year 11 (14/15 years)	49	28	77

LONGITUDINAL STUDIES OF DRUG USE AMONGST NON SCHOOL ATTENDEES

Longitudinal school based surveys are invaluable for assisting us understand the drug use behaviours of young people over the developmental period of adolescence than single cross-sectional studies from which much of the drug use prevalence estimates for school aged young people, particularly school excludees, are obtained. The main advantages of these studies are that they provide repeated measures of the same respondents at a number of time intervals and enable researchers to describe patterns of change as well as the direction of change and more accurate interpretation of causal relationships.

However, there are a number of disadvantages with longitudinal studies. Due to the time taken to complete a longitudinal study, they are time consuming and can be expensive compared with cross sectional research studies and once started offer limited opportunities for modification. There are also issues around the accuracy of the information provided over a period of time due to missing data which may result from the failure of participants to remember past events, behaviours, or from unwillingness by the them to divulge some information, as well as the inability of researchers to locate co-operation from some respondents.

Also over the duration of the study there is increased probability of study attrition resulting from a refusal to co-operate from participants who may for example move to other locations outside the study area.

The BYDS used a repeated cross-sectional study approach to investigate drug use behaviours of the school exclusion sample from the age of 11-16 years. This research design was used in the early days of adolescent drug use and in locations where adolescent drug use was studied over a period of time where it was difficult to identify and survey the same individuals each year as in a traditional longitudinal study. Due to the difficulties associated with tracking young people who stop attending school, this approach was considered the most effective approach for studying the school excludees who participated in each stage of the BYDS. Using this research approach data collected on the same set of variables (and perhaps *at*) on two or more periods, but includes non-identical (but comparable) cases in each period.

The data may be regarded as a separate cross-section at each datasweep, but because the cases are comparable from one period to another, we may make comparisons between the groups. In this paper findings from the school exclusion sample of the High Risk Booster Sample of the BYDS are analysed to explore the extent to which the specific needs of school aged young people vary in relation to drug education and prevention initiatives whilst they remain part of the statutory education system even if they are not attending mainstream school.

DRUG USE AMONGST YOUNG PEOPLE WHO HAVE STOPPED ATTENDING SCHOOL WHO PARTICIPATED IN THE BYDS

The drug use behaviours of the school exclusion sample of the BYDS from the age of 11-16 years will be presented in this section. It will begin by presenting the level of exposure to illicit drugs, followed by lifetime use, more recent use at each stage of the study and then the frequency of use of each substance. Comparisons will be made with data from the mainstream sample of the BYDS in order to provide a context for the drug sue behaviours of the school exclusion sample.

At each stage of the BYDS the school exclusion sample reported higher levels of exposure to illicit substances compared with the mainstream school sample. This was in response to the question *have you ever been offered ..., or been around when it was being used or you could have had some?* The level of exposure to each substance was at a relatively high level at each stage of the research. This is particularly noteworthy during the first two years of the research before the participants had reached the teenage years. Perhaps the most important finding is the level of exposure to illicit substances with nine out of ten reporting exposure to cannabis, more than had (56%) exposed to ecstasy and one fifth (19%) exposed to cocaine by the age of 14 years at the third annual data sweep pf the study even though the levels of exposure to ecstasy and cocaine continued to rise during the subsequent years of the study. This is also the stage at which exposure to solvent abuse reached a high level at around one third.

The lifetime drug use prevalence estimates for the school excludees participating in the school exclusion sample of the High Risk Booster Sample of the Belfast Youth Development Study show much higher levels of use for these young people at all stages of the research compared with those who remained in mainstream school. In particular the school excludees had reached a relatively high level of lifetime use of these substances form the beginning of the study. In the second year of the study in particular, when the young people were aged 12/13 years nearly two thirds (62%) had used cannabis and one quarter has used ecstasy. The levels of use of these substances continued to rise with more than eight out of ten reporting lifetime use from the third year of the study when the participants were aged 13/14 years. By age 16 years, more than half (53%) had used ecstasy, one fifth (19%) had used cocaine. The majority had used tobacco and alcohol from the age of 11/12 years at the beginning of the study. The levels of lifetime use remained at this level throughout the study, compared with the mainstream school survey for whom the levels of drug use appeared to increase significantly from the age of 14 onwards form the their year of the BYDS.

The school exclusion sample reported higher levels of more recent use as measured through 'last year' use. This may provide us with evidence for ongoing use once it began, particularly in relation to cannabis use as well as tobacco and alcohol.

Table 3. Drug Use Patterns for School Excludees and Young People Attending Mainstream School

Substance	Year 1 School Sample *	Year 1 School excludees**	Year 2 School Sample *	Year 2 School excludees**	Year 3 School Sample *	Year 3 School excludees**	Year 4 School Sample *	Year 4 School excludees**	Year 5 School Sample *	Year 5 School excludees**
Tobacco	38	84	53	93	62	90	68	96	69	96
Alcohol	70	67	79	83	87	92	91	94	69	96
Been Drunk	15	33	32	64	46	81	59	77	69	94
Solvents	6	33	10	28	14	48	15	36	14	38
Cannabis	8	33	20	62	32	81	43	82	46	87
Ecstasy	2	17	4	25	6	27	9	30	12	53
Cocaine	2	0	3	0	4	6	5	14	7	19
Heroin	1	8	2	7	2	0	1	0	1	0

* School Sample; ** School excludees

Table 4. Exposure to Drugs of School Excludees and those Attending Mainstream School

Drug	Year 1 School Sample*	Year 1 School excludees**	Year 2 School Sample *	Year 2 School excludees**	Year 3 School Sample *	Year 3 School excludees**	Year 4 School Sample *	Year 4 School excludees**	Year 5 School Sample *	Year 5 School excludees**
Solvents	14	50	23	48	28	65	31	77	31	58
Cannabis	17	67	32	76	47	90	57	90	59	89
Ecstasy	6	33	11	35	16	56	24	63	30	4
Cocaine	5	17	8	14	10	19	13	28	18	37
Heroin	3	8	5	10	5	4	6	14	5	6

* School Sample; ** School excludees

Table 5. Last year use by school excludees and those attending mainstream school

Drug	Year 2 School sample*	Year 2 School excludees**	Year 3 School sample*	Year 3 School excludees**	Year 4 School sample*	Year 4 School excludees**	Year 5 School sample*	Year 5 School excludees**
Tobacco	34	83	42	81	47	86	47	89
Alcohol	68	69	77	85	84	84		
Been Drunk	27	45	41	68	55	69	66	87
Solvents	8	28	10	27	9	12	8	21
Cannabis	17	55	28	75	37	78	42	82
Ecstasy	3	7	5	19	8	22		
Cocaine	2	3	3	2	4	8		
Heroin	1	0	1	0	1	0		

* School Sample; ** School excludees

From the second year of the research the majority of cannabis users were using this drug at least on a weekly basis. This increased to more than three quarters (77%) of all cannabis users in the fourth and fifth (81%) years of the study. Nearly half of all cannabis users were using the drug each day during the last two years of the study. In the fourth year of the study when the participants ere aged 14/15 years this was 41 per cent of cannabis users rising to 48 per the following year when aged 15/16 years.

Alcohol intoxication became more frequent amongst the young people who had stopped attending school as the study progressed two and three. This increased to two thirds (62%) in year 4 and three quarters (75%) in fifth year of the study when the young people were aged 15/16 years.

THE MESSAGE FOR DRUG EDUCATION AND ERADICATION

A range of existing research including overview and meta analysis have indicated that drug education and prevention should be tailored to the lifestyle of its target audience (Tobler et al, 2000; Van Gageldonk and Cuijpers, 1998; White and Pitts, 1998). This is not always the case, particularly for young people who stop attending mainstream school before the age of 16 years (EMCDDA, 2003). Vander Laenen and De Wree (2008) argue that drug education would be more successful if it incorporated the experiences of young people as a starting point for educating them about drugs. They suggest that ignoring such experiences of young people will result in them questioning the relevance of drug education. The findings from the research undertaken with the young people who had stopped attending school but participated in the BYDS show the higher levels of substance use by them. These findings also highlight the different needs of these young people in doing so and provides data for informing drugs education and eradication initiatives for school aged young people who are no longer attending mainstream school. In particular it shows that such initiatives are required at an earlier stage compared with those attending mainstream school. The higher levels of drug use during the pre teenage years highlight this period as one of the particular significance for young people who have stopped attending school during this period. However these findings do not provide insights into the procedures for delivery of such initiatives but the BYDS has shown that if the required resources are applied it is possible to target and track these young people throughout the period of adolescence, a key factor in the effective delivery of drugs education and eradication measures.

At a general level the analysis of the school exclusion sample of the High Risk Booster Sample of the Belfast Youth Development Study shows that as young people age through adolescence the numbers who find themselves outside mainstream school before the age of 16 years at the end of compulsory schooling increases each year. This is also a period when the numbers who begin to experiment with illicit drugs also increases and therefore the role of education and eradication initiatives become particularly crucial. Therefore the number and frequency of delivery of these initiatives will increase as these young get older. These findings have an important role to play in the area of drug education and eradication amongst all school aged young people, particularly as it presents a unique opportunity to present drug use estimates for the onset and development of drug use amongst young people who have stopped attending school. They may also provide a contribution to the debate on the accuracy of drug use prevalence estimates for school aged young people which are often based only on those who attend mainstream school. In addition the findings have demonstrated that with the appropriate investment of resources and commitment from the appropriate agencies, it is possible to produce an important and valuable resource for the design, development and delivery of such initiatives. In doing so this can go some way to addressing the limited information base which has lead to insufficiently tailored drug education and eradication practices for the specific needs of vulnerable young people including those who are excluded from school (Vander Laenen and De Wree, 2008). The level and frequency of drug use estimates presented in this paper also shows the importance of maintaining a contemporary evidence base of the drug use behaviours of these young people.

More generally the early introduction of drug preventative ad eradication measures to combat the risk factors associated with school exclusion may also lead to further general savings in public finances. Investment in early prevention and eradication programmes has the potential to reduce the need for more expensive intervention programmes for disaffected pupils, and may also lead to both fiscal savings to the economy and a reduction in the level of social exclusion. This would be achieved by reducing the potential link between of school exclusion and social exclusion which has been linked to illicit drug use in adolescence. Research from Northern Ireland has indicated that these young people are marginalized or socially excluded following their exclusion from mainstream school and often suffer lower levels of self-esteem, low expectations and with little ambition are more at risk of being unemployed when they are adults (McVicar, 2000). Successful prevention and eradication strategies tailored to their needs could lead to increased employability and subsequent employment leading them to participate in more productive and healthier lifestyles, a factor linked to reducing the long term impact of both early onset drug use and exclusion form school.

In general the findings from the school exclsuin samples of the BYDS suggests that drug prevention should be more extensive than is the case today (Franzkowiak, 2002; MacMaster et al, 2005; Guzys and Kendall, 2006). This will assist the reduction of 'risk' factors (Hawkins et al, 1992) to illicit drug use particularly around exclusion and marginalisation in adolescence and beyond. Social inclusion has become a political and educational issue, which focuses on the need to address division and exclusion in learning, while aiming to promote participation in learning activities, either formally or informally. In this perspective extending the range of possible interventions to include planned cultural and structural changes in the learner's social and political circumstances, within and without the formal learning situation will assist the delivery of drug education and eradication initiatives for those who have stopped attending school before the age of 16 years. As such, there has been a move away from interventions based on the individual to those that take the social situatedness of the problem into account and move towards inter-agency, multi-component approaches. Indeed, as previously highlighted, the SEU (1998) advocates 'joined up solutions to joined up problems'. Intervention programmes should be directed towards the analysis of barriers to learning and to the social personal development of the young people in the context of lifelong learning that offers opportunities for them to return to tailored learning and development, an important protective factor to ongoing drug use and abuse beyond adolescence.

Before concluding this paper it is important to highlight potential limitations of the school exclusion survey of the BYDS. Whilst questions are often raised about the accuracy and value of self-report drug use measures, longitudinal studies provide opportunities to overcome this potential pitfall through developing a familiarity between the young people and the researchers over a number of datasweeps. A further potential limitation may be associated with the repeated cross-sectional nature of the research design. This means that unlike traditional longitudinal designs where the study cohort contains the same participants each year, the repeated cross sectional design used for the school exclusion sample of the BYDS targeted all those who met the criteria for inclusion at each data sweep regardless of their participation in early stage of then research. However, each datasweep included the same drug use measures across all stages of the study, similar to a longitudinal research design. In this way cross sectional research design provides insights to the drug use behaviours of young people excluded from school throughout adolescence.

In conclusion, this paper has highlighted the drug use behaviours of young people who stopped attending mainstream school over a five year period. It shows that these young people begin using both licit and illicit substances at a much earlier age that those who continue to attend mainstream, school. It appears they may move beyond experimental; use to more frequent use of these substances. This information provides important data for the design and delivery of targeted education and eradication initiatives. It also suggests that such initiatives should be delivered at an earlier stage than they are for those who remain in school and that with the appropriate resources this is achievable to hard to reach groups such as those excluded form school.

ACKNOWLEDGMENT

The Belfast Youth Development Study is funded by the Health and Social Care Research and Development Office, Public Health Agency, Northern Ireland

REFERENCES

Audit Commission (1996) *Misspent Youth: Young People and Crime.* London: Audit Commission.

Beinart, S., Anderson, B. Lee, S. and Utting, D. (2002). *Youth at Risk.* London: Communities that Care.

Birch, S. H., & Ladd, G. W. (1998). Children's interpersonal behaviors and the teacher-child relationship. Develop- mental Psychology, 34, 934-946.

Botvin, G.J., Baker, E., Dusenbury, L., Botvin E.M., Diaz, T. (1995) Long-term follow-up results of a randomised drug abuse prevention trial in a white middle-class population. *Journal of the American Medical Association,* 273 (14), 1106-12.

Bryant, A.L. and Zimmerman, M.A. (2000). Examining the effects of academic beliefs and behaviours on changes in substance among urban adolescents, *Journal of Educational Psychology,* 94, 3, 621-637.

Catalano, R.F., Haggerty, K.P., Gainey, R. R., Hoppe, M.J., and Brewer, D.D. (1998). Effectiveness of prevention with youth at high risk of drug abuse. In W.J. Bukoski and

R.I. Evans (eds). *Cost benefit/Cost effectiveness Research of Drug Prevention: Implication for Programming and Policy.* Rockville: NIDA Research Monograph 176.

Dolcini, M.M. and Adler, N.E. (1994). Perceived competencies, peer group affiliation, and risk behaviour among early adolescents. *Health Psychology,* 13, 496-506.

Eastwood, C. (2000). Who is 'out of school'. *Child Care in Practice,* 6, 1, pp. 9-26.

Ellickson, P.L. and Bell, R.M. (1990). Drug prevention in junior high: multi-site longitudinal test. *Science,* 247, 1299-1305.

Elliot Huizinga and Ageton (1985) *Explaining delinquency and drug use.* Beverly Hills, CA: Sage.

EMCDDA (2003). Selective prevention: First overview on the European situation. Lisbon: EMCDDA (European Monitoring Centre for Drugs and Drug Addiction). Reteieved from:

http://www.emcdda.eu.int/index.cfm?fuseaction+public.ContentandnNodelD=1569andsLanguageISO=EN (20/10/04).

Everett, S.A., Malarcher, A.M., Sharp, D.J., Husten, C.G., and Gioviona, G.A., (2000). Relationship between cigarette, smokeless tobacco, and cigar use, and other health risk behaviours among U.S. high school students. *Journal of School Health,* 70, 234-240.

Flood-Page, C., Campbell, S., Harrington,V., and Miller, J. (2000). *Youth Crime: findings from the 1998/99 Youth Lifestyles Survey.* Home Office Research Study 209. London: Home Office.

Franzkowiak, P. (2002). Primary Drug Prevention: Developments in Germany since the 1970s. *Journal of Drug Issues,* 32, 491-502.

Gottfredson, D.C. and Gottfredson, G.D. (2002). Quality of school-based prevention programs: results from a national survey. *Journal of Research in Crime and Delinquency,* 39, 3-35.

Gold, M. and Reimer, D.J. (1975). Changing patterns of delinquent and behaviour among Americans 13 through 16 year olds: 1967-72. *Crime and Delinquency Literature 7*: 483-577.

Goulden, C. and Sondhi, A. (2001). *At the margins: drug use by vulnerable young people in the 1998/99 Youth Lifestyles Survey.* London: Home Office Research Study 228.

Grant, B.F. and Dawson, D. A. (1997). Age at onset of alcohol use and its association with DSM-IV alcohol abuse and dependence: results from national Longitudinal Alcohol Epidemiologic Survey. *Journal of Substance Abuse,* 9, 103-110.

Griffin, K.W., Botvin, G.J., Doyle, M. M., Diaz, T. and Epstein, J.A. (1999). A six-year follow-up study of determinants of heavy cigarette smoking among high-school seniors. *Journal of Adolescent Health,* 22, 271-284.

Guzys, D. and Kebndal, S (2006). Advocating for a harm-minimization approach to drug education in Australian schools. *The Journal of School Nursing,* 22, 259-263.

Harris, N. (2000) Education law: excluding the child. *Education and the Law,* 12, 1, pp. 31-46.

Hawkins, J. D., & Weis, J. G. (1985). The social development model: An integrated approach to delinquency prevention. *Journal of Primary Prevention,* 6(2), 73-97.

Hawkins, J.D., Catalano, R.F. and Miller, J.Y. (1992). Risk and protective factors for alcohol and other drug probems in adolescence and early adulthood: implications for substance abuse prevention. *Psychological Bulletin,* 112, pp. 64-105.

Hawkins, J.D., Catalano, R.F., and Arthur, M. (2002). Promoting science-based prevention in communities. *Addictive Behaviours*, 27, 951-976.

Hayden, C. (1997). *Excluded from Primary School: Debates, Evidence Responses.* Buckingham: Open University Press.

Hayden, C. and Dunn, S. (2001). *Outside looking in. Children and families experiences of exclusion from school.* London: The Children's Society.

Health Advisory Service (HAS) (1996). *Children and young people: substance misuse services and substance of young need.* London: Stationary Office.

Hibell, B., Anderson, B., Bjarnason, T., Kokkevi, A., Morgan, M. and Narusk, A. (1997) *The European Schools Survey Project on Alcohol and Other Drugs (ESPAD) Report.* Swedish Council for Information on Alcohol and Drugs 1997.

Johnston, L.D., O'Malley, P.M., and Bachman, J.G. (2001). *Monitoring the future national survey results on drug use, 1975-2000. Volume 1: Secondary school students.* Bethesda, MD: National Institute on Drug Abuse.

Kandel, D.B., Simcha fagan, O., and Davies, M. (1986). Risk factors for delinquency and illicit drug use from adolescence to young adulthood. *Journal of Drug Issues,* 16, 67-90.

Kilpatrick, R., Barr, A., and Wylie, C. (1999) *Northern Ireland Suspension and Expulsion Study (1996/97).* Bangor: Department of Education for Northern Ireland.

Lloyd, C. (1998). Risk factors for problem drug use: identifying vulnerable groups, *Drugs: education, prevention and policy,* 5 (3) pp. 217-232.

Lynam, D.R., Milich, R., Zimmerman, R., Novak, S.P., Logan, T., Martin, C., Leukefeld, C., and Clayton, R. (1999). Project: DARE: no effects at 10-year follow-up. *Journal of Consulting and Clinical psychology,* 67, 590-593.

Social Exclusion Unit (2001). *Preventing Social Exclusion. Report by the Social Exclusion Unit.* London: The Stationary Office.

McMaster, S.A, Holleran, L.K. and Chaffing, K (2005). Empirical and theoretic support for the inclusion of non-abstinence-based perspectives in prevention services for substance using adolescents. *Journal of Evidence-based social work,* 2, 91-111.

McVicar, D. (2000). *Young people and Social Exclusion in Northern Ireland: 'Status 0' Four years on.* Belfast: NIERC.

Melrose, M. (2000). *Fixing it? Young People, Drugs and Disadvantage.* Dorset: Russell House Publishing.

Mensch, B.S. and Kandel, D.B. (1988). Dropping out of high school and drug involvement. *Sociology of Education,* 23, 325-31.

Miller, P. and Plant, M. (1996) Drinking, Smoking and illicit drug use among 15 and 16 year olds in the United Kingdom, *British Medical Journal,* 313, 394-397.

Miller, P. and Plant, M. (1999) Truancy and perceived school performance: an alcohol and drug study of UK teenagers, *Alcohol and Alcoholism,* 34(6): 886-93.

Newcombe,M.D. and Felix-Ortiz, M. (1992). Multiple protective and risk factors fro drug use and abuse: cross-sectional and prospective findings. *Journal of Personality and Social Psychology,* 63, 280-96.

Newcombe,M.D., Maddahian, E., and Bentler, P.M. (1986). Risk factors for drug use among adolescents: concurrent and longitudinal analysis. *American Journal of Public Health ,* 76, 525-30.

Oetting, E.R. and Donnemeyer, J.F. (1998a). Primary Socialization Theory: The Etiology of Drug Use and Deviance. *Substance Use and Misuse,* 33 (4), 995-1026.

Oetting, E.R. and Donnemeyer, J.F. (1998b). Primary Socialization Theory: The Influence of the Community on Drug Use and Deviance. *Substance Use and Misuse,* 33 (8), 1629-1665.

Osler, A., Street, C., Lall, M., and Vincent, K. (2002). *Not a Problem? Girls and school exclusion.* York: Joseph Rowntree Foundation.

Nation, M., Crusto, C., Wandersman, A., Kumpfer, K.L., Seybolt, D., Morrissey-Kane, E., and Davino, K., (2000). What works in prevention. Principles of effective prevention programmes. *American Psychologist,* 58, 449-456.

Park, J., Kosterman, R., Hawkins, J.D., Haggerty, K.P., Duncan, S.C., and Spoth, R. (2000). Effects of the "Preparing for the Drug Free Years" curriculum on growth in alcohol use and risk for alcohol use in early adolescence. *Prevention Science,* 1, 125-138.

Petraitis, J., Flay, B. R., & Miller, T. Q. (1995). Reviewing theories of adolescent substance use: Organizing pieces in the puzzle. *Psychological Bulletin, 117,* 67–86.

Powell, J., Hardoon, K., Derevensky, J. L., & Gupta, R. (1999). Gambling and risk-taking behavior among university students. *Substance Use & Misuse, 34,* 1167–1184.

Powis, B., Griffiths, P., Gossop, M. Lloyd, C. and Strang, J. (1998). Drug use and offending behaviour among young people excluded from school, *Drugs: education, prevention and policy,* 5 (3), pp. 245-56.

Rhodes, T., Lilly, R., Fernandez, C., Giorgino, E., Kemmesis, U.E., Ossebaard, H.C., Lalam, N., Faasen, I. And Spannow, K.E. (2003). Risk Factors associated with drug use: the importance of 'risk environment'. *Drugs: Education, prevention and policy,* 10, 303-329.

Rutter, M., Maughan, B., Mortimer, P. and Ouston, J. (1979). *Fifteen thousand hours: secondary schools and their effectiveness in children.* London: Open books.

Rutter, M. (1990). Psychological resilience and protective mechanisms. In J. Rolf, A.S. Masten, D. Cicchetti, K.H. Neuchterlein, and S. Weitraub. *Risk and Protective Factors in the Development of Psychopathology.* Cambridge: University Press.

Rutter, M., Giller, H., and Hagel, A. (1998). *Antisocial Behaviour by Young People.* Cambridge: Cambridge University Press.

Schulenberg, J., Bachman, J.G., O'Malley, P.M. and Johnston, L.D. (1994). High school educational success and subsequent substance use: A panel analysis following adolescents into young adulthood. *Journal of Health and Social Behaviour,* 35, 45-62.

Sloboda, Z. (1999). Problems for the future? Drug use among vulnerable groups of young people. *rugs: education, prevention and policy,* 6 (1), 195-201.

Smith, R. (1998). *No Lessons Learnt. A Survey of School Exclusions.* London: The Children's Society.

Snow, P. C., Wallace, S.D. and Munro, G.D. (2001). Drug Education with Special Needs Populations: identifying and understanding the challenges. *Drugs; education, prevention and policy.* 8(3), 261-273.

Social Exclusion Unit (1998) *Truancy and Social Exclusion: Report by the Social Exclusion Unit ,* Cm 3957 (The Stationary Office).

Sussman, S., Dent, C.W., McAdams, L.A. Stacy, A.W. Burton, D. and Flay, B.R. (1994) Group self-identification and adolescent cigarette smoking: A one year prospective study. *Journal of Abnormal Psychology,* 103 576-580.

Sylva, K., 1994. School influences on children's development. *Journal of Child Psychology and Psychiatry* 35, pp. 135–170.

Tobler, N.S., Roona, M.R., Ochshorn, P., Marshall, D.G., Streke, A.V. and Stackpole, K.M. (2000). School-based adolescent drug prevention programs: a998 meta-analysis,. *Journal of Primary Prevention*, 20, 275-336.

United Kingdom Anti-Drugs Co-ordination Unit (UKADCU) (1998) *Tackling drugs to build a better Britain: second national plan 2000/2001.* London: Cabinet Office.

Vander Laenen , F and De Wree, E. (2008). Why the preventyion of cananbsi does not work: vulnerable young people's analysis. In: Korf, D. (Ed) *Cannabis in Europe: Dynamics in Perception, Policy and Markets.* Berlin: Pabst Science Publishers.

Van Gageldonk, A. and Cuijpers, O (1998). Effecten van verslavingspreventie. Utrecht: Trimbos-Instituut.

Voelkl, K.E. and Frone, M.R. (2000). Predictors of substance use at school among high school students. *Journal of Educational Psychology*, 92, 583-592.

Warr, P. (1987). Psychology and Work. Chichester:Wiley

Ware, S. R. (1999). Editorial: Imprisonment - is this is the only way society can deal with vulnerable and excluded people with alcohol and drug problems. *Drugs: education, prevention and policy*, 6 (1), 5-6.

Werner, E.E. (1989). High risk children in young adulthood: a longitudinal study from birth to 32 years. *American Journal of Orthopsychiatry*, 59, 72-81.

White, D. And Pitts, M. (1998). Educating young people about drugs: a systematic review. *Addiction*, 93, 1475-1487.

Willis, T.A., Vaccaro, D., and Bensen, G. (1995). Coping and competence in adolescnet alsohol and drug use. In J.L. Wallander and L.J. Siegel (Eds), *Adolescent health problems*, (pp. 160-178). New York: Guildford Press.

Wisely, C., Gledhill, N., Cyster, R., and Shaw, H. (1997). *The New Young Heroin User.* Unpublished Report.

INDEX

T

U